Annotation and Its Texts

PUBLICATIONS OF THE UNIVERSITY OF CALIFORNIA
HUMANITIES RESEARCH INSTITUTE
Mark Rose, *Director*

Annotation and Its Texts
Edited by Stephen A. Barney

Annotation and Its Texts

Edited by

Stephen A. Barney

New York Oxford
OXFORD UNIVERSITY PRESS
1991

Oxford University Press

Oxford New York Toronto
Delhi Bombay Calcutta Madras Karachi
Petaling Jaya Singapore Hong Kong Tokyo
Nairobi Dar es Salaam Cape Town
Melbourne Auckland

and associated companies in
Berlin Ibadan

Published by Oxford University Press, Inc.,
200 Madison Avenue, New York, New York 10016

Library of Congress Cataloging-in-Publication Data
Annotation and its texts / edited by Stephen A. Barney.
p. cm. — (Publications of the University of California
Humanities Research Institute)
Papers from a symposium held Apr. 8–10, 1988 at the University of
California, Irvine, and sponsored by the University of California
Humanities Research Institute.
ISBN 0-19-506301-5
1. Transmission of texts—Congresses. 2. Manuscripts—Editing—Congresses.
3. Criticism, Textual—Congresses. 4. Annotating,
Book—Congresses. 5. Marginalia—Congresses. I. Barney, Stephen A.
II. University of California (System). Humanities Research
Institute. III. Series.
Z40.A56 1991
001.2—dc20 90-42549

9 8 7 6 5 4 3 2 1

Printed in the United States of America
on acid-free paper

Contents

Introduction

In April of 1988 the University of California Humanities Research Institute sponsored at Irvine a symposium on the topic "Annotation and Its Texts." This volume gathers most of the papers, in revised versions, delivered at the conference, together with one paper, Peter W. Cosgrove's, solicited separately and not presented at the symposium.

Given the subject of the symposium, I laid down a rule that the published papers would appear unadorned by notes. The scholarly instincts of some of the contributors, however, made adherence to this rule impossible. Yet the papers retain such traces of oral presentation as add to their *enargeia*, and the last three papers especially, presented by "respondents" at the symposium, give some idea of the lively colloquies our various disciplines and points of view engendered.

Jacques Derrida wittily speaks of the "law" of this symposium, a little document I sent to the speakers as I invited them, which aimed to stimulate their thinking on our topic. Because several of the papers refer in some fashion to this document and volunteer to stand before the law, I reproduce it here:

Notes Toward a Symposium on Annotation

In connection with particular writers, periods, cultures:

- Where does a text stop and a footnote begin? What is hors d'œuvre?
- In the Knight's Tale, Chaucer writes epexegetically:

  Ther saugh I Dane, yturned til a tree—
  I mene nat the goddesse Diane,
  But Penneus doghter, which that highte Dane.

What is the effect of self-annotation?

- Commentary accommodates a text to a presumed audience. Do we blaspheme in commenting on sacred writing? What is a fundamentalist commentary?
- When is footnoting a critical activity? When is it a political activity?
- What do we mean in saying philosophy is footnotes to Plato and Aristotle?
- Can an event be footnoted? What do historians do? What are the writings of Gibbon and Carlyle?
- How can we distinguish footnotes, commentaries, essays, new texts? What are Blake's marginalia? What is Gregory's *Moralia in Job*? *Pale Fire*? *Glas*? *The Shepherd's Calendar*? *The Rime of the Ancient Mariner*? *The Waste Land*? *Ficciones*?
- Are there good and bad footnotes?
- Which comes first, the text or the footnote?
- Is any text unannotatable? Is any footnote uncriticizable?
- Can writers control or deny annotation?
- Does annotation require a writing culture? What is an oral footnote? What is teaching?
- How do we distinguish a scholiast from an exegete from an editor from a critic? Do texts require repair?
- What effect has the format of annotation upon its text?
- What's the difference between a symposium and a footnote?
- Have footnotes a logic? Does annotation classify?
- Do any texts originally ask for annotation? *Finnegans Wake*? *Paradise Lost*? The *Divine Comedy*?
- How does a computer annotate?
- Does annotation presume method? a grammar? presume that a text has meaning? presume what its readers need to know? presume to limit the incomprehensible or the ugly or the bad?
- What do legal annotators do? Can unwritten laws be annotated? Do annotations have more force than their texts?
- When may annotation be described as emulation, competition?
- What connection has annotation to information retrieval?
- When is annotation unnecessary? Do we annotate a lyric? a logic

text? a textbook? a modern novel? a senate hearing? another footnote?

- How does annotation differ from intertextuality?
- From what communities does annotation emerge? Who needs notes?
- What communities are especially bookish: rabbinic? medieval scholastic? legal? academic? right-wing? geological? And why? Are there schools of annotation?
- Does it matter who annotates? A smarter writer annotating a dumber? an enemy? our own marginalia to ourselves

In arranging these papers I finally decided that a roughly chronological order of their subjects did the least harm, while I invite the reader to notice the many ways in which they speak to each other. Hence the first paper deals with annotation within the Bible, and the seventh with a contemporary author's struggles with self-annotation; the last three were responses, delivered in this chronological order, to the other papers at the symposium. In between, the speakers treat of Origen, of Old English manuscripts, of fourteenth-century commentaries, of a sixteenth-century reader, and of eighteenth-century exploiters of the bottom margin.

Continuing his seminal series of essays on the Bible, James C. Nohrnberg speaks, if I may adopt his idiom, of how glossing generates prose, and of how the two larger instalments of the Bible generate a glossolalia of accountability or registration. He concludes, if I understand him, by urging that the tail of the biblical gloss wags the dog of the text because the Bible particularly commands us to have faith in what is not present, what is unseen. Stephen G. Nichols in a way speaks to the same point, noticing the iconic and ecphrastic, as it were rhetorical, function of formatting and rubrication on the medieval manuscript page, the ways in which the visual, fancied, and imagined can reequip the castrated body of the text when received only literally and logically.

By looking at annotation that is just barely *there*, those uninked, scratched glosses in Anglo-Saxon manuscripts, codicological instances, so to speak, of Derridean traces, Thomas E. Toon puts into question what we see when we look at a book. Like Austin but at another level of literary perception, he invites us to look at the *uses* of books in a scribal politics: how to do things with pages. Traugott Lawler likewise studies the politics of medieval annotation, from the example of a twelfth-century self-annotating author and his fourteenth-century commentators. These peculiarly schoolish productions display sometimes the petty and often irrelevant arrogance of emulous scholarship, but sometimes a serious rivalry that at least amounts to good pedagogy, a technique of accumulation that is complementary rather than destructive.

Examining a diligent sixteenth-century reader's multiple sweeps through the text of a classical author, Anthony Grafton develops the theme of a politics of annotation in a new key. In the special social order of Tudor England, he observes, the evidences of critical reading as found in marginalia take place in an arena never wholly private, and the gifts of eloquence and copiousness could grant one power in the great world. A reader like Harvey connects Livy to life and life to Livy. Peter W. Cosgrove, the absent *alazon* of the symposium, the late-coming canon's yeoman of our pilgrimage, brilliantly continues the exploration of the rhetoric of annotation by finding, in the footnotoclast Pope and the notolator Gibbon, contrary movements that undermine their opposed claims to authority.

Thomas McFarland offers a footnote to his own life as a scholar, a confession by a demonstrably learned man of his radical unknowingness and its vicissitudes in the marketplace, and a satire on the footnote's presumptuous and fraudulent effort to stand thereunder as a sign of an intertextual culture that itself is no more than a soothing myth. So we move from an essay on the gloss as the founding registration of the Word of God to an essay on the footnote as the proud emblem of the post-Leibniz wasteland.

This darker side of the contemporary politics of annotation forms the theme of Ralph Hanna III's first response to the symposium. He speaks of the annotator's engagement in a suppression of certain guilty knowledge—namely, that annotation pretends to mediate an alienated text and its readership, whereas in fact it aggressively creates a reader who never will be and an author who never was. He leaves it for us to surmise whom the annotator serves.

Annotatio: id est lex—so, Laurent Mayali reminds us, wrote the great glossator on the great medieval collection of canon law. He finds the principle of legitimization, as represented by annotation, in the principle of genealogy: "as there is no father without a child, there is no text without annotations"; his metaphor resembles Nichols's metaphor of the memberless body. Hence the annotator is truth's vicar, and annotation is the imitation (the term is thought to be etymologically connected with the term "emulation") of a text—Derrida might call it at once a mime and a graft, a parasite and a tattoo. Like the semipublic readers of whom Anthony Grafton speaks, Mayali speaks of annotators as partakers of a community of power lying between oral and literate cultures, the priests of writing.

The third response had to be, as in the fairy tale, the final one. This text from Jacques Derrida illustrates in its production, as he observes, some of the mutuality and alienation, the double bind, inevitable in commentary. Its present form, "approved by the author," is a kind of translation derived from two imperfect sources: a computer-mediated text "entered" by the author—a text that mingles two national languages—together with the text of a garbled transcription of the author's oral presentation, in clear but accented English, a transcription prepared by a person who could not speak or hear the language of the symposium, that is, academic literary English. Hence the text before you includes an invisible commentary by the editor (and his collaborator, Michael Hanly) in his role as translator and tidy-upper and desperate preserver of the serious play in the language of the originator. Only because of the accident of deferred mortality was the editor able to relegitimize and reauthenticate this mediated text by the simple expedient of returning to the author and asking him, "Is this what you meant?—still knowing that, because the author's first language is not that of the present text, he might well reply, "Have you said what I meant?" I will not, then, presume to tell you what Jacques Derrida means, trusting that you will read his work and the other papers in this volume in that magical way you have of reading texts without glosses while knowing it cannot be done "in the strict sense."

I would wish, the contributors willing, to dedicate this first volume from the Humanities Research Institute to its only begetter, Murray Krieger.

Annotation and Its Texts

1

Justifying Narrative: Commentary within Biblical Storytelling

James C. Nohrnberg

We can read a text only insofar as some primitive or putatively original member of that text—a donnée—has attached to itself a saturation of glosses: every isolatable unit in a given discourse functions as a comment on, supplement of, or gloss upon some prior instance of that discourse, right back to the original clearing of the throat in advance of the externalizing of articulation. Clearing the throat glosses the silence that precedes it; silence is a kind of pre-text that is erasable, and as if in want of revision, improvement, editing, and abridgment. The text itself starts out as a gloss imposed or inscribed upon silence or blankness; it becomes readable—makes sense and makes sentences—when sounds, marks, words, phrases, clauses, and propositions serve to explain their being copresent in a way conformable to coherence—that is, conformable to the prior experience and training of the reader: when, so to speak, the text has reached the margins. The reader is one who is experienced and trained in the coherence of other, prior texts, which is to say, experienced and trained in the production of his own supplementary glosses. Everything we read is thus a gloss upon, or translation of, some original improvement upon silence. Prose is ideation that has assimilated to itself a continuous running gloss, and that has thereby become self-sufficient in the sense of self-explanatory. Yet it is the margins as much as anything that tell us that this point of repletion has been reached: the point at which the text has the completeness of a corpus of glosses. "See Spot run," for example, is a text, but it is also a gloss: that is, it is a caption for a picture that the child is asked to "read," as it were, in the translation provided by the words.

In the sense developed above, the Bible is decidedly "prosaic," for the text is characterized by its own intratextual exegesis at almost every level, from the lexical to the theological, and including the propositions that are prescriptive (law) and future-oriented (prophecy). Our question here is, how does this self-exegesis of the text comport with the nature and purposes of biblical story-telling?

Characters, for example, belong to story-telling. In his *Poetics of Biblical Narrative*, Meir Sternberg postulates an "epistemological revolution" that replaced the depiction of a literary character's existence with the depiction of his knowledge.[1] Prime examples of this 'in-forming' of character are the stories of David the schemer

1. Meir Sternberg, *The Poetics of Biblical Narrative: Ideological Literature and the Drama of Reading* (Bloomington, Ind.: Indiana University Press, 1985), chapt. 1, esp. pp. 12–13, 46–56, and again pp. 87–89 (cf. p. 88: "It all goes back to an epistemological revolution, which shifted the center of gravity from existence to knowledge"). Perhaps the work most relevent to the project of the present essay is Michael Fishbane's magisterial and exhaustive *Biblical Interpretation in Ancient Israel* (Oxford: Clarendon Press, 1985). Again and again Fishbane shows how biblical material has been reprocessed by the text to bring its meaning up to a current theological standard. For example, the battlefield exhortation at Joshua 1:6, 18, "be strong," meaning "be of good courage, play the man," has been supplemented (Deuteronomistically) to mean "be strong *in the torah*," by the intervening verses at 7–9 (Fishbane, *op. cit.*, p. 384).

For an interesting perspective on the "dialogical" approach to the biblical text taken here, compare the univocal rule (from Maimonides) governing traditional Torah interpretation, as discussed by Jon D. Levenson, "The Eighth Principle of Judaism and the Literary Simultaneity of Scripture," *Journal of Religion*, 68 (1988), pp. 205–25. (Three different biblical laws regarding the manumission of the slave necessarily issue in a fourth law, when the texts are synchronized in the Talmud.)

The 'literary' consequences of the compoundedness of the biblical text are broached in Nohrnberg, "On Literature and The Bible," *Centrum* (University of Minnesota), II:2, Fall, 1974, esp. pp. 5–10, 14–27. See similarly Northrop Frye, *The Great Code* (New York and London: Harcourt Brace Jovanovich, 1981), pp. xxi, 201–27.

The author wishes to thank Stephen Barney, Daniel J. Kinney, and Rev. Mark Olsen for the suggestions that got the present essay started.

and Joseph the interpreter. But the knowledge in which the biblical figures participate can seem rather less Jamesian and rather more "prosaic," in our sense, when the characters are embedded in a text which they are also portrayed as productively collaborating with. We are often denied the illusion of their autonomy or inner-life apart from the articulation of the text, since the narrator feels free to make the characters forespeak a variety of psalms, laws, oracles, blessings, and versified formulae, and in general makes the characters participate in counsels larger than their own.

Biblical characters, it follows, regularly name their children prophetically and interpretatively. In this light we may consider the following passage from the Book of Ruth: "the women said, 'Is this Na'omi?' She said to them, 'Do not call me Na'omi, call me Mara, for the Almighty has dealt very bitterly with me. . . . Why call me Na'omi, when the Lord has testified against me . . . ?" (Ruth 1:19–21, RSV). "Why call me 'my sweet'?" Naomi asks sourly, casting herself as an intra-biblical exegete, a critic of the relation between name and vocation. Ruth might well be the one to draw the reader's attention to the characters' names in her book, for the names found at the outset of her story are indeed generated allegorically. But at the end of this same book the allegorical names are replaced by a list of much more 'historical' persons, a list which is anonymously supplied in the voice of an authoritative genealogical gloss: "These are the descendents of Perez . . ." (Ruth 4:19). The end-note asserts the descent from Perez to David, without mentioning the intervention of Ruth or Naomi at all. This descent is the one that the story interrupts in order to explain the hazard in which a given lineage stood, between the descendents of Perez and the ancestors of David. But from the genealogist's point of view, it is the *genealogy* that is the true story, while the story itself is more truly a fictionalized and 'aggadic' *gloss*.

Let me give a more fine-textured example of the text watching itself, polishing itself, and reflecting on itself in the glass of its internal glosses. Despairing of her barrenness, Hannah secretly vows to give her son to the service of God, if God will only give her a son. The priest Eli pronounces a reassuring benediction over her and she is dejected no longer. After the birth of Samuel, Hannah offers a prayer of praise to God, an exultation of her heart in

Yahweh's power to save. "There is no Holy One like Yahweh," she says parallelistically, "no Rock like our God" (1 Sam. 2:2:, The New Jerusalem Bible, hereafter NJB). The comparatives in Hannah's hymn credit God with an incomparable holiness and reliability, but when the song rhetorically prefers God over the sanctuaries and stones belonging to other gods, those other gods are conceivably given a momentary purchase on existence. There *are* "no other gods before [Yahweh]," a monotheistic glosser might like to insist, and so he seems to interpolate a remark between the two lines I have quoted—switching from the third and first persons to the second—"indeed, there is no one *but* you" (NJB). The "gloss" is almost an aside to God, and it "demythologizes" some imaginary contest for priority among the gods with homiletic "no contest." The rest of the gods not only do not amount to anything, they don't exist at all. The pious gloss has gone inside the text, so it is no longer much of a gloss, but nonetheless we may ask where it came from. In one sense, it came from inside as well: from the Bible's reflection on itself—from, for example, the arguments against idolatry in the long prose gloss in Isaiah 44, which follows on the verses declaring that God is the supreme revealer: "besides me there is no god. . . . There is No Rock [besides me]; I know not any" (44:6, 8 RSV).

In another sense the gloss comes from Hannah herself, since she is credited with the whole hymn. But the hymn is in verse and sounds like other hymns and texts, such as the one from Isaiah 44 just cited. Thus the hymn is itself an interpolation, put in Hannah's mouth because the hymn turns to celebrate Yahweh's power to reverse wordly expectation, to fill the famished and make the barren to bear seven, and to humble the proud and exalt the humiliated. (Hannah will bear a total of six, so she actually will come up one short. In the Bible, six-sevenths is perhaps the part originally taken for the whole, as good as the seven sons that Naomi has, vicariously, in the devotion of her daughter-in-law Ruth [Ruth 4:15].)

Yet even if Hannah's hymn aligns itself with the advent of Samuel and Samuel's priesthood, it also says that Yahweh "endows his *king* with power" (1 Sam. 2:10 NJB). But what king? Presently there is no king in Israel, nor will there be, until Samuel has grown up and anointed him: through Samuel "[Yahweh] raises up the strength of his Anointed," as the hymn concludes (1 Sam. 2:10 NJB). And why do the people ask Samuel to appoint a king for them? Because, according to chapter 8 of 1 Samuel, Samuel has grown old and his sons do not walk in his ways, the very situation in the priesthood that Samuel was born into in the first place. The royalist content of the hymn, curiously enough, aligns it with the etymology that Hannah has previously supplied for her newborn's name; "I have asked him of the Lord" (1 Sam. 1:20 RSV). This is an etymological gloss on a name that in Hebrew can only be that of the name of the future King *Saul*, whom indeed the people ask for, not of the Lord directly, but of the Lord through Samuel their mediator. In getting Samuel born through Hannah, the narrator is also treating, more remotely, of the elect and diselect King Saul, and of the diselection of the old priesthood and the election of the new office of the prophet.

The story has begun from the woman whom Yahweh has made barren and who therefore refused to partake of the festivities of the sacrifice. Thus she might well choose a psalm about Yahweh's omnipotence and uncontrollable intent, as an accompaniment for the dedication of her son Samuel back to the God from whom he was asked. And she might particularly and more personally confess that "there is none besides thee," because she has put nothing "before God," as the prose of the preceding narration has emphasized: "she . . . took her stand before Yahweh. . . . She prayed before Yahweh. . . . She prayed before Yahweh. . . . [She] was pouring out [her] soul before Yahweh. . . . [She and her husband] . . . worshiped before Yahweh" (1 Sam. 1:8, 10, 12, 15, 19). "'I am the woman,'" she tells the priest Eli, "'who stood here beside you, praying to Yahweh,'" that same Yahweh whom Hannah will say that there is none besides, and the Yahweh who intends the raising up of a new priesthood after his own heart and who intends the beggaring of the old overweening priesthood deriving from Eli (1 Sam. 1:26, 31–36).

The priest of the story has been no real mediator between Hannah and God, whose prayers have been private and remain undisclosed to Eli. The interpolations she makes in the hymn, like the insider's view of the story, open her communication with God to a reader's scrutiny. "For it is not by strength that man triumphs," as a possible second gloss by Hannah insists (1 Sam. 2:9, NJB); rather, Hannah has triumphed solely through the intervention of God.

Even if we could confidently identify the glosses as not belonging to the original hymn—and we cannot—we surely cannot identify them as not belonging to the original story. For Hannah's prayer could consist of precisely no more than the two Jerusalem Bible parentheses: "there is none besides thee, ... : . . . not by might shall a man prevail" (RSV). Hannah's putative supplementations of the psalm actually condense its essential import for her.

The poem glossing Hannah's situation presumes the theology of the "poor of Yahweh," and the glosses on the poem guard even further than the poem itself against any underestimating of Yahweh's transcendent reality. The glosses do not make Hannah's hymn over in the image of Hannah's situation, but God has made Hannah's situation over in the image of Hannah's hymn, and so it is natural for her to further appropriate the hymn by means of the little comments that make it even more insistent upon Yahweh's singularity for her and for the glosser. The priest, we remember, has misinterpreted Hanna's original prayers before Yahweh as evidence of public drunkenness. Hannah's own possible additions seem to murmur corrections into her hymn's text in a way that reminds us of Hannah's corrective responses to the decadent priesthood hanging over her shoulder while she prayed. Her hymn glosses or gives tongue to her original "speaking in her heart; only her lips moved, and her voice was not heard" (1 Sam. 1:13 RSV). The priesthood cannot hear or read her original prayer, and yet her subsequent magnification of the Lord constitutes a resounding acknowledgment of her prayer's having been heard. Even more complexly, Hannah has not only glossed the conception and birth of Samuel with a hymn celebrating Yahweh's support for the anointed king, but has also glossed his name with an etymology suggesting that the son she asked for was named Saul, the Hebrew word for "ask" (*shaal*). Her prayer seems to have been overheard by the future.

The text can thus be represented as a tissue of glosses. The hymn of the rejoicing Hannah has been inserted into the story to gloss the silent prayer of the despairing Hannah, and to gloss her blubbering drunkenness as alleged by the priest. The internal gloss on the hymn glosses and insists upon the hymn's incipient monotheism, and it personalizes the hymn as Hannah's. But the royalism of the hymn glosses the asking for and the naming of *Samuel* as the election of *Saul*—Saul is thus found "among the prophets" before his very introduction—and so the whole story, and not only the hymn, glosses the calling into being of the kingship, since the act of asking for Samuel seems to be glossed by the act of asking for Saul. The priest wishes that Hannah may have the thing that she *asked* for, thus he is the first to gloss the name of Saul, the king that the people will *ask* Samuel for (cf. 1 Sam. 1:17 and 12:19 RSV; "'we have added to all our sins this evil, to *ask* for ourselves a king'"). They get what they ask for, when Samuel "hearkens" unto their request (1 Sam. 8:7, 9, 22; 12:1). Hearkening is what God asks for, and the sons of the priest Eli do not hearken to their father's voice when he upbraids them with what he has heard of their evil dealings (1 Sam. 2:25). They have made their heart as well as their persons *fat*, and Hannah's hymn tell us that the Lord will destroy the fat.

Despite the significant doubling of Samuel and Saul, Samuel is not the king himself, but his eventual nemesis. He is a prophet called from the womb—ultimately from the tomb as well—and so the story also glosses the constituting of prophecy as the adversary of the royalist state, insofar as the state will prove itself disloyal to Yahweh. "How long?" the priest asks about Hannah's supposed drunkenness, inadvertently causing us to hear the kind of question that the prophets were going to be asking a heedless nation or a delaying God: "O Jerusalem, wash your heart from wickedness, that you may be saved. *How long* shall your evil thoughts lodge within you?" (Jer. 4:14 RSV; see also Rev. 6:10, Ps. 4:2, 79:5, Zech. 1:12). Indeed, we may think that the careful description of how Hannah prayed ("she spoke in her heart; only her lips moved, but her voice was not heard") answers to Jeremiah's demand, "Put away the foreskins of your heart" (Jer. 4:4), as well as his original in Isaiah, "Wash you, make you clean; put away the evil of your doings from before my eyes" (Isa. 1:16). Hannah accordingly consecrates her unconceived son to Nazirite vows. The preceding Nazirite annunciation was that of Samson, who was forbidden strong drink. But Samson was not called as a prophet, while Samuel is credited with prophecy's fundamental message, delivered by Samuel to Saul, that what the Lord wants is not cultic sacrifices, but hearkening (1 Sam. 15:22).

The word "hearkening," Prof. Herbert Marks has pointed out, can suggest Samuel's own name. For the message in question is in verse, again an indication that the recombinant intertextuality of text and gloss is to be invoked. Hearkening, from the verb *shamea* ("to hear"), is the heedfulness that requires the sacrifice of the contrite heart. Hannah, who refused to eat of the sacrifices that the priests have been gobbling up, will indeed sacrifice the child for which she has asked, yet her sacrifice will, in the language of her hymn, make her full. She will have as many children as Leah had sons, for "God *hearkened* unto Leah" (Gen. 30:17). God hearkened unto Leah because she was despised, and like Hannah, the name of one of her sons seems to be glossed in terms of the asking–hearkening complex of our text: "And she [Leah] conceived, and bare a son; and said, Because the Lord hath heard that I was hated, he hath therefore given me this son also: and she called his name Simeon" (*shama*, "he has heard"; AV Gen. 29:33). Does such a wordplay gloss the story, or does the story gloss the wordplay? For the wordplay itself goes back beyond Simeon to the naming of Ishmael in the womb: "Behold, thou art with child," says the angel of the Lord to Hagar, "and shalt bear a son, and shalt call his name Ishmael; because the Lord hath heard thy affliction" (AV Gen. 16:11). As these examples suggest, almost everything coming into being in the Bible is compounded with the tremendous fatality of its also coming into utterance—the Bible itself included. The Psalmist says, "God has spoken once, twice I have heard this" (62:11), a distich that speaks not only for the ethos of biblical parallelism, but also for the ethos of biblical textuality itself.

It is hard to know what constitutes the so-called "saturation point," that is, the point at which the glosses upon an original paucity of information can be construed as closing out further glosses as unneedful or superfluous incorporations into the text-in-the-making—a text that comes into existence or repletion at exactly the point when further glosses can be distinguished from it. This point of repletion, the point at which the intratextual parts company with the intertextual, is the point at which the text-in-the-making becomes (if I may put it this way) canonic to itself. At such a point enough of the questions and expectations raised by the gloss upon the aboriginal waste and void have been met and satisfied for the proposed discourse to self-enclose. Further glossing interferes with what has been sufficiently glossed, and the text thereafter will become overdetermined. This relation between the initiative of the text and its completion is suggested by the rabbinic legend that in the beginning God was fruitlessly pondering how he might commence the creation, until he finally turned for help to the Talmud.[2]

Let us imagine that there is such a thing as an overglossed text. The gloss that specifies redundantly and tautologically is somehow self-evidently defined or differentiated as being otiose. But the gloss also defines itself as different from the text by its seeming to hail from a different plane of explanation than that occupied by those explanations required to establish the initial coherence of the text, its univocality, which is to say, by its seeming to come from a different text or a rival rhetorical organization or rival pattern of coherence.

An example of a gloss that seems to overdetermine a text is the text of the law concerning the indemnification of a woman who miscarries as a result of male violence. If she suffers further harm, beyond the miscarriage itself, "then you shall give life for life, eye for eye, tooth for tooth, hand for hand, foot for foot, burn for burn, wound for wound, stripe for stripe" (Exod. 21:22–25

2. The gloss as a phenomenon belongs to the drive towards intelligibility found in all interpretation. This purpose is described, for example, in Hans-Georg Gadamer, *Truth and Method* (translator not stated) (New York: The Seabury Press, 1975), pp. 262 and 301, as implying a distrust of the text as it stands uninterpreted, or a distrust of its wholeness. We may note in passing that the literary gloss is often the citation of another literary text. Insofar as the Bible imitates the totality of a literature, the allusion in question simply tends to be a reference to another verse of the Bible.

For an example of how a text—especially an inwrought one—is the type of its own interpretation, consider the apparently unintelligible language that Dante puts into the mouth of the giant Nimrod: *Raphèl mày amèch zabì almì* (*Inferno* 28.67). The words might prompt the gloss (mine, I'm afraid) that Nimrod is praying to the giants' god (Heb. *raph-* + *el*) who has forsaken him, using a distorted rendition of the words from the cross ("*Eli, Eli, lama sabachthani*, that is to say, My God, my God, why hast thou forsaken me?" [Matt. 27:46]). But this gloss is prompted by a feeling for the innate congruity between the present text of Dante and the adduced one of scripture, for Jesus' words in a 'foreign' language were themselves doubtfully and incorrectly interpreted by "some of them that stood there" (Matt. 27:47), even while these same words aptly gloss the crucifixion with the first line of Psalm 22 (hence Dante's rhyme word "salmi", cf. *Purgatorio* 23.73–74, ". . . the tree which made Christ gladly cry Eli"). In a sense, Nimrod's idiolect isolates him in a community of one: in terms of the conclusion to my essay, a community that lacks the gift of glosses.

RSV). This text is not very "univocal," for the most complete enunciation of the principle of retaliation in kind has been attached to the least susceptible case. For who can know the exact extent of the effects of the miscarriage? Who can translate female damage into male damage, who can say which of the brawling males, apart from the husband, hurt the woman? And who can relate all these traumas to abortive childbirth while ignoring the life of the fetus, as the father must do even when he sets the fine for causing the miscarriage? The law seems to make nonsense of the law, through its glossing of retaliation as retaliation in kind. Yet where in the Bible is retaliation in kind enunciated as a policy? In connection with Cain, the first Lamech, and Noah, of course, but also the pregnancy of Hagar.

When Sarah drives out her rival Hagar, the angel announces to the fugitive that the future Ishmael's hand shall be against every man and every man's hand against him: he shall be a wild ass of a man (Gen. 16:12). The *talio*-gloss in Exodus seems to have gotten attached to the wrong troubled pregnancy, the one in the law (i.e., in the statutes), rather than the one in the narrative. And yet the Mosaic law as a whole comes into existence in conjunction with a defense of the weak: the welfare laws in particular are glossed, explained, and justified as so many forms of sanctuary, as an extending of legal protections to the otherwise unprotected. Furthermore, the narratives are all to be glossed as providing clues to the law, given their inclusion in the text containing the laws: they are thus a corpus of case law. It would be hard to miss, for example, the fact that the law disallowing disinheritance (violation of the rights of primogeniture, Deut. 21: 15–17) cries to be glossed by the exceptions taken to such a law by the stories of diselection in Genesis. The statutes, in effect, gloss the cases.

A text, then, is a tissue of glosses that render the unreadable as readable; but these glosses are not perceived as glosses, because they have fallen into a prior pattern of coherence that establishes their unity as discourse and therefore marginalizes attempts to supplement that unity—or that coalescence of discourse—as glosses. The unity of the group of glosses now forming the text is "artificial," insofar as any member gloss can be marginalized without raising more questions than keeping the gloss answers; and the unity is "natural," insofar as any given member of the text is necessary to bridge between any two others.

Glosses bring the reader into a mindfulness of what other minds found or wished to be found in—or wished to be remembered by—the text's more primitive members. The text's more primitive members are those to which the drift represented by the whole most readily attaches, what that drift most readily would gloss. These primitive members are, so to speak, the text's kerygma, the nuclear form of the drift or intention the text expands upon. Text and gloss, then, are seen to be mutually oriented upon each other, like the sexes, or like figure and ground. There are no texts without glosses in the sense of internal self-modification, there are no lines without the betweenness between the lines, the interlinearity that makes them readable and glossable. Thus the two most significant texts for thinking about the literary phenomenon of glosses are perhaps the Bible and *Finnegans Wake.* They are, I should suppose, the most self-enclosed of texts, yet paradoxically they are the ones most open to the labor of the glossator. The reason must be sought in their constitution and construal as precisely that kind of text that reveals any text whatsoever to be a prose fabrication, in the sense of a tissue of glosses.

Although virtually anything in a text that is isolated for particular scrutiny will present itself as a gloss upon some other part of the text, one has to speak as if we can distinguish the text from the glosses, which are typically identified as instances of inconsonant specification, parenthetical or interpolated comment, internal but nonetheless extracontextual reference, overdetermined prose discourse, editorial cross-referencing, and the like. But a text that has attracted such things out of its margins and into its texture, and that has accommodated if not wholly assimilated them internally, has been as much redacted as glossed. Perhaps no better illustration of the indistinction in question is the comment that such and such has happened in the history recounted by the narrative *in order that the word of the prophet might be fulfilled.* Such a remark does not so much bracket itself, as bracket the whole hiatus between forecast and enactment, a hiatus that reverberates in the words of the psalm, "Once God has spoken; twice I have heard this" (Ps. 61:11 RSV). Only in the performative utterance of God Himself is there no room for this temporal interpolation: "God said, 'Let there be light,' and there was light"—and yet what God says nonetheless gets said again, thus opening up that "meantime" between utterance and its registration, or between the intending and the achieving of meaningfulness, or the positing of the sign and the depositing of its significance. Glossing emerges as a kind of registration in this sense.

In what follows, the posteriority of the gloss has something of the status of a legal fiction, like the background of a painting that is painted to foreground into existence an object that is thereby absented from the background, and yet remains there diacritically, so to speak, as a silhouette. The processes of reading are the processes of prioritizing glosses, deciding what is in explanatory apposition to what; but almost every etiological narrative tells us that at some originary point the dog did not wag the tail except insofar as the tail wagged the dog. For example, there are so many biblical references to Esau's association with the color red—the color phonetically associated with the name Edom—that one begins to lose any sense of whether the color has determined the gloss provided by the story, or the story has been glossed by the addition of the references to the color. Each element seems to be a function of the other, or they have cooriginated in a way that throws an emphasis upon the priority of one of any two textual members without decisively according it to either one or the other. The language of "Edom" and "red" seems to have turned the text into the story of the language. "We call them Edomites because they are ruddy" seems as logical a deduction as "We tell stories about their ruddiness because they are settled in a land with a red-sounding name, and are identified ethnographically by a red-sounding patronym." Such reading is glossing, because it is the supplementation of writing without which the writing would not have come into existence.

Doubtless such a reciprocity exists between the narratively prior members and the intratextual glossing activity, as we will presently see in our example of the biblical account of Abraham and the Hittite landowners. But which will be the narratively prior members? Whatever we decide is a "given"—or a premise—in the text will turn whatever remains into evidence of a glossing activity. And this particular rule may be less "exceptionable" than it looks. For example, the explanation of a foreign word must surely qualify as a gloss. Yet if the alienation or marginalization of the word in question is itself understood as a subject of the text, then the activity of glossing that word—the activity of bridging back to it—is the text's very raison d'être: namely, to create a context for understanding the exchange of—or between—the two words, or their respective contexts. This is the case, for example, with the gloss explaining what prophets used to be called in Israel, before the career of the charismatic Samuel (I Sam. 9:9).

How much less decidable is the case for priority when we meet specifications that appropriate the text for "contemporary" or putatively postbiblical readerships, readerships first brought into existence by the text's creation, but a people itself being brought into existence by its memories and conservation of the things in the text. Such and such a place *x* is now such and such a place *y*. But it would not be a place at all, had it not been the site for such and such a narrative attaching to it and leading to its enshrinement first in the collective memory and then in the text. The earlier portions of the narrative abound in such displaced foundation stories, stories that in effect reclaim the promised land for subsequent generations of claimants. Such glosses contemporize the action of a story by restaking the original claim made within the story by its actors and agents. This recuperative catechizing of the present moment, or this retrieval of the record of the past for contemporary reference, makes the stories glosses on questions of historical identity, identity the stories transmit and lead up to. For example, Rachel's tomb is in Israel "today," meaning that this tomb is still maintained, meaning that Rachel's memory is not dead, meaning that Rachel continues to exist collectively in her descendents, meaning that the Ephrath that was is identifiable with the Bethlehem that now is (Gen. 35:20), and suggesting to us that the child named after the dying Rachel's sorrow—Ben-oni—is one with the child of her husband Jacob's name-revising blessing—Ben-jamin. The geographical glosses thus incorporate and transmit something of the same ethnographic information that the story itself does.

For a full-blown example of the glossing activity pertaining to the "prosaic" activity of a biblical character, we may study Abraham's initial obtainment of real estate in the Promised Land. The point will be to see the working out of the paradoxical relations between the intratextual gloss and the allegedly primitive text members: to see, in other words, the so-called kerygma change places with the so-called gloss, and thus to support our intuition that a given text could not be read as a coherent whole, or "canon," if this apparently subversive exchange did not take place.

Both the second and the penultimate verses of the story of the purchase of Sarah's place of burial gloss the site in question as *Hebron*: that was where Sarah died, "at Kir'iath-ar'ba (that is, Hebron) in the land of Canaan," and that is where she was entombed, "in the cave of the field of Mach-pe'lah east of Mamre (that is, Hebron) in the land of Canaan" (Gen. 23:2, 19 RSV). Hebron is the place where the men of Judah will one day anoint David their king, so we may thus imagine the tomb of the patriarchs as having something like the moral force of the stone of Scone in tribal Scotland. In Hebrew dying is virtually to go and sleep with one's fathers, and so Hebron is also roughly identified with the Abraham's bosom of Luke 16:22.

The story is internally framed with the references to Hebron. But it is externally framed as well, with the information pertaining to the patriarchal pedigree: the information that Abraham's brother's wife Milchah had borne eight, one the father of one Rebekah, and with the account of the sending for this Rebekah, whose kinsmen commend her marriage with Isaac with the blessing or wish that her "descendants possess the gate of those who hate them" (Gen. 24:60 RSV)— an echo of the angelic blessing of Abraham that precedes the announcement of Rebekah, the promise to Abraham that his "descendants shall possess the gate of their enemies" (Gen. 22:17 RSV). This blessing of Abraham was the consequence of Abraham's offering up of Isaac, which resulted in the consecration, as it were, of his patriarchy: the blessing itself becomes a part of the patriarchal inheritance, and its transmission across the gap between Abraham and Rebekah is an earnest upon its later transmission to Jacob and the sons of Jacob. Thus the dying Jacob is able to promise his son Judah—Leah's lastborn—that "your hand shall be on the neck of your enemies," and that "the scepter shall not depart from Judah" (Gen. 49:8, 10 RSV); this is the kingship that Judah seems first to get in Hebron (2 Sam. 2:1–7), upon the death of Saul and the crowning of David. But this blessing passes to David through his ancestress the Moabitess Ruth, who is blessed at the gate of the society into which she is adoptively incorporated in Bethlehem, with the wishes that she should be made "like Rachel and Leah, who together built up the house of Israel," so that she should "prosper in Eph'rathah and be renowned in Bethlehem," and that her house should "be like the house of Perez, whom Tamar bore to Judah" (Ruth 4:11–12 RSV). (Ruth bore her children to Boaz, whose father was Salmon, Salmon thus being an ancestor of David's son Solomon, one of the two pillars of whose house bore the name Boaz. All this takes us a long way from the tombs of Rachel and Sarah and Rebekah and Leah, but it helps explain what Joyce implies by telling us to wipe our glosses with what we know, which seems to mean that one should gloss one's glosses with the text. In that case, which seems to be the biblical one, glossing is a critical form of crossreferencing, the most common form taken by biblical marginalia.)

To gloss the two Abrahamic sites as Hebron is obviously to make a claim upon these places, or vice versa, to assert Hebron's claim upon them, that is, upon their Abrahamic associations and legacy. Hebron would be claiming to be the original nucleus of Israel, the proto-Israel of the pre-Israelite patriarchs. This claim-making activity is not posterior to the activity portrayed within the story, however, for in the story Abraham successfully appropriates a piece of Canaan to his dead family, and so to his unborn descendants. On the one hand, we can say that Abraham gets no more of the Promised Land than he can lay claim to by dying on it; on the other hand, this limited space is nonetheless a recognizably potent claim upon the territory in question, since one's native land is the place where one is born precisely because it is also the place where one's progenitors have lived, procreated, died, and been buried.

This claim upon the land is honored and revalidated, so to speak, generations later by the repatriation of the body of Jacob for burial with Abraham and Isaac, and by the final deposition, in Israel, of the bones of Joseph with the remains of Joshua, the actual conqueror of the Promised Land. Abraham was not born in Canaan, and so his obtaining of a burial site here makes a very good partner chapter with the story of Abraham's obtaining of a wife for his son abroad in the East, the Old Country. In consenting to come west, Rebekah is recruited for the tomb that Abraham has just purchased; and in letting their kinswoman go, Rebekah's relatives are conceding this marriage to Abraham (or rather to his go-between), just as Ephron the Hittite has conceded to the other Hittites the surrender of his piece of property to their Eastern guest—that is, to Abraham's need for a place to bury his dead out of his sight (Gen. 23:4). The Hittites keep assuring Abraham of his burial rights in the land to which he has come, but Abraham keeps insisting that these be formalized by payment or exchange, and specified in the hearing of witnesses. By having Ephron accept the (probably exorbitant) price that Ephron just happens to have mentioned, ostensibly by way of forgiving it (but likelier by way of putting the purchase quite beyond Abraham's means), Abraham backs the Hittites into giving up the land for good and ever. It is here that the characters and the glossing narrator are brought to a likeness, for Abraham asks the Hittites to make good on their offer by specific means of "the cave of Mach-pe'lah, . . . at the end of [Ephron's] field"; "I give you the field," Ephron finally says to Abraham, but he says it now in a way rather at odds with the previous reluctance of the Hittites to do more than make a vague promise that they will probably resist actually making good on: "and I give you the cave that is in it; in the presence of the sons of my people [i.e., future witnesses] I give it to you" (Gen. 23:11 RSV). Following the even more formal transaction that secures this already official-sounding bestowal of the land on Abraham, the narrator practically attaches a map to the deed or act of deeding, along with a clause specifying mineral and timber rights:

> So the field of Ephron in Mach-pe'lah, which was to the east of Mamre, the field with the cave which was in it, and all the trees that were in the field, throughout its whole area, was made over to Abraham as a possession in the presence of the Hittites, before all who went in at the gate of his city. After this, Abraham buried Sarah his wife in the cave of the field of Mach-pe'lah east of Mamre (that is, Hebron). The field and the cave that is in it were made over to Abraham as a possession for a burying place by the Hittites. (Gen. 23:17–20 RSV)

Through the narrator's glosslike repetitions, substitutions, and specifications, we could say that Abraham got the land in hearing and got it in writing, just as he took possession of it both de jure, by purchase for a consideration, and de facto, by occupation and use.

In Genesis and Exodus a kind of linguistic, etymological, and etiological claim-staking, by way of glosses, attaches to sites that are not otherwise appropriated, that is, that are not conscripted politically or ideologically. A place name may be shown to get its meaningfulness through its connection or contact with a scriptural character, or a place may get is name itself in the same way. The stories attaching to God's old or new name Yahweh (the novelty or antiquity of the name depends upon whether we take the historicist, revolutionary point of view of the story—"E"—or the alternative evolutionary and ethnocentric point of view of the readership—"J") have as their point that God is thusly to be called upon (Gen. 4:26) or remembered (Exod. 13:15)—that is, as Yahweh. The "Elohist" or "E" story in Exodus 3 glosses the name memorably, and intends to enable a memory of the name's innovative or inaugural character for religion and for Israel in the same momentum. God seems, indeed, to discover his own name, and thus in a way to remember it himself. The stories that remember Israel's history are similarly stories that imply the irruption of memory. The reason that remembering always implies forgetting doubtless derives from the very nature of consciousness, which is conscious of some one thing to the exclusion of some other one, and which is therefore conscious and unconscious both alternately and simultaneously, as well as intermittently. Thus the glosses in Scripture fall into a more general motif of text recovery within Scripture, and a more general motif of history recovery, since a history cannot, by our principles of consciousness, be remembered, unless that history is also subject to a forgetting. The prophets, suffering from disregard, wrote their prophecies down in order that their words might be remembered in the latter day, and thereupon be found to agree with what, in the long run, had come to pass. The glosses likewise conserve a connection between a past and a present Israel: thus if the grave of the patriarchs is contemporary Hebron, then the "memorials" of the past are not in disrepair. Therefore the formula for the grave site recurs at the end of Genesis—the patriarchal prefix to the history of Israel—no longer as part of a story of the grave's acquisition, but now as part of Jacob's last will and testament, uttered with his dying breath:

> I am about to be gathered to my people. Bury me with my ancestors, in the cave in the field at Machpelah, facing Mamre, in Canaan, which Abraham bought—the field [which he bought]—from Ephron

> the Hittite as a burial site of his own. There Abraham and his wife Sarah were buried. There Isaac and his wife Rebekah were buried; and there I buried Leah—the field and the cave in it which were bought from the Hittites. (Gen. 49:29–32 NJB, but modified to include the Hebrew phrase "—the field [which he bought]—")

One concludes from this that Jacob, like Abraham, is a careful legalist concerning not so much his funeral arrangements as his inheritance and estate. His strict repetition "remembers Abraham," as God Himself had indeed promised Abraham to do regarding Lot (Gen. 19:29; see God's motivation in blessing Isaac at 26:24, and Isaac's wish for Jacob at 28:4); Jacob's speech understands the tomb as a kind of family registry where one checks in when one checks out. But note again the apparently redundant phrase "the field"; I would suggest that it is a gloss, for it recurs in a repetition of this formula at the actual burial scene of Jacob in the next chapter (Gen. 50:13), where other glosses, specifying the trans-Jordanian location of another mourning site, attest to the glossator's activity in this particular neighborhood of the text.

Now why "the field"? Because the text wants to specify that, although a given patriarch is buried in the cave, reference to what Abraham originally purchases is correct only if it is to a somewhat larger or more visible tract of land than an "out of sight" cave: the tract includes a *surface*, one that can stand for the Promised Land itself. This fact is not, the gloss might insist, to be forgotten, which is to say, it is to be reclaimed or recovered from not being known: it should not be buried, even if the space of the cave itself is necessarily buried space (being a place for the dead, who are to be kept "out of sight"). Again we see how the activity of glossing a particular narrative comports with the internal activities of that narrative, and how the glossing of the text comports with the text's own establishing of its intention to function not only as a story, but as a kind of registry of story, or witness.

The gloss is constitutive, and belongs to a chicken-and-egg circularity that attaches Hebron to Abraham by founding Hebron upon Abraham's remains, but it can do this only by finding Abraham's remains sited upon the future Hebron. Abraham exists because the collectivity Hebron adopts him as its representation or patron saint, even as sojourning Abraham adopts Hebron as his legal resting place and his reliquary, the shrine for his remains. Abraham forsees the future value of Hebron, and so the price, however steep by biblical standards (Meir Sternberg has suggested that one compare the much lower price—fifty shekels versus four hundred—that David pays for the future Jerusalem altar site at 2 Samuel 24:24), is a good deal when viewed from the point of view of the future—that is, when viewed as an investment in that future.

In such a process Abraham is not only constituted as a proto-historical Hebronite, he is also constituted as an adopter. How central adoption is to the character of Abraham appears in his family, which is a tissue of legal relations, for "Abraham," collectively considered, is himself a kind of "registry." Sarah is perhaps Abraham's barren half-sister, adopted as his wife (in this case she is not so unlike his niece Milchah, daughter of his dead brother Haran, and adopted as his brother Nahor's wife); Lot is Abraham's nephew, adopted to be his sharer in the land of promise; Hagar is his wife's bondwoman, adopted to be the bearer of his first child; Eliezar of Damascus is his servant, originally adopted to be his male heir; Ishmael is his son, thereupon adopted (through the rite of circumcision) to receive the legacy of the blessing. Terah is his father, adopted into his household upon the departure from Ur to Haran. The adoptive homeland, as localized in Hebron, adopts the adopter, appropriately enough: for every adoption adopts both parties to it.

Even rather egregiously intrusive glosses, once we have acknowledged this cooperative relation between the glossing of the story elements and the constituting of the narrative, seem to justify themselves, and to do so by explaining what the narrative is—so to speak—about, or rather, *also* about. For example, when Laban sets out to substitute Leah for Rachel in the bride bed of Jacob on the evening of his wedding celebration, the text tells us that Laban gave Leah his slave girl Zilpah for a handmaid. When all is said and done, this is a gloss, one lodged in the middle of the sequence that has Jacob bedding the bride and finding her, come the dawn, to be the bride's sister. "A busy night," the waggish Sternberg comments amusingly in his *Poetics*, but Laban can hardly be providing Leah with her handmaid in the same motion that he is sticking Jacob with an unrecognized Leah, though the point of his action is approximately the same: namely, that Laban takes very good care of his daughters, and provides a husband and a handmaid for each—the older one first—whereas Isaac did not succeed in providing a blessing for both his sons. For the gloss is paralleled by Rachel's being supplied with her handmaid in an identical supplement seven years and a few lines later. Yet this parallelism testifies to the glossator's entry upon the processes of Biblical composition, and even if the first gloss jumps the narrative gun by imposing a list of the dramatis personae on the reader in the midst of the drama itself, the gloss also shows us that the narrative is about how Jacob came to be a polygamous yet endogamous corporation, and how to be engaged to Rachel was to acquire or adopt four wives in the deal. That was what came with Rachel, and it came, so to speak, in the wrong order. Jacob, the usurper upon primogeniture, has jumped the gun in seeking to marry Rachel first, he is told, and thus the glossed narrative has him acquiring everyone in the wrong order: he gets the slave girl before he gets the wife, and he gets the wrong wife before he gets the right one, and he gets her slave girl before he finally beds this right one.

The narrative as now glossed hardly puts this sequence to rights, but it shows us that to get one of the wives is to get them all. This package deal is there to justify, in our terms, the confession of the future brothers that they are twelve sons of one man, if not exactly of one busy night. If you marry one, you marry them all, and thus Israel affirms its unity of national consciousness. The various substitutions of one wife for another, as detailed in the subsequent narrative, insist upon the original interchangeability of the wives by repeating it. "Love me, love my sister"—"and," the glosser preemptively is adding, "also my handmaid, and my sister's handmaid." The gloss saddling the groom with Leah's handmaid even before the story has saddled him with Rachel's older sister—Leah herself—manifests this intratribal condition of interpolated interrelatedness at the textual level. A sister, genetically speaking, is her sister's keeper.

Yet the sons of the wives of Jacob are tribally distinct. For Jacob's tangle of endogamy issues in the eponymous ancestors of the twelve exogamous tribes: marriage in Israel is intratribal, and the tribes do not intermarry. This separation of the tribes is symbolized by the only patriarchal generation of a daughter, namely Dinah. One does not marry one's sister, any more than one marries an outlander or Canaanite, and the brothers thus jealously prevent Dinah's assimilation to the outlander Schechem; therefore the narrative can find for Dinah no husband without incest or rape, in a reversal upon a narrative that could find for Jacob no wife without her handmaid and sister also making their way into the bed, the bargain, and the prose.

As it turns out, then, the glosses have their contribution to make to any biblical poetic that recognizes a proper basis in a poetics of this text's particular and particulate textuality. In focusing on the glosses, we are also focusing our attention on the scrupulosity of a text that annotates itself especially where something we have called a "registration" is wanted: legal and genealogical registration have been important in the examples so far cited. Thus the reasons for telling the story—namely, to preserve it and to establish the continuity of memory over the interpolations of the forgetfulness that obliges us to remember restoratively, repetitively, and intermittently—these reasons are one with the reasons for the glosses.

There is something paradoxical here: sometimes it seems that we are wiping our glosses with something we cannot confidently know, the site or situation of the past. The text is insistently referential and historiographic, and it never throws into prominence, as *Tristram Shandy* does, the fictionality of the text's completeness, reliability, authenticity, and knowability, or the delusionary character of the story's recordability or recoverability. But nonetheless the biblical story is attached to an esoteric revelation and comes from an anonymous narrator who is revealed to the reader only as a glossator.

For example, the garden of Eden is elaborately glossed, one might suppose, precisely because it is not found on any map: the gloss tells us that the site was the source of four rivers, and that these rivers negotiate the space of something like the ancient known world. This gloss functions to bridge the gap between the premise of performative utterance—roughly speaking, let there be utterance, "Let there be a God who says let there be"—and the human situation of situatedness and territoriality and nativeness—"let there be a world to whose anteriority we can recur." It remembers what we can have only on report—where we came from. But nowhere does the text concerning Eden say, "it is said that." The glosses never offer an internal critique of the story's judgments and assertions. As surely as the existent rivers have headwaters, and as surely as a land has a geology, Eden specified a specific, irrigated locale.

But why, we may still wish to ask, does the featuration of Eden's landscape appear in terms of its hydrology? Rivers are, of course, mapmakers, and are a good way of indicating the reality of the territories being mapped. Yet the glossator's use of headwaters to refine upon the territorial specificity implied by Eden's having a name is not just another example of the narrator moving from the abstract to the concrete, as, for example, he moves from light to day, to evening and morning, to the Sabbath and Babylonian Standard Time. One of the rivers "winds all through the land of Cush" (Gen. 2:13 NJB), its meandering implying a geographical survey of the place in question. Thus the glossator has introduced into Eden a feature of the landscape that not only can make Eden landscape, but that recalls us to those lands relevant to an ethnographic intention of the text, namely that of registering lands that are native territories and that promise landedness and boundaries to the peoples.

And what about the other intention of the text, the genealogical intention of registering the lineages that issue in the patriarchal family saga? Is Eden's landscaping by the glossator's rivers and headwaters relevant to that? It should be, for the Bible is a wonderfully totalized text: the genealogies tell the story, as well as the stories telling the genalogies; the text glosses the glosses, as well as the glosses glossing the text. Does, therefore, the glossing of Eden as the headwater of the territories' irrigation have any particular genealogical import?

The answer is to be found in a relation between landedness, water sources, and contracting—or leasing. The use of a land's wells, for example, constitutes a claim upon that land, and in proceeding to the Promised Land the Israelites, when they are obliged to pass through foreign territories, specifically disavow the use of the natives' wells. But Isaac's relations with the "locals" in Canaan entail deals made concerning the use and maintenance of the land's wells, because, while the foreigner may disclaim title to the wells, the guest and sojourner cannot really afford this luxury.

Throughout the patriarchal saga the class of wells within Canaan is subject to either naming glosses or naming stories. When the well is in the East, it is appropriated quite differently; namely, by means of a betrothal proposed or engaged for at the site of the local well, by a suitor from abroad. The story that begins with the irrigation of the earth from Eden goes on to the creation of the man and thence to the promulgation of the first law, and the story that begins from the situating of man in the garden goes on to the creation of the animals from earth-stuff and the creation of the woman from man-stuff, and thence to the first marriage engagement and the breaking of the God-given law. While the biology is genealogically oriented, the law—because the law in question is a law against mixing good and evil in one meal—is ethnographically oriented: it is a Jewish dietary law. Such a law is primally broken, the story implies, even while the story also implies that the marriage contract is universally recognized and honored. But just as the law is broken in a way doubly recognizable to a post-Mosaic audience, so the marriage contract is celebrated in a way that underwrites the dialectic of endogamy and exogamy as we subsequently meet it in Genesis, where it governs the patriarchal marriage saga.

Eden, according to our account, names a place as the headwaters of the territories, and as the former native territory of the primal couple. Thus the extent and commonality of the rivers is reproduced in the exogamy and endogamy of the primal marriage, which is both universal and incestuous, both an estrangement from and conjunction of the man with his own "flesh." This flesh is therefore appropriately glossed; "Therefore does a man leave his father and his mother and cleaves [*sic*] to his wife, and they become one flesh" (Gen. 2:24 RSV). He leaves his flesh before rejoining it, and so he does not know it as his own, that is, as that of his daughter or sister, and therefore the couple is not ashamed of the parties' nakedness before each other as kin. But, on the other hand, neither are they not-kin; for they belong to the same "flesh," as later progenitors of Israel belong to the same tribe, or race, and as the man and the animals do not. The animals are therefore ineligible for the marriage to the man, as the Hittite women were later offensive in the marriage of the Abrahamic Esau.

What the man first said to the woman in the garden—"this is my flesh"—is what Laban will later say to his kinsman Jacob at the well: "you are my flesh" (Gen. 29:14). Equally important has been the discovery in the preceding generation that Rebekah is the flesh of Abraham's brother, at the analogous Eastern well in Nahor-land: the well-betrothal scene has thereafter become part of this tribe's ethnic inheritance.

The reclaiming of these wells by the act of telling and retelling stories about them is of course a story in its own right: this would be the story of the exile in Babylon—exile in territories where the storytellers habituated themselves by discovering or inventing sites associated with a Semitic origin at, and a homecoming to—as well by projecting an emigration from—"Ur of the Chaldeans" (Gen. 11:28). Thus Eden may qualify both as an ideal, paradisal homeland from which the subject has been historically exiled, and a real Eastern locale from which the subject will emigrate.

In the generation immediately before Rebekah's, however, there has been no well of betrothal, unless we are willing to consider the wells of divorce and alimony associated with Hagar. But these are wells in the wilderness, and so wells that must first serve as landmarks and halfway houses, rather than as symbols of the establishing and rejoining of family life. These lonelier sites, I would like to argue, are partly distinguished from Rebekah's and Rachel's wells precisely by their being glossed geographically. A well in the wilderness would have to be named, in such a case, because it would naturally be associated with exile or a sojourning that could not be, in itself, repatriatory (nobody can wholly or exclusively own a desert). Thus the solitary pilgrimage that takes Hagar out of Sarah's reach finds her by a spring in such a desert, namely "the spring on the road to Shur" (Gen. 16:5). But the angel's question "'where have you come from, and where are you going?'" is not wholly answered until the angel's annunciation of Ishmael, who is named on the basis of *God's having heard* Hagar's cry. The attention Hagar has commanded from a just God prompts further naming activity: "Hagar gave a name to Yahweh who had spoken to her, 'You are El Roi,' by which she meant, 'Did I not go on seeing here, after him who sees me?' This is why the well is called the well of Lahai Roi; it is between Kadesh and Bered" (Gen. 16:13–14 NJB).

The story of Hagar's expulsion is renewed and/or repeated, after Sarah has borne Isaac. Essentially Abraham must now sacrifice Ishmael, and on this occasion the father sends Hagar away provisioned with a container of water; it is exhausted after she has wandered off into the desert of Beersheba, but God opens the despairing

Hagar's eyes and she sees a well and gives her son a drink. Thereafter the boy grows up and learns, as Hagar has, to survive—as an archer—in the desert of Paran, and his mother takes him a wife *from Egypt*: that is, from her original territory, as opposed to her mere stock (i.e., the text does not say "from the Egyptians"). Hagar put her son a bowshot away under a bush when she despaired of his life, and Ishmael's profession is one that allows him to close the desert-measure of distance between the desert dweller and his sustenance. After the tribal independence announced in the first story, in the second story the disinheriting of the more adoptive and less Semitic half of Abraham's family issues in its further joining with an ethnic and territorial identity of its own.

The name Beersheba itself has not, so far, been glossed etymologically, as Lahai Roi was, but by way of compensation it is domesticated in the very next story about Abraham. This is a story about Abraham's establishing his right to a well in Beersheba, against the claim of Abimelech: like the cave of Mach-pe'lah, the well is surrendered for a valuable consideration. Furthermore, "this was why the place was called Beersheba: because there the two of them swore an oath" (Gen. 21:31 NJB). Thus the domestication of the wilderness landscape for Hagar in the first story of her pregnancy is displaced from the Hagarenes to the Semites in the appendix to the second story of the well. The same thing happens with the landscape for the sacrifice of Ishmael in the second story of the divine providing, for the landscape is domesticated for the sacrifice of Isaac in terms carried over from the first story of Ishmael: "Then looking up, Abraham saw a ram caught by its horns in a bush. . . . Abraham called this place 'Yahweh provides,' and hence the saying today 'On the mountain Yahweh provides'" (Gen. 22:13–14 NJB). These etiologies have the appearance of glosses, but the glosses themselves form a dialogue, a complex texture of exchanges and substitutions, whereby which of the two sites (Ishmael's Lahai Roi or Isaac's Moriah) is going to get called "God Provides" is in question, precisely because biblical election, or the chosenness and endowment and landedness of peoples, is also in question. Once again the activity of the putative glossator is hand in glove with that of the narrator, which is presumably why the glossator is only putative.

(There are, one should add, notably revisionary glosses in the Bible: they are especially found in prophecy, for example at Isaiah

9:13–16, where the interpolated glossing verse, verse 15, attempts to specify the identity of the "head" and "tail" that Yahweh has cut off from Israel: the verse says they are elder and prophet. It seems likelier that the leaders ["head"] and the followers ["tail"] of verse 16 were once meant. Sometimes prophecy has been fine-tuned after the event to take account of a not wholly anticipated eventuality: see, for example, the specification of the date "within sixty-five years" for the ruin of Ephraim, at Isaiah 7:8. Such specification seems consonant with the actual conditions of prophecy, for we are pretty much told that the prophets wrote down what they had to say because it was being disregarded: in this way the prophecy could be shown to have been correct when, in the latter day, its forecasts should have come to pass. Later prophets had secretaries, and secretaries are professional personnel entrusted with getting straight what others have to say.)[3]

It seems, then, that the glosses on the narrative occur in certain predictable places, where a geographical place comes into territorial question, or where a nomenclatural usage dating from time immemorial can be assigned a plausible origin by being used to

3. For the intra-textual exegesis of prophecy, see Michael Fishbane, *Biblical Interpretation in Ancient Israel*, esp. pp. 465–489, and the same author's essay, "Inner Biblical Exegesis: Type and Strategies of Interpretation in Ancient Israel," in *Midrash and Literature*, ed. Geoffrey H. Hartman and Sanford Budick (New Haven, Conn: Yale University Press, 1986), pp. 19–37. Cf. pp. 22–23 of Fishbane's essay for an analogous example of politicised identifications at Isaiah 29:9–11. In the present piece I am reading the activity of glossing somewhat metaphorically, so that different members of the text are said to gloss each other, and thus to generate the full form of the text, or of a story. An example, one relevant to the revisionary explanation of glossed prophecy, might be the verse oracle that Elijah pronounces in 1 Kings 17:14. Taken alone, the oracle could be read as optimistically promising that a given dry spell would end shortly, before (any household's small) current supplies of meal and oil should run out. But in the surrounding narrative the drought proves to be a long one, perhaps much longer than expected or predicted. Thus the story of Elijah and the nearly destitute widow 'glosses' (or explains or justifies) the oracle as having promised that small or depleted jars would miraculously supply (a very large amount of) meal and oil—that is, to the divinely elected widow. For despite the drought the woman had faithfully consented to share her family's substance with the oracle-giver. She had done as she was told, as God planned for her to do, and she had not been anxious for the morrow. Thus "the jar of meal was not spent nor the jug of oil emptied, just as Yahweh had foretold through Elijah" (1 Kings 17:16).

reinforce or cap the denouement of a particular narrative.[4] We will want to ask if a "dialogue of glosses" similar to the one just observed also pertains to the assigning of Abraham's burial site to Hebron, where we saw the issue was one both of a shrine site ("George Washington slept here") and of the landedness of the immigrant ("the Indian wants the Bronx"—wants it back). As we have seen, landedness is not to be considered without considering displacement along with it, and so we can begin to guess where to look to find a gloss answering to the identification of sojourning Abraham's final resting place. We will expect to find a monument to a point of departure, to a separation of those chosen and patrilineally destined to inherit in the Promised Land from those who are not so chosen. We are scripturally advised to remember Lot's wife for exactly these reasons: because she is unable to extract herself from the destruction of the cities of the plain. Lot's own escape is similarly arrested in Zoar: "'That town over there is near enough to flee to, and is small,'" he pleads: "'Let me flee there—after all it is only a small place—and so survive.' . . . That is why the town is named Zoar" (*mitze'ar*, "a trifling thing": NJB gloss) (Gen. 19:20, 22 NJB). Though we cannot be sure that the etiological explanation for the place name of this city of the plain constitutes a genuinely belated gloss, we can see that a "before" and "after" pertaining to

4. Because the theme of the Old Testament narrative is the claim of a people upon its genealogical, historical, ethnic, and national identity, the nexus of gloss and text turns up in the Bible regularly in the explanation of personal names, of places and place-names, of antiquities, and of (customary) sayings. For an example of this last, sayings, David's alleged hatred for the lame is used to gloss a saying at 2 Samuel 5:8 (or, conversely, the saying is used to gloss the story), in a footnote to the account of the conquest of Jebus/Jerusalem. Even the disabled will be an impediment to David's attack on the city, the Jebusites promise: "'The blind and the lame will hold you off' (That is to say: David will never get in here)." Then we read, "as for the blind and the lame, David hated them with his whole being. (Hence the saying: the blind and the lame may not enter the Temple.)" [2 Samuel 5:6–8, NJB, which supplies the parentheses].) Perhaps this 'tissue of glosses' is quite "dialogic" enough as it stands, but we can hardly help adding that one of the lame sat at King David's very table in Jerusalem: "one of Jonathan's sons," to which the speaker introducing him at 2 Samuel 9:3 adds, "he has crippled feet." Thus we go on to read, "Meribbaal ate at David's table like one of the king's sons . . . Meribbaal lived in Jerusalem, since he always ate at the king's table. He was crippled in both feet" (2 Sam. 9:12–13, NJB). Does the "gloss" on the saying of 2 Samuel 5:8 know the "gloss-like" identifications of Meribbaal made by both the speaker and the narrator in 2 Samuel 9?

this particular landscape has prompted glossing activity elsewhere, since the landscape itself seems to have disappeared under the Dead Sea and since Zoar's antiquity has provided it with the earlier name Bela ("consumption"; see Gen. 14:2-3 for this tradition).

Lot dare not stay in such a marginal place long, but retreats to a cave in the hills where his daughters get him drunk and father on him Moab and Ben-Ammi: Moab "is the ancestor of the Moabites of our own times," and Ben-Ammi "is the ancestor of the Bene-Ammon of our own times" (Gen. 19:37-38 NJB). The daughters sleep in a cave with their father, like the patriarchal family they are, but ordinarily you do not sleep with your father until you are both dead. These sisters have been their father's genetic keeper, but Lot's cave—unlike Hebron—is not exactly found on the register of historical places, nor are the concerned personages enrolled in the family Bible, unlike the patriarchs interred at Hebron. Rather, the offspring of the incest of Lot's daughters are contemporized by the gloss: they are people "of our own times"—they sure got here fast, one is tempted to say. The apparently historical note really observes the lack of a true history or chronology, and that is not at all beside the point. The question we will want to ask is: what does the activity of the glosser have to do with the incestuous activity of the internal agents? In the dialogue of glosses, the gloss speaks to the listing of the genealogical contents of the cave of Mach-pel'ah. But there is no such listing in Lot's case because, in the "allegory" of the gloss, the point is that the Moabites and the Ammonites have to be told who their father is. Their names can never tell them anything but the tautologous relation and collapsed genealogy of incest and self-fathering, since *me'ab* means "from (my) father," and *ben'amni* means "son of my kinsman." The *tribe* is their father, the name of their eponymous ancestor. The etymologies of their names are parodies of the name Abraham ("father of many"), and their genealogy is a short-circuiting of the genealogies of those people who call Abraham their father.

Thus Lot has escaped from Sodom and the sterility that overtakes his wife, but not from tautologous sexual relations, and his subsequent offspring cannot know who they are patrilineally, but only tribally and generically. But that is exactly the case where the incest taboo does not obtain; genealogy, lineage, and story—the Hebrew word is the same for all three—all break down and come to an end. Lot may not die in his cave, but he is not heard of again, and the implication is that the sons of Ammon—"the Bene-Ammon of our own times"—do not know their father Lot precisely because he unwittingly knew his daughters in the biblical sense, as he formerly offered his daughters to be known, in the same sense, by the Sodomites. If the Sodomites in the plain were a bunch of abusive city homosexuals and rapists who preyed on strangers, the Ammonites are a bunch of drunken, incestuous, cave-dwelling hillbillies who can't tell the difference between family members. Thanks to the intervention of Abraham, Lot is delivered out of the threat of assimilation and deracination in the cities; but only in the second marriage of Ruth, the Moabite ancestress of David, will some part of Moab be delivered out of the lack of a genealogy—a protodynastic sequence that connects the past to the present historically and patrilineally and so builds up the house of Israel.

The naturally annotative style of the Bible precludes any strong distinction of the glosses from the discourse: "the well was used for watering the flocks" (Gen. 29:2)—gloss or narrative? "Thus did Esau despise his birthright" (Gen. 25:34)—gloss or narrative? "In those days there was no king in Israel; every man did what was right in his own eyes" (Judges 21:25)—gloss or narrative?

Anyone who has studied traditional verse, let us say Middle English popular poetry, has learned to recognize little pieces of the diction that mainly supply the composition with "metrical putty." We could define many of our glosses in an almost opposite way. They are not metrical putty intended to fill out a line of verse with the prescribed number of metrical units, but rather bits of prose that almost do the opposite: they prevent metricality, and theefore create prose, by pushing the lines of discourse out to the edge of the page, and by preventing the discourse from falling into the rhythm of parallelism that seems endemic to traditional storytelling. The glosses deviate into senses a little beyond the progression set up by the story, and interrupt the rhythm of repetition in favor of a rhythm of association (in terms taken from Frye's *Anatomy of Criticism*), and so create a progressive recognition—of subject matter, continuously accessioning new subject matter. To a greater or lesser extent this happens in all discourse whatsoever, but clearly the annotative style favors the rhythm of association, which tends to justify what is being said not by repeating the sound and varying the sense, or varying the sound and repeating the sense—these are the means of poetry—but by adding to the sense and supplementing it contextually, and dissociating the sense from the sound, phonologically considered, and associating the sense with secondary content.

Contrary to Molière's Monsieur Jourdain, we do not speak prose on a daily basis, any more than we speak verse. Yet anyone who has heard himself lecturing from memory or notes will notice that he or she relies on a certain kind of "putty," crutches that are neither prose nor verse, but that belong to both rhythm and thought: phrases like "well, now," "so to speak," "that is to say," "it occurs to me," "as if," "something like," "kind of," "sort of," "furthermore," "hopefully," "what I mean is," "this is related to," "given what I've said," "this brings us to." We take these things out of our students' prose, but they are essential to the back-and-fill of discoursing aloud on one's feet, and I am suggesting that putting something analogous in—to effect an annotative modification of what is being said by means of nascent glosses or parentheses—is equally essential to the composition of prose.

Thus the glosses belong to the poetics of a biblical prose in a particularly telling way, because they belong to its invention and development. They are virtually a means to prose, as a continuously self-annotating discourse like that of Burton's *Anatomy of Melancholy* shows. Printers setting prose type bring the lines over to the far margin by means of spacers, which is called justifying the line; far from marginalizing the glosses, the writing of prose glosses to the margins. As metrical putty justifies the line of verse, so glosses seem to me to justify the line of prose: if glosses are the spacers of prose, then they are prosaic in a deeper sense than initially supposed.

By these lights, verse is a form of singing, and prose is a form of editing: in the case of the Hebrew, editing includes punctuation, vowel points, capitals, and glosses. Notice again the "Dick and Jane" books. They were teaching not only reading, but also a very odd form of rendering discourse telegraphically: "SEE SPOT RUN STOP." "S.O.S." This stripped language, somewhat like that of the then current Tarzan movies, is initially deprived of the spacers and justifiers of running discourse: "Hey, look at Spot doin' his thing—runnin', I mean." This last sequence is neither prose nor verse, but it is much more recognizably and authentically self-contextualizing discourse than "See Spot run." The initial "Hey" is for signaling and initiating communication (like the "Lo" stuck in at the beginning of *Beowulf*); another such phrase, roughly speaking our "lo and behold," belongs to Hebrew narrative discourse, and it naturally makes its way into the bed in the example we have considered: "And behold! it was Leah."

The biblical glosses that begin "This is why" seem to me to belong to the mind of the narrative, the mind of the prose, and the mind of the Old Testament—all three—because of what has been called the Jewish predilection for justified law (the subtitle for David Weiss Halivni's *Midrash, Mishna and Gemara*),[5] and because of what can be called the Hebrew writers' penchant for etiology. This is to say that the "glosses" have, in a sense, caused the "text," rather than the other way round. I can think of two good examples of biblical texts where the narrative cannot be well understood without an analysis that takes such a reversal upon an etiological understanding into account. Yet they are radically different examples, if only because the second is from the New Testament.

The first example, from the Old Testament, is that of Jacob wrestling with the angel, where the narrative concludes that Jacob left the arena limping and that is why the Israelites to this day do not eat the tendon attaching to an animal's hipbone. This anthropological note sounds like one made by a good ethnographer, but whether the story is told to enforce a dietary taboo—"step on a crack and break your mother's back"—or is annotated to explain one, the inclusion of the custom proves essential to our knowledge of Jacob's identity, and not extraneous to it: for Jacob is a twin, and yet a twin who limps—which is to say, that much less a twin. Thus in this story he is renamed Israel. The individualizing of ethnic identity, and the privileging of this ethnic identity over the patrilineal identity of Jacob's rival Esau-Edom, is accomplished precisely in the observance of unique dietary customs. Jacob's sticks his diselect relatives (Esau in comparison to Jacob himself, and Isaac in comparison to Rebekah) with diselect eating habits, and recruits his house's wealth from the marked sheep and goats of the rival relative's flock. God has hired the handicapped, and thus his prophets predict that he will save the lame and gather the outcast (Zeph. 3:19), and gather those that halt into Zion, the tower

5. David Weiss Halivni, *Midrash, Mishna and Gemara: The Jewish Predilection for Justified Law* (Cambridge, Mass.: Harvard University Press, 1986). See esp. pp. 13–14, 16.

of his flock (Micah 4:6–8). Thus Jacob's handicap in the story is turned to Israel's advantage in the gloss.

A second example of a glosslike sentence occurs in the middle of the ninth chapter of John, which is the narrative of Jesus' healing and then his converting of the man born blind. The story "breaks" very much according to this two-part description, for at the beginning the man does not know very much about Jesus, "the sent one," and at the end he is virtually a pre-Christian Christian: he is a man who has seen and believed—really the only believer that the miracle yields, and so initiated into a kind of esoteric Christian gnosis. At the middle of the story the Pharisees and the Jews have questioned first the man and then his parents about his cure, and his parents have referred the questioners back to their son: "'Ask him. He is old enough: let him speak for himself.'" Here the text adds, by way of explanation; "His parents spoke like this out of fear of the Jews, who had already agreed to ban from the synagogue anyone who should acknowledge Jesus as the Christ. This was why his parents said, 'He is old enough; ask him'" (John 9:22–23 NJB). The intratextual glosses in the Old Testament seem to work to recover, conserve, and appropriate received traditions. In the New Testament such glosses seem to work to mark the point at which the Gospel or the "new tradition" began, which is to say, where there has been a break with the former tradition. In what follows I propose to examine this narration in some detail, in hopes of getting a more exact sense of both this difference and this exception-taking quality as found in one particular gloss and its placement.

The Rev. Mark Olsen, a graduate student currently at my university, has pointed out to me that the "anachronistic" gloss—as John's reference to the quarrels in the first-century synagogues may be alleged to be—exhibits not only a contemporizing intention and explanation, but also a certain keystone position in this narrative. Its centrality appears in the chiasmic symmetricality in the frame for the passage:

"'Ask Him. He is old enough:' . . . 'He is old enough; ask him.'"
{--------[{--------------[{{. . .}}]---------------}]--------}

The core passage—indicated here by "(. . .)"—then explains that the parents did not want to incriminate themselves with the synagogue authorities by acknowledging Jesus as the Christ: that is, by confessing the Christian kerygma, the confession that Jesus is "the sent one," or the Messiah, or the Lord, or the Light. The gloss seems to speak to the exclusion of the Jewish disciples of Jesus from synagogues after the death and "messiah-fication" of Jesus, but of course such ostracized disciples were also among the authors of the New Testament; thus it is less important to think of these Christians as having read their current situation into the story of the man born blind and his parents, than to think of their situation as itself generating the man born blind—and as generating his parents' resistance to confessing the blind man's redeemer. The subject of the story in John 9, the blind man, reaches his spiritual majority with a kind of excommunication from his own past context: his alienated neighbors, clergy, temple, people, and family.

For the story as a whole is arranged symmetrically around the gloss, as Reverend Olsen suggests. The story is composed of a series of concentric askings and identifications. The parents in the story have never seen Jesus: they do not know who opened their son's eyes or (at the least) they're not telling. The former blind man also says he does not know something: that is, he does not know Jesus' whereabouts and cannot tell his neighbors. Furthermore, his neighbors do not know whether he is the former blind man, or a man who looks just like him. The disciples also do not know something—the source of the evil of the man's blindness: Who sinned, they want to know, this man or his parents? Jesus answers that neither party is guilty, but that one must carry out one's work as long as one is in the world, and adds that he himself must do so while he is himself the light of that world (i.e., in it).

The neighbors have offered the curious idea that the blind man might have a "sighted" double abroad in the world, somebody who looks just like the blind man but can see. Jesus himself might be indicted for a similar fraud, for Thomas the Twin was absent when Jesus returned from the dead to give his testimony that he had overcome the world. It is this same Jesus who will be made to praise that faith which is the substance of things unseen: "Jesus said to [Thomas], 'You believe because you can see me. Blessed are those who have not seen and yet believe'" (John 20:20 NJB). This narrative of Jesus' postmortem confrontation with Thomas the Twin gives the lie to any assertion that Jesus has been replaced by a look-alike substitute, even while it commends subsequent reliance on hearsay originating from the Apostles—secondhand testimony about Jesus.

A somewhat similar conclusion to this story of a doubtful double is attached to our story of the Blind Beggar: guilty are those who have heard and yet will not see and witness. For in our story the neighbors now bring the former beggar before the Pharisees, who ask him how his cure was done. Such a cure would convict Jesus of Sabbath breaking, and a Sabbath breaker cannot be from God. Nonetheless, the Jews are divided by doubt, and the blind man is prompted to opine that the man who opened his eyes is a prophet. The prophet Elisha did cures, of course, but the prophet Isaiah heard God telling him to deafen and blind his audiences (Isa. 6:9-10, 29:9-14) in a remarkable apperception of the efficacy of the prophet's word even when the word was not being received. Jesus may be becoming a prophet, at least in this latter-day sense of a prophet as a hardener of unheedful or unhearkening hearts. (See Gerhard von Rad, *Old Testament Theology*).[6]

The Pharisees now check the story with the man's parents: Is the man telling the story really the same one who was born blind? The parents do indeed acknowledge that the man in question is their son, but they do not know how the witness or storyteller sees, or who has opened his eyes. Then comes the supplemental remark about their fear of being banned from the synagogue if they should make some further acknowledgment of Jesus' identity: the Jews should ask their son, his parents now say. We already know that Jews will not hear, and thus we sense that they are on the way to being *unable* to hear as well.

In "part 2" of this story the Jews send for the man born blind "for the second time," and tell him to confess to some mendacity or error or other, since they are convinced that Jesus is a sinner. Again the man has to answer that he doesn't know about this, all he knows is that he can see. How did Jesus do it? the Jews ask, and the man born blind asks back why they want to hear it all again: "'Do you want to become his disciples yourselves?'" For to hear the man's story *repeated*—to seek to hear it repeated—is to be evangelized, and the Jews are, inadvertently, turning the former blind man into their reluctant evangelist: a missionary, or "sent one." Thus the Jews now insist that it is rather the former blind man who is the disciple of Jesus, while they themselves are the disciples of Moses: "'as for this man [Jesus], we

6. Gerhard von Rad, *Old Testament Theology: Volume II, The Theology of Israel's Prophetic Traditions*, trans. D. M. G. Stalker (New York and Evanston: Harper & Row, 1965), pp. 87-96, with pp. 152-55.

don't know where he comes from.'" We hear an echo from the inauguration of John's Gospel, "'Can anything good come out of Nazareth?'" (John 1:46; Nathanael's response to the protoconvert Philip, who claims that Jesus is the one that Moses wrote about in the Law—e.g., the Mosaic prophet of Deut. 18:15-19—"as the Prophets did also"). The Jews lack, so to speak, the circumstantial nativity story for Jesus that they have for Moses, and the Gospel of John itself also lacks this nativity story. However, in that story's place John has the metaphysical generation of Jesus, the story that he derives from God's Word: John's Jesus is begotten, as it were, in one's hearing about him, as Nathanael hears about him from Philip in John's first chapter.

The former blind man says that the Pharisees' incomprehension is amazing: to be able to do what Jesus has done, the doer in question must be one from God. The narrative has now put the blind man in the position of those who in the future will acknowledge Jesus as the Christ in the synagogue, and the Jews summarily and preemptively eject the man as a born sinner—eject him from their company, we must assume, but also from their conversation or sect. The Jews are becoming the Jews, and the Christians the Christians, that is, each is becoming the alienated essence of the other. The story is anachronistic, in that the protowitness is being scapegoated for a Christian identity he cannot yet quite have, but it is an identity that he is in the process of acquiring by becoming the object of untoward attention because of his remarkable difference from his erstwhile community. For in being asked to glorify the giver of his gift of sight—"Give God the praise"—the blind man is being led to make his difference concerning the sight-giver public, and a matter of record. Is it blindness that is being cured, or tongue-tiedness?

Jesus himself, taking a kind of proprietary interest in this future Christian, now finds the ex-communicated man out and asks him if he believes in the Son of Man. The man asks who this Son of Man might be, so that he might believe in him, and Jesus says the former blind man has seen the Son of Man and that he is speaking to him presently. The man now calls Jesus "Lord" and confesses his belief in him worshipfully. Jesus then declares that he has come into the world "so that those without sight may see and those with sight may become blind" (John 9:39 NJB), and tells the Pharisees who are present that it is not their blindness itself that makes them guilty, but rather their presumption that they can see in spite of it. Here we might suppose that the man's parents were not guilty for their son's blindness, but that that they have subsequently become guilty for their own. The Jews, so to speak, are "parents" who are not acknowledging their "son" Jesus as the sign of God's power that he manifestly is. The "son" must do what the "parents" will not do, and is thus brought to speak on his own behalf. That is what eventually happens, because Jesus himself now presumes to speak to the man on Jesus' own behalf. Jesus' self-spokesmanship seems to me to be critical in the tale: it is a model for the initiative that the Christian must take as a proselyte who is to become a proselytizer.

The usual idea is that the propositional structure of the kerygma that "Jesus is the Christ" may be mapped onto the narrative structure of "Jesus is risen." Jesus is the Christ by virtue of the resurrection of faith in Jesus that took place in his followers after his death. I don't disagree with this at all, though it is a curious faith, in view of the more quizzical historical original at the grave site: "Jesus is not here"—Jesus is missing, Jesus is stolen away. The Easter faith nonetheless does seem to me to demand some sort of precedent of the kind depicted in the story of the man born blind, a demand made by the historical Jesus as it was made by the prophets before him, a demand that what was being rejected should nonetheless be acknowledged, remembered, or witnessed: "for"—as the "gloss" says—"the Jews had *already* agreed that if any one should confess [Jesus] . . . , he was to be put out of the Synagogue." The adverb "already" anticipates the objection that the gloss is, narratologically and historiographically speaking, an anachronism; the word also betrays an anxiety that it does not make sense for the Jews to have "already" organized an opposition to the novel idea of a "Christian confession." The Jews know too much about the kerygma for it to have the novelty of the kerygma.

Yet the story insists that, from the outset of his ministry, Jesus polarized a reaction that compelled those who were for him to commit themselves to a confession of some sort, one that precipitated them into becoming his interpreters, explainers, and glossers. The return of Jesus to the man born blind is, so to speak, the first second coming, and thus Jesus comes to the man, the way we have said significance does: belatedly, when it comes to be registered as having been implicit in what has preceded it. The healing miracle of the story is thus displaced to the giving of sight to the company receiving the miracle, since the blind man thinks that it is a miracle that the Jews *don't* believe: after all, nobody has heard of the curing of congenital blindness since the beginning of the world.

In general, the Johannine Jesus is revealed as the revealer (as Bultmann says in his *Theology of the New Testament*),[7] and what Jesus reveals, tautologically, is that he is the revealer. Thus Jesus does not reveal the world to the blind man; rather, he reveals to the man that he, Jesus, is the revealer of the world, or rather, the revealer of a *new* world. For the world Jesus reveals is a different and changed world, a world with Jesus—the Revealer—in it: Jesus-in-the-world is now the principal thing to be seen there, the thing that was formerly not seen. Thus Jesus cures the man's congenital blindness on the model of the primal *fiat lux*, when God alleviated the original darkness on the face of the deep, in an act of mercy towards non-entity. This act likewise "revealed the revealer": that is, it revealed God to be the Creator and Revealer of a new heaven and a new earth.

Even my retelling of this tale suggests how symmetrical its pattern is, with a pair of callings of the man to account being placed on either side of the centralized examination of the man's parents. The duplicated Greek phrasings of the story halves make the overall symmetries—centering on the catechizing of the parents—even easier to see. Perhaps the single most important theme of the Bible is accountability; the gloss puts us at the heart of the New Testament version of such a theme, the demand for an account of one's encounter with the Christ. This is an encounter that the parents have only experienced secondhand, and that can *only* be experienced, at first, "secondhand," if the promulgation of the Gospel itself has any point at all: Paul was, so to speak, the first second Peter. First the neighbors quiz the man, then the Pharisees do so; the parents are presently queried; then the man is quizzed by the Jews, and finally he is catechized by Jesus himself—Jesus, the enlightener of the world who makes the self-enlightened blind while he illuminates the ignorant and benighted. The situation alluded to in the "gloss"—that of crypto-Christians in the synagogue seeing or

7. Rudolf Bultmann, *Theology of the New Testament*, trans. Kendrick Grabel (New York: Charles Scribner's Sons, 1951, 1955), sec. 48.2 and 3, in vol. 2, pp. 61–69.

not seeing their way to a deeply self-redefining and potentially self-compromising acknowledgment of the Christ and his works in them, and thus seeing or not seeing their way right out of the synagogue—has created the ring structure that radiates out from the balked confession, and that enables us to reread the initial miracle, that the man can see, as the renewed miracle showing the man the Christ that can make one see. The concentric structure of the text well illustrates that the "testimony" provided by Jesus' works—works that are doubles for his words about himself—therefore "is identical with that which is to be substantiated" (Bultmann, ibid.):[8] the man can truly testify that Jesus has made him see only if he can "see"—or attest to—the power of Jesus.

The poetic miracle of the re-creation of the blind man's eyes by a healer becomes the prosaic miracle of the re-creation of a confused man's beliefs about what there is to see in Jesus. Thus the prosiest bit of the story—what the fearful *parents* had as a reason for not witnessing to Jesus (the "this was because of")—has uncovered the story's whole second impetus, toward the figurative and hermeneutic. The storyteller's signature (that is, the signature of the community preserving the story) is found in the very parents who are authored into the story precisely in order to balk at the leap of faith and the act of witness required to cross the gap that the story opens between the externalized and interiorized kinds of seeing. Somebody in that temple had to see as the parents refused to, had to speak as "witnesses," in order for the story to be told: somebody had to have resisted the parents' refusal to tell such a tale, in order to overcome the obstacle to the blind man's "good news" being got out or about.

Thus the man who had been made to see is revisited by Jesus himself, in order to prompt him to say what his parents have not been able to say, that he has witnessed nothing less than the power of God. Only this second coming of Jesus to the man can realize or actualize the first one, and it is this posterior actualization of Jesus as Christ that the parents refuse to either sponsor or cooperate in. Not only has the tale been written to explain what presents itself as an explanatory gloss on the tale, but the tale has also been written so as to make this originative gloss appear to be merely an explana-

8. Bultmann, *Theology*, edn. and trans. cit., vol. 2, p. 66.

tory, self-bracketing aside, and thus neither terminal nor germinal. But the appearance is deceiving: from the point in the story where the parents refuse to become accessory to the Christian confession, the story's midpoint, the tail has begun to wag the dog.

The story not only re-creates an esoteric, spiritualized *fiat lux*, but also an Adamic origination or realization. In the mud daubed on the blind man's eyes, the man's visual organs are remade according to a Genesis original for the creation of man (Gen. 2:7). But given the Gospel context, one can go further and say that the man's eyes are, as it were, resurrected from the dead. It is the claim that Jesus resurrected Lazarus from the dead that mobilizes the chief priests toward his execution (John 11:53). Thus the Gospel goes on to say, after the culminating sign of the raising of Lazarus:

> Though he had done so many signs before them, yet they did not believe in him; it was that the word spoken by the prophet Isaiah might be fulfilled:
>
> "Lord, who has believed our report,
> and to whom has the arm of the Lord been revealed?"
>
> Therefore they could not believe. For Isaiah again said,
>
> "He has blinded their eyes and hardened their heart,
> lest they should see with their eyes and perceive with their heart,
> and turn for me to heal them." (John 12:37–40 RSV)

But what would it have been like if the parents in the synagogue had, in fact, begun to offer witness like that finally offered by their son? That is, if the congregation had not hardened its heart? It would have been something of a miracle, in the New Testament sense of a messianic sign to Israel. But there can be no sign without an interpreter, and the only interpreters around in John 9 are Jesus and the man born blind himself. The revelation contained in the sign is therefore necessarily secret. The Messianic healer of blindness is revealed as the revealer only to the reader, and not to Israel.

In the Gospel of Matthew the nativity of the new king is a somewhat similar secret, for the magi are divinely counseled not to share it. In Luke, however, Jesus' nativity is not only a sign, but also a kind of public event. The result is more ecumenical and the sign therefore calls into existence a remarkable number of interpreters: a whole community of inspired persons like the Old Testament Hannah. Their activity, somewhat unlikely as a matter of straight history, can nonetheless be glossed historically, by referring it to the Church office of "interpreter," as that office appears in 1 Corinthians 14:26–33. A rather different example of this office is offered by Jesus himself, at the other end of Luke, on the road to Emmaus: "And beginning with Moses and all the prophets, he interpreted to them in all the scriptures the things concerning himself" (Luke 24:27 RSV).

The end of Luke's Gospel, however, is really only the middle of the Lukan oeuvre as a whole: "part 2" is the book of Acts. Thus the end of Luke and the beginning of Acts frame what emerges as a kind of narrational "intertestamental interval," like the one mediated by Matthew's magi—in this case, the interval between the silencing of the Jewish prophet (cf. Luke 22:64) and the announcing of the Christian community. The activity of Luke's postmortem and self-interpreting Jesus mediates this intertestamental space, with which we have also been identifying the narrator's humble parenthesis in John 9. Thus Jesus' mid-Lukan exposition of scripture can signal a turn toward the scripture-searching origins of the New Testament, even while directly anticipating the Pentecostal community at the opening of the book of Acts, where the outburst of prophetic and interpretive activity originally surrounding the birth of Jesus, at the beginning of Luke's Gospel, bursts out again, after the day when Jesus was taken up. Such a reborn community has received the gift of tongues, which is to say, the gift of glosses.

2

On the Sociology of Medieval Manuscript Annotation

Stephen G. Nichols

Imperial splendor and annotation seem strange bedfellows. And yet when Gibbon speaks of the fateful transfer of Roman law to the person of the emperor as one of the most striking—for him, aberrant—manifestations of imperial power, annotation is the mark of that power. A creation of post-Augustan Rome, *annotatio* designated a ruling, grant, or privilege by the emperor written in his own hand in purple ink ("a compound of vermilion and cinnabar," says Gibbon) and conveyed in rescripts. Rescripts were "replies to the consultations of the magistrates," direct appeals to the emperor for judgment that bypassed offical deliberative processes. The rescripts with their purple autograph decrees were "transmitted to the provinces as general or special laws which the magistrates were bound to execute and the people to obey."[1]

Gibbon deplored the embodiment of legislative power in the person of the emperor represented by rescript and annotation. "The pleasure of the emperor has the vigour and effect of law, since the Roman people, by the royal law, have transferred to their prince the full extent of their own power and sovreignty" (quoted by

1. Edward Gibbon. *The History of the Decline and Fall of the Roman Empire.* A New Edition with Notes by Dean Milman, M. Guizot, and Sir William Smith. 8 volumes. (London: John Murray, 1903), 5, p. 271.

Gibbon, 5:270). "The will of a single man, of a child perhaps," complains Gibbon, "was allowed to prevail over the wisdom of ages and the inclinations of millions, and the degenerate Greeks were proud to declare that in his hands alone the arbitrary exercise of legislation could be safely deposited" (5:270).

Over several centuries, rescripts and annotations multiplied to the point where compilations of these rulings were required. In 438 Theodosius II ordered a compilation of the laws and decrees issued since 313, in the reign of Constantine. The Theodosian Code arranged these rulings in sixteen books. This code survives today, the principal source of our knowledge of rescript and annotation. Representing the voice and the hand—writing and orality—"divine annotation" and "sacred imperial oracle" convey the imperial will: "by the authority of a sacred imperial oracle or through the sacred annotations of Our Divinity."[2]

In the first of Constantine's edicts preserved in the Theodosian Code, dating from 314, Constantine specified the relationship of rescript and annotation as symbols of the emperor's own person in imperial courts:

> 1.2.1. Emperor Constantine Augustus to Julius Antiochus, Prefect of the City Guard. It is Our pleasure that Our annotations shall not be admitted without a rescript. Therefore the office of Your Gravity shall observe, just as has always been observed, that you shall consider that Our rescripts and letters shall be heard [in court], rather than Our annotations alone.

The rescripts and annotations did not simply address matters of state. The Code offers a privileged picture of the cultural construction of life under the empire and the emperor's role in confirming social attitudes. The emperors Gratian, Valentinian, and Theodosius Augustus, for example, pronounced firmly against precipitate remarriages by newly widowed women:

> 3.8.1. If any woman who has lost her husband should hasten to marry another man within the period of a year (for We add a small amount of time to be observed after the ten months period, although We consider even that to be very little) she shall be branded with the

2. *The Theodosian Code and Novels and the Sirmondian Constitutions.* Translated by Clyde Pharr. (Princeton: Princeton University Press, 1952), 11.21.3 (p. 314).

> marks of disgrace and deprived of both the dignity and rights of a person of honorable and noble status. She shall also forfeit all the property which she has obtained from the estate of her former husband, either by the right of betrothal gifts or by the will of her deceased husband. She shall know also that she shall expect no help from Us through either a special grant or imperial favor or an annotation.

Perhaps the example that comes closest to illustrating Gibbon's view of annotation and rescript as the exercise of capricious tyranny occurs in an edict promulgated by two emperors successively in 414 and 415:

> 15.7.13 Emperors Honorius and Theodosius Augustuses to the Most Noble Diogenianus, Tribune of Amusements.
>
> We decree that actresses of mimes who have been freed from their bonds by divine imperial annotations shall, with the greatest insistence, be recalled to their compulsory public services, so that the usual display cannot be absent from public amusements and on festal days.

The decrees regulating procurers suggest a chilling view of the risk of women without the protection of powerful husbands or families, and shed light as well on the deemphasis of celibacy among late imperial clergy. The fate of at least some religious women and the imperial edict disposing of their case strike the modern reader as grotesque, although some sort of rough palliation of their violation seems intended:

> 15.8.1 Emperor Constantius Augustus to Severus, Prefect of the City. If any man should wish to subject to wantonness the women who are known to have dedicated themselves to the veneration of the holy Christian law and if he should provide that such women should be sold to brothels and compelled to perform the vile service of prostituted virtue, no other person shall have the right to buy such women except either those who are known to be ecclesiastics or those who are shown to be Christian men, upon the payment of the proper price.

The annotated rescript became both sign and icon of the imperial wisdom resolving a knotty legal problem that had been referred to the emperor by one of his magistrates for resolution. In these decrees, *annotatio* was both *personificatio* and *translatio* of imperial power into a document that would be conveyed from the court, to represent the emperor's person, his imperial dignity. Annotation thereby became, like the saint's relic, an artifact imbued with the power of an absent presence: in short, metalepsis, in the sense of substituting an indirect expression for a direct one. In making a preceding thing understood by a *translatio* of it—the emperor's physical presence by his autograph—the annotation turns out not simply to be a trope, yet another rhetorical figure, but a note, a gloss on the emperor's presence. Like the sandals of Empedocles—the footnote by which Empedocles' self-immolation in the crater of Mount Etna was revealed and which, in a modern annotation, served as a titie for an excellent book by Claude Edmonde Magny some years ago—the annotation suspends the emperor's body, his physical being, in a tension of potential representation.

The annotation is a decorporealization, a substitution for the body, that yet remains, like the sandals of Empedocles, as a reminder of the body's presence in the text, at least in its rhetoric. This association of rhetoric with corporeality may be what Aristotle had in mind when, so it is said, he called Empedocles the father of rhetoric. In this sense, the annotated rescript is also a compressed *apostrophe*, the voice of the body. The emperor's signature and comments on the rescript make it a form of direct address to an absent official communicating moral and legal reflections. Finally, *annotatio* implies intertextuality in both a discrete and a more global sense: discrete in the incorporation of a subtext—the imperial magistrate's request for imperial guidance; global in that the very terms "rescript," "*annotatio*," and so on evoke a bureaucracy predicated upon rhetoric and letters as a foundation for the vast political edifice that was the Roman empire.

What we need to retain from this reverie on the late imperial use of annotation is the understanding that the practice originated in the very centers of power, that it had judicial consequences, was philosophically pragmatic, and intervened in all aspects of social and political life. Annotation was a cultural construction that may be studied as a sociology of imperial legislative practices. The attributes that marked this activity as a product of Roman rhetoric—*translatio*, apostrophe, *personificatio*—are all categories of what medieval arts of rhetoric call "amplification," *amplificatio*, the intervention and enlarging upon a prior subject. Medieval annotation did not forget its cultural roots in the late Roman empire, even when the emperor's hand became a footnote to history.

Annotation and the Medieval Manuscript Culture

Annotation was central to the forms of cultural expression that have come down to us from the Middle Ages. Yet in modern times annotation has been undervalued and insufficiently appreciated as a problematic that can help us to recognize the symbolic role of graphics in a manuscript culture. By raising the question of annotation, we place the study of medieval literature in its medieval context as a cultural artifact. We also insert the study of medieval symbolic expression into its preprint cultural materiality, often obscured by the preconceptions underlying critical editions of medieval works. This is precisely the problematic that Walter Benjamin evokes in *The Work of Art in the Age of Mechanical Reproduction*, and to some extent in his essay "The Sociology of Language."[3]

The focus on annotation—I will be more precise about my use of the term shortly—allows us to study the literary work itself within the context of the manuscript matrix, that is, the medieval mode of production. Our study of medieval literature will thus also encompass artistic and intellectual forms of expression that necessarily accompanied literature in a manuscript culture. Literature was not simply discourse, it also implicated the body and a whole sociological infrastructure of production: the scribe in the scriptorium, the rubricator, and artists specializing in decorated initials and miniatures. Beyond that—and also beyond the purview of my paper—there were, at different ends of the social spectrum, the socioeconomic elements implicated in the production of materials—paper, parchment, inks, colors—and patronage.

By the simple act of focusing on annotation—that is, on aspects of the medieval work extrinsic to the narrative itself—we resituate the work in a context not of text but of artifact production. Anno-

3. Walter Benjamin. "The Work of Art in the Age of Mechanical Reproduction." *Illuminations* (London: Fontana/Collins, 1979): 219–53. "Problème de Sociologie du langage." *Essais* 2: 1935–40 (Paris: Denoël/Gonthier, 1983): 5–36.

tation, whether of the "formal" kind that clearly constitutes part of the manuscript production, exemplified by rubrics and illuminations, or of the informal kind found added on the margins of manuscripts and the *bas de page* that J. J. Alexander and Michael Camile have studied so effectively, reveal that the medieval work was always a multiphase product. Literary vernacular works, the subject of my study, were divided between what Emmanuèle Baumgartner has called the textual space and the manuscript space.[4] Such a designation calls attention to the fact that the space of annotation and the textual space of the literary work, however coextensive they may appear as we look at a manuscript, are culturally and historically composite.

One need only compare a manuscript to a critical edition to discover how radically ahistorical and fundamentally logocentric the latter is by its insistence on rendering the medieval artifact as primarily a phenomenon of narrative. This denies the fact that there was no one version of a medieval work, no "ideal" text, and no such thing as a "pure" text, a text reduced to its verbal essence. For the medieval work, within the manuscript matrix, reveals a series of creative tensions between what we may call the nuclear work, composed at some prior point in time by one individual possessing a specific aesthetic, philosophical, linguistic, and historical point of view, and the "extended work," the text with all its extradiegetical, illustrated, interpolated, and abbreviated manifestations produced by one or usually more individuals often decades or even centuries after the writer composed.

It is in the context of the extended work that we find the annotations, written or visual signs that are adventitious to and asynchronous with the production of the hypothetical Urtext. In any given manuscript, the nuclear work exists in tension with the accretions and annotations—a culturally imposed surplus—from a later period.

The relation of the nuclear work to its manuscript context goes beyond questions of alterity or historicism to raise issues such as the relationship of text and image, the rapport between dominant cultural thought—"official" culture—and the various ways by which artistic expression could support or contest dominant views

4. *Écritures*, 2 (1985): 95–116.

by invoking marginal cultural forms. It also raises questions of the mixing of artistic and intellectual modes we associate with fictional literature and philosophical inquiry. The literary work viewed within the context of the manuscript matrix also raises questions about medieval notions of closure, as well as the writer's status as *auctor*, since the manuscript places the task of completion in the hands of others. Similarly, this perspective places us in a dramatic confrontation with the cultural layers of learning, the rich mixture of historical, philosophical, and literary perspectives coming from a profoundly multilingual culture.

One might argue that many, if not all, of these elements permitting us to view the work as a product of cultural expression might be gleaned from what formalists would call "the text itself." The text of a work remains essential as the principal locus of attention, but it is precisely in studying the text that we understand the "surplus" that annotation in the medieval context brings to our understanding of the work on the one hand, while on the other we discover the extent to which the processes of text production, particularly rhetoric and dialectic—and especially such rhetorical tropes as *amplificatio*—facilitated and even encouraged extradiegetic annotation.

By studying the text in relation to the symbolic surplus with which a manuscript culture surrounded the nuclear work, we recognize how tightly the two were linked in the economy of text production. Above all, we discover the extent to which the same impulses that generate processes of literary expression also control the extradiegetic network of the extended work, particularly rubrication. Rubrication, as we shall see, belongs resolutely to the linguistic matrix of the text, and therefore participates in the rhetorical and dialectical network established by it. Despite the heightened visual dimensions of rubrication, heightened by the elements of color—rubrics are red—rubrication extends the hegemony of writing into the domain of the symbolic surplus that constitutes the extended work. Rubrication, in short, privileges writing over visual expression, text over image, even though, as we shall see, it is also text-as-image to an important extent.

As Georgio Agamben has argued in his book *Stanze*,[5] phantasms, the formation of mental images, play a key cognitive role in

5. *Stanze: La parola e il fantasma nella cultura occidentale* (Turin: Einaudi, 1977).

Western thought. At the same time Western philosophy, both classical and Christian, resisted the image, with its associations of sensuality and libido, in favor of rational forms of expression. In many ways the impulse to rubricate texts arose from a need to impose a philosophical schema on them, to show the dialectical progression of rational thought in a work, particularly a philosophical one. The English scholar M. B. Parkes showed some years ago in his article, "The Influence of the Concepts of *Ordinatio* and *Compilatio* on the Development of the Book," that between the twelfth and thirteenth centuries "thinking became a craft" as the process of monastic meditative reading to oneself was transformed into scholastic *lectio*. As Parkes reminds us:

> scholastic reading was a process of study which involved a more ratiocinative scrutiny of the text and consultation for reference purposes. The two kinds of reading required different kinds of presentation of the texts, and this is reflected in changes in features of layout and in the provision of apparatus for the academic reader.[6]

Glossing, rubrication, and other apparatus we still associate with scholarly writing came to surround the main text on the folio page. The headings or rubrications within the text, however, assumed progressive importance as techniques for representing the rational ordering and logical development of the argument. In effect, processes of rational thought, dialectic, and rhetoric found within the main work came to be extended to a deictic framework that became part of the textual presentation. Rationality, the tight control of the work by linguistic logic—the fourth branch of philosophy, as Hugh of St. Victor reminds us—motivates the development of book presentation.

At some level, the development of a set of rationally motivated diectics—rubrics—within the manuscript matrix argues an underlying antagonism toward cognitive imaging triggered by the language of the work. To control the propensity toward imaging, rubrication used rhetorical and dialectical techniques associated with logical analysis to segment and label textual elements. The result offered something like a structured analysis of an ongoing "argument," that

6. *Medieval Learning and Literature*. Ed. J. J. G. Alexander and M. T. Gibson (Oxford: Oxford University Press, 1976), p. 115 and (above) 117.

is, an analytical exposition of the kind illustrated, for example, by Hugh of St. Victor in his *Didascalion.*

Hugh links logic and rhetoric[7] and defines "rational" or "argumentative knowledge," also called "the Theory of Argument," as the branch of "linguistic logic" concerned "with the conceptual content of words."[8] In Hugh's scheme, "demonstration consists of necessary arguments and belongs to philosophers." Probable argument is the branch of linguistic logic belonging to dialecticians and rhetoricians, which is the part that concerns us.[9] It is divided into *dialectic*—which he defines as "clear-sighted argument which separates the true from the false"—and *rhetoric*, "the discipline of persuading to every suitable thing."[10] For Hugh, each stage of the cognitive tree of the theory of argument contains *invention*, which "teaches the discovery of argument and the drawing up of lines of argumentation," and *judgment*, which "teaches the judging of such arguments and lines of argumentation."[11]

In keeping with the change in the sociology of literacy that Parkes identified, Hugh composed the *Didascalion* in the 1120s as a

7. Hugonis de Sancto Victore. *Didascalion: De Studio Legendi.* Ed. Charles H. Buttimer (Washington, D.C.: The Catholic University Press, 1939): 2:18, ll.13–18 (p. 37). "et merito ab his tribus tantum sapientia vocabulum sumit, quia, licet tres reliquas, id est, ethicam, mechanicam, logicam, congrue ad sapientiam referre possimus, expressius tamen logicam, propter vocis eloquentiam, mechanicam et ethicam, propter circumspectionem morum et operum, prudentiam sive scientiam appellamus." (And the name of wisdom belongs to these three [theology, mathematics, and physics] alone: for although we can without impropriety refer to the remaining branches (ethics, mathematics, and logic) as wisdom, still these are more precisely spoken of as prudence or knowledge—logic because of its concern for eloquence of word, and mechanics and ethics because of their concern for works and morals.) Hugh of Saint Victor. *The Didascalion: A Medieval Guide to the Arts.* Translated from the Latin by Jerome Taylor. (New York: Columbia University Press, 1961): 2:18 (p. 73).

8. *Didasc*: 2:28: "ratio disserendi agit de vocibus secundum intellectus."

9. *Didasc*: 2:30: "demonstratio est in necessariis argumentis et pertinet ad philosophos"; "probabilis pertinet ad dialectos et ad rhetores."

10. *Didasc*: 2:30: "dialectica, disputatio acuta verum a falso distinguens. rhetorica est disciplina ad persuadendum quaeque idonea."

11. *Didasc*: 2:30: "probabilis dividitur in dialecticam et rhetoricam, quarum utraque integrales partes habet inventionem et iudicium. quia enim ipsum genus, id est, dissertivam, integraliter constituunt, necesse est ut in compositione omnium specierum eius simul inveniantur. inventio est quae docet invenire argumenta et constituere argumentationes. scientia iudicandi, quae de utroque iudicare docet."

treatise on reading. Hugh's preface unambiguously articulates the analytical orientation of reading: "The things by which every man advances in knowledge are principally two—namely reading and meditation. Of these, reading holds first place in instruction and it is of reading that this book treats, setting forth rules for it. . . . This book, moreover, instructs the reader of secular writings as of Divine writings."[12] The cognitive tree, moreover, maintains a dual approach calculated to balance the imaging that must invariably accompany cognition with a rational control at every level of the cognitive process: dialectic balances rhetoric and within each of these, judgment is set off against invention. Furthermore, the definitions of invention and rhetoric stress rational rather than imaging processes: "invention teaches the discovery of arguments and the drawing up of lines of argumentation," and so forth (2.30). It is not surprising, then, that rubrics should provide a kind of exoskeleton segmenting works into units and identifying them in a kind of logical schema for rational reading akin to, but not necessarily identical with, Hugh's.

Now this was to be expected in the kind of scholastic texts Parkes dealt with, yet he notes the inevitable extension of the procedure into vernacular works, and Hugh himself held that his treatise on reading was as much for secular as for divine works. We can see for ourselves that this is so with a work like the *Roman de la Rose*. First, however, by way of underlining the strength of the imaging mechanisms in the text, we should not forget those other manifestations of formal annotation that constitute so important a part of the extended work, the miniatures. Like the rubrics, miniatures are generated by rhetorical and dialectical processes within the literary work. In a sense, one might think of them as literalizations of the verbal imaging mechanism, an extension of the concept of "flowers of rhetoric." Geoffrey of Vinsauf, in his *Poetria Nova* (c. 1200), helps us to see just how vividly the concept of rhetorical imaging was understood in the early thirteenth century:

> Whether it be brief or long, a discourse should always have both internal and external adornment. . . . First, examine the mind of a

12. Duae praecipue res sunt quibus quisque ad scientiam instruitur, videlicet lectio et meditatio, e quibus lectio priorem in doctrina obtinet locum, et de hac tractat liber iste dando praecepta legendi. [. . .] instruit autem tam saecularium quam divinarum scripturarum lectorem.

> word, and only then its face; do not trust the adornment of its face alone. . . . Let the mind's finger pluck its blooms in the field of rhetoric. But see that your style blossoms sparingly with such figures, and with a variety, not a cluster of the same kind. From varied flowers a sweeter fragrance rises; faulty excess renders insipid what is full of flavor.[13]

But even if illumination as annotation literalizes radically the verbal imaging mechanisms, one should beware, as I have suggested elsewhere, of seeing manuscript miniatures as unproblematic or "simple" illustrations.[14] Illuminations are annotations that engage the verbal text by juxtaposing real images to metaphorical ones. Where and how the *transsumptio* of word into image takes place depends not on the text, but on the dialectics of illumination. Even though poetic texts may encourage imaging, illuminations choose their texts, texts do not choose their images.

Rubrication and the Politics of Reading: the *Roman de la Rose*

Medieval manuscripts did not have the variety or the convention of typographical variation that we are accustomed to and that constitute a form of implicit annotation. They did use two common forms of graphics to highlight text: decorated initials and rubrication (rubrics). These two forms have long been recognized as the kind of extradiegetic intervention that we associate with annotation. Both involve the use of colors different from the color of the ink used for the main text—indeed, "rubric" comes from Latin *rubrica*, "red," the traditional color for rubrics—and both constitute posterior intervention in the text by a nonauthorial consciousness. While

13. *Poetria Nova of Geoffrey of Vinsauf.* Ed. and trans. by Margaret Nims. (Toronto: Pontifical Institute of Mediaeval Studies, 1967). Bk 4, ll. 736-41, 1225-29. "Sit brevis aut longus, se semper sermo coloret/Intus et exterius . . . Verbi prius inspice mentem/Et demum faciem, cujus ne crede colori./ . . . Sic igitur cordis digitus discerpat in agro/ Rhetoricae flores ejus. Sed floreat illis/Sparsim sermo tuus, variis, non creber eisdem./ Floribus ex variis melior redolentia surgit;/Quod sapit, insipidum vitiosa frequentia reddit." *Poetria Nova*, ed. by Edmond Faral. *Les arts poétiques du xii*[e] *et du xiii*[e] *siècle* (Paris; Champion, 1962), pp. 220, 235.

14. "The Image as Textual Unconscious in Medieval Manuscripts," *Esprit Créateur* 29 (1989):7–23.

decorated initials and rubrics may appear in most manuscripts of the same work, they need not and often do not occur in exactly the same way or place in two different manuscripts, even when the same material is rubricated. This variation helps in identifying annotation as an artifact of intentionality distinct from convention. Indeed, one of the fascinating aspects of the whole question of annotation seems to be its ambivalent relationship with conventionality.

Decorated initials and rubrics, while both graphic signs on the manuscript folio, stand in quite different relationship to the text they set off. The decorated initial appears to be a relatively straightforward way of marking a passage with minimal intervention by the scribe in the original text. The rubric, on the other hand, constitutes a scribal insertion, an interpolation of metacritical perspective, even with simple rubrics. But let's look quickly at how the system works in the *Roman de la Rose*, using a late-fourteenth-century French manuscript completed about one hundred years after Jean de Meun finished the work begun some fifty years earlier by Guillaume de Lorris. This manuscript belonged to William Morris before J. Pierpont Morgan acquired it; the inscriptions on the flyleaf constitute in themselves an interesting footnote to the conjunction of antiquarianism and high capitalism in the late nineteenth century.[15]

The Bounded Space of the Manuscript: the Incipit

First note how the manuscript matrix identifies the narrative as a bounded text with a beginning and ending that have terms specific to the manuscript medium: "incipit" for the beginning, "explicit" for the end. These are rhetorical conditions imposed on the nuclear

15. The Pierpont Morgan Library, New York. Morgan M132, *Le Roman de la Rose et le Testament Jean de Meun.* Ms. vellum, Paris, c. 1370. 190 leaves of two columns with 34 lines. Grisaille miniatures. Morgan Library Catalogue of Manuscripts (1906), no. 112. Morgan M185, *Le Roman de la Rose.* Ms. vellum, Paris, 14th c. 108 leaves of which the first 82 have two columns with 36 lines originally part of a 154 leaf *Rose* manuscript of the 14th c. Miniatures. The manuscript belonged to Richard Bennett prior to the Morgan acquisition. No. 111 in the Morgan Library Catalogue of Manuscripts (1906).

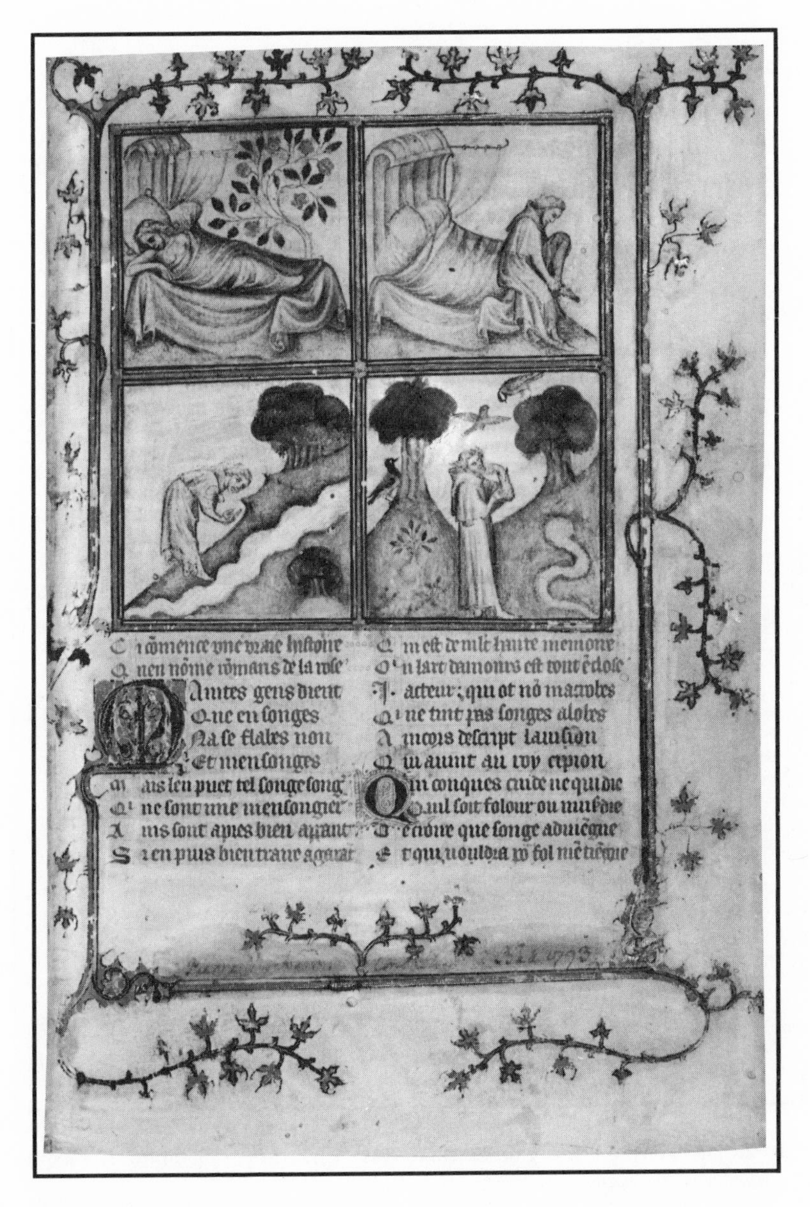

Fig. 1. The Pierpont Morgan Library, New York. Ms. 132, Folio 1: Incipit/ *Romance of the Rose*.

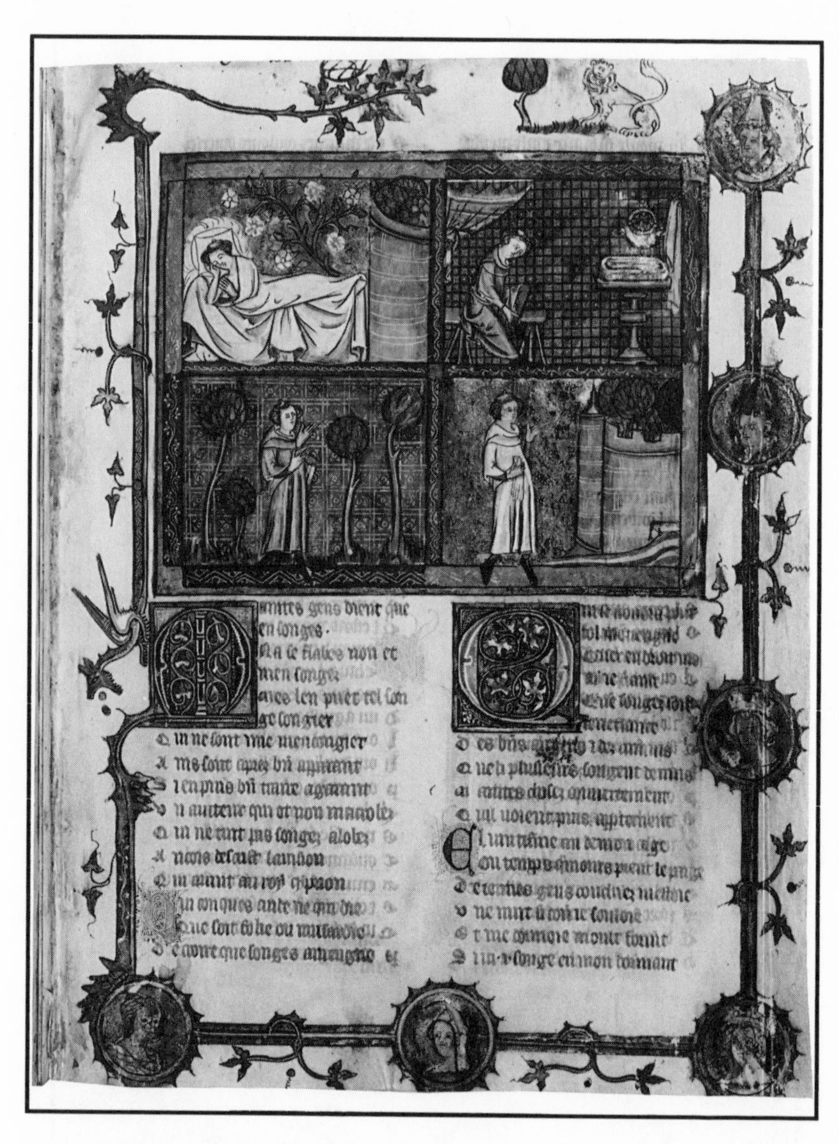

Fig. 2. The Pierpont Morgan Library, New York. Ms. 185, Folio 1: Incipit/ *Romance of the Rose*.

156

Mais de tant fui ie si bon fis
Conques nul mal gre ne men sot
Li doulz qui nul mal ni pensot
Ains me consent a sueffre faire
Quanque il scet qui me doie plaire
Si mapelle il de couuenant
Cil fais grant desauenant
Si sui trop outrageux ce dit
Si ny met il nul contredit
Que ne preingne main et cueille
Boutons et roses rains et fueille
Quant en si hault degre me vi
Que iay si noblement chevi
Que mesperance nert pas fable
Pour ce que fuis et agreable
Fusse vers tous mes bienfaiteurs
Si que doit faire bons debteurs
Car mult estoie a eulz tenus
Quant par eulz ier deuenus
Si riche que pour voir affiche
Richesse nestoit pas si riche
Au dieu damours et a venus
Qui moreut aidie miex que nulz
A bel acueil et a amy
Cui mot estre si bon amy
Et a tous les barons de lost
Dont ie pri dieu que ia nes ost
Des secours aus fins amoureux
Entre les baisiers sauoureux
Rendi graces .x. fois ou .xx.
Mais de raison ne me souuint
Qui tant gasta en moy de paine
Malgre richesse la villaine
Qui onques de pitie nusa
Quant lentree me refusa
Du sentieret quelle gardoit
De cestui pas ne se gardoit
Pour ie suy ceanz venuz
Repostement les saulz menuz
Malgre mes morteulz ennemis
Qui tant moreut arriere mis
Especialment ialousie
A tout son chapel de soussie
Qui des amans la rose garde
Mout en a or fait bone garde
Ains que dillec me remuasse
A mon vueil encor demourasse
Par grant ioliuete cueilli
La fleur du bel rosier fueilli
Ainsi oi la rose vermeille
A tant fu iour et ie mesueille

Explicit

Fig. 3. The Pierpont Morgan Library, New York. Ms. 132, Folio 156: Explicit/*Romance of the Rose*.

Fig. 4. The Pierpont Morgan Library, New York. Ms. 132. Folios 1v–2. The Formal System: Decorated Initials.

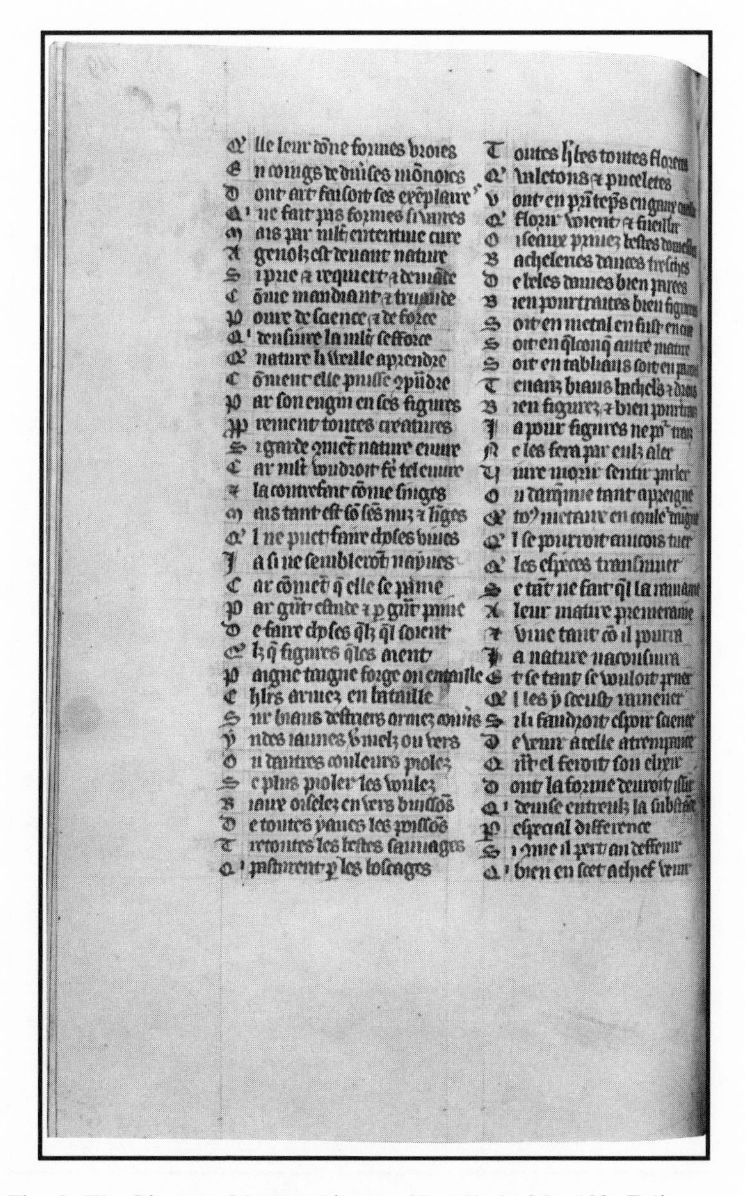

Fig. 5. The Pierpont Morgan Library, New York. Ms. 132, Folio 119v: "Neutral" Page.

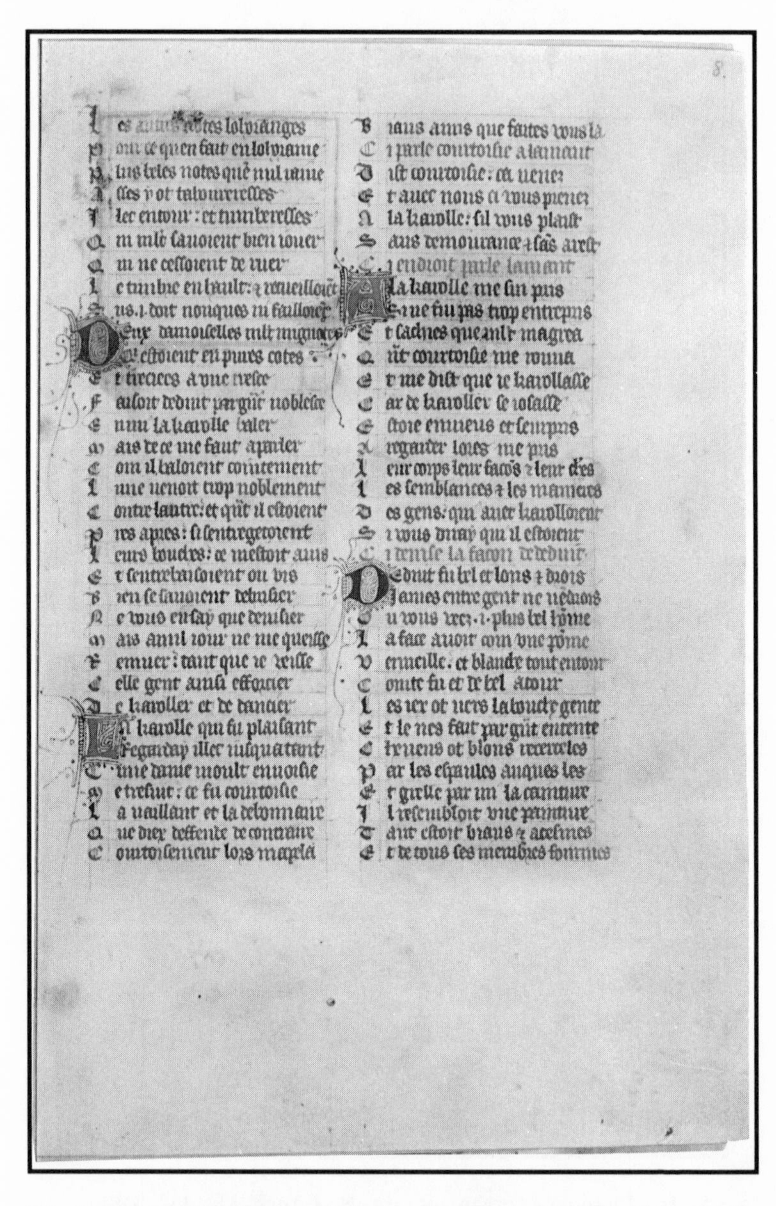

Fig. 6. The Pierpont Morgan Library, New York. Ms. 132, Folio 8: Discourse Annotation.

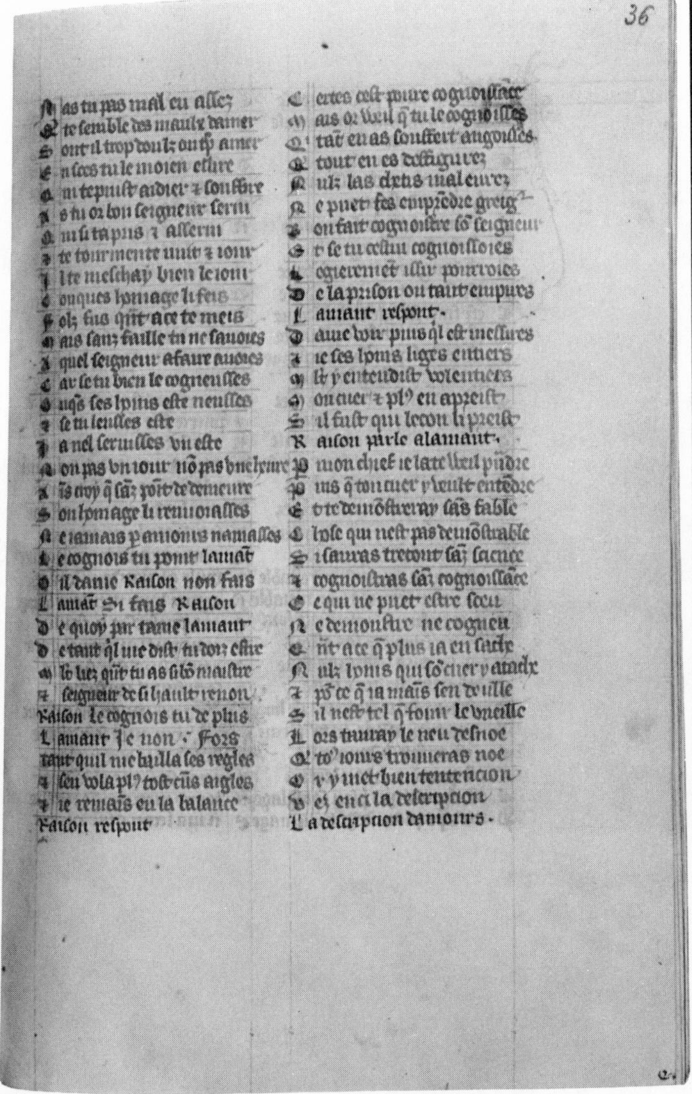

Fig. 7. The Pierpont Morgan Library, New York. Ms. 132, Folio 36: Discourse Annotation.

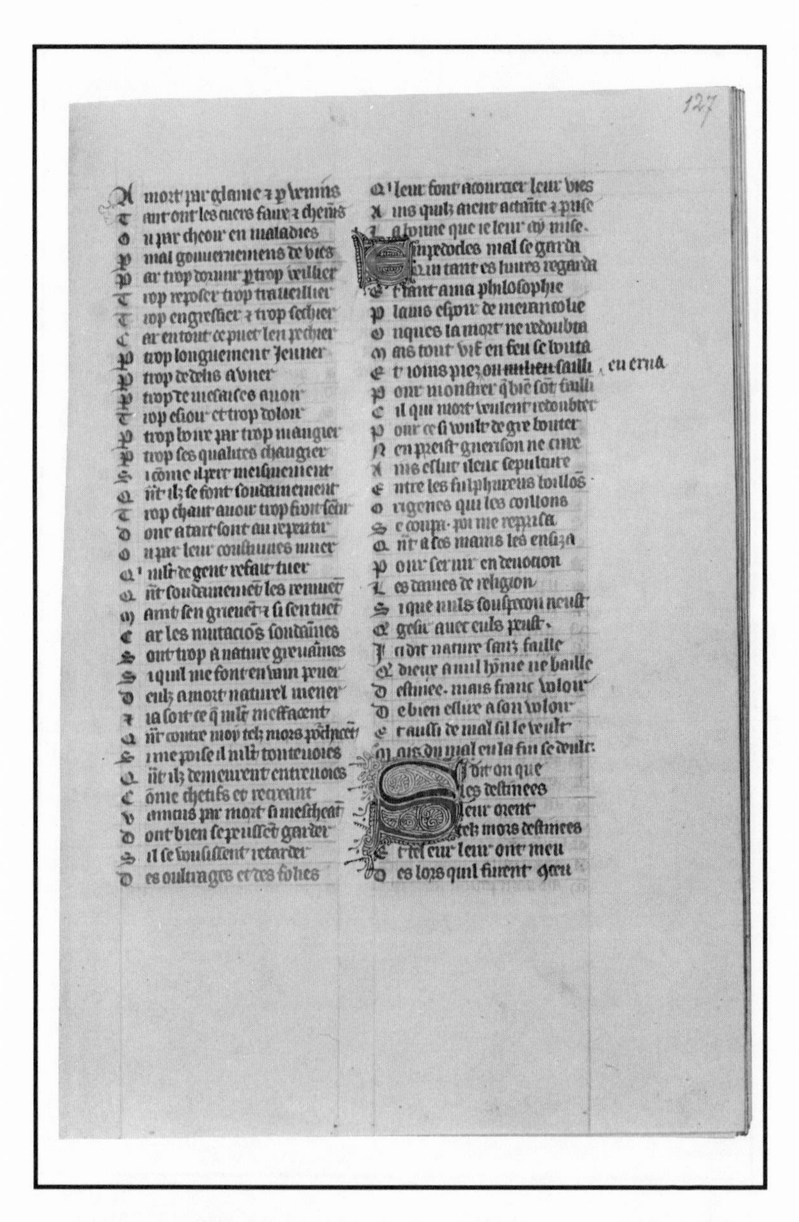

Fig. 8. The Pierpont Morgan Library, New York. Ms. 132, Folio 127: The "Transgressive" Rubric: Empedocles and Origen Passage.

work by the manuscript culture and frequently have little to do with internal narrative economies.

The difference between textual space and manuscript space is both prominent or dialectically marked in the incipits of manuscripts with important illuminations at the head of the work. The *Roman de la Rose* has a rich tradition of such incipit illuminations. Morgan 132 and 185 (the latter another fourteenth-century Paris manuscript of the *Rose*) suggest at once the conventionality and yet the variety of manuscript incipits (figures 1, 2).

The space of annotation dominates massively, as both verbal and visual representation—in the form of rubrics, decorated initials, miniatures—and as purely decorative convention in the form of the vine motifs. Yet it would be a mistake to look only at the picturely qualities of the folio in each case. Morgan 132 may seem the less dramatic, since the grisaille of its artwork appears eclipsed by the gold leaf and brilliant blues and reds of Morgan 185. But Morris chose well in acquiring Morgan 132; it's more interesting.

Morgan 132's space divides into a textual register and an annotative one: the two systems literally move in different directions. One reads the visual narrative horizontally from left to right on top, then from left to right again on the bottom. The rubric uses the same convention, thereby identifying with the image field. But the text must be read first vertically in the left-hand column, then vertically in the right. Note how the two-column layout—similar to modern textbooks—facilitates a presentation that encourages annotative intervention.

More interesting, the text of the rubric, which is a gloss on the beginning of the work, lays out its rhymes horizontally:

Ci commence une uraie histoire   Qui est de molt haute memoire

Qu'en nomme romans de la rose   Ou l'art d'amours est tout enclose

One literally cannot read the text vertically without violating poetic conventions, that is, without winding up with nonpoetry. I would suggest that we have in this very first rubric a quiet allegory of the appropriation of the textual space by the annotative system. Space permitting, we could linger over the actual text of the rubric to appreciate how in so succinct a space it manages to provide a philosophical vocabulary, a set of terms—*vraie*, *histoire*, *haute mémoire*, *nommer*, and so on—for critically juxtaposing the literal and the symbolic.

We receive a clear demonstration here that the issue is not one of analogy between two expressive spaces, text and annotation (despite their contiguity), but rather the breaking of analogy. Commentary, whether visual or verbal, miniature or rubric, will metaphorically repredicate the text, however minimally. From that perspective the miniatures are interesting, for they appear to reinforce the concept of the dream as a referential event, a mimetic account, by offering a visual summary of the first part of the narrative. And yet the upper left-hand image showing the lover asleep—a conventional way of representing dream visions—with the rosebush hovering next to the bed, depicts the symbolic components of the allegory more provocatively than the text. For the image boldly rends the pretext of mimetic referentiality by conflating symbols the narrative naturalizes. The rosebush in the bedroom, the emphasis on the young lover's body, and the vaguely sexual natural shapes bespeak an erotic symbolism that the allegorical trappings only accentuate. They also energize the cliché of the rubric's first line, *Ci commence une uraie histoire*, with new meanings that destabilize our sense of the conventional.

The Bounded Space of the Manuscript: the Explicit

If we turn to the end of these two manuscripts, the situation appears very different, indeed almost banal. In M132, folio 156 (figure 3), the narrative ends thus:

> Par grant ioliuete cueilli
> La fleur du bel rosier fueilli
> Ainsi oi la rose vermeille
> Atant fu iour & ie m'esueille
>
> & Explicit &
>
> [With great delight I picked
> The flower of the beautifully-leaved rosebush
> And so I had the carmine rose
> Then it was day and I awoke.]

The narrative reaches a double closure: first, with the plucking of the rose, which ends the quest for sexual gratification while signaling the transparence of the allegory, and second, by the lover's awakening, which constitutes the natural ending to the dream allegory. Taken together, the double ending parodies the high seriousness of the allegorical mode by suggesting that we have more to do with an adolescent erotic dream and noctural emission than with the high seriousness Guillaume de Lorris claims for his project. Such thoughts, however, take us too far afield. All we need to see here is the narrative's obvious ending.

Separated by a clear space and decorative conventions, we find a one-word rubric, the conventional "explicit." The narrative does not need the gloss. But the rubric is not in the narrative space. Like the rubric at the head of the work, it distances itself from the textual space and is both a written and a visual sign. But even as a written sign, it also differentiates itself from the text. It won't do simply to say that a Latin word at the end of a vernacular text is a pure convention, without meaning. "Explicit" evokes its counterpart, "incipit," to remind us that the technical terms for describing the manuscript boundaries containing the text were not vernacular, but Latin. Two systems of cultural expression confront each other and whoever looks at this folio. No matter how conventional, how frozen, the Latin word distinguishes between the vernacular language of romance narrative and the Latin scientific language, the language of analytical thinking.

Along with the Latin goes the culturally marked concept of closure, the ideology of closure, as in alpha and omega, the beginning and the end; in the end was the beginning and the beginning is in the end. The explicit/incipit linking in this manuscript exhibits that kind of cosmic narrative circularity. For the first panel of M132's incipit (figure 1) contains the elements—though not the action—of the final lines, showing that the illuminator was an analytical as well as a doctrinal reader.

By way of contrast, the explicit to Morgan 185 (not shown) merits comment. This manuscript that began so exquisitely ends in something of a farce, but an instructive farce. Like the scribe of M132, M185's scribe came to the end of the narrative, skipped the requisite spaces, and wrote his explicit, amplified by the addition of the rhymed couplet that serves as a long title to the work: "Explicit le romans de la rose/Ou l'art d'amour est toute enclose." But then came the rubricator, who wrote exactly the same explicit in the space originally left blank by the scribe, the space of the manuscript. It is indeed the place where the rubricator would customarily insert a rubric, if needed. But here the rubric glosses the explicit, which is already a rubric—a wonderful example of mimetic desire, of the rivalry between scribe and rubricator, and, in terms of the modern labor movement, of fourteenth-century featherbedding in the scriptorium.

At the same time, this specular confrontation of explicits uncannily betrays processes of appropriation fundamental to the work itself. From the opening lines evoking Macrobius's commentary, we find a work in which texts read other texts. Jean de Meun appropriates Guillaume de Lorris's unfinished work of 4,000 lines and grafts onto it an 18,000-line rewriting that never ceases to refract and reformulate the host. Quite unconsciously, and in the same vein, the rival explicits enact the parable of ambivalent possession and ambiguous closure evoked in Jean de Meun's ending.

Parenthetically, one might also speculate that the doubling of the explicit distich in M185 suggests that the incipit/explicit distich had assumed something like the status of a genre, that is, a formal element whose absence would somehow be seen as a solecism to be corrected. In B.N. 1565 in Paris, at the top of the first folio, over a three-quarter-page miniature preceding the opening, the rubricator wrote across the width of the folio: "Ci commence le roman de la rose. ou lart damours est tout enclose." At the end of the work, however, the manuscript contains only "Explicit et complet. anno .Lii." In a later hand, an annotator who has been an active contributor of marginal variant readings throughout the manuscript, has added the canonical distich, "Explicit le Roman de la Rose . . . ," followed by another in Latin. The annotator then notes: "Ces distiques se trouvent souvent a la fin de quelques mss. de ce Roman."

The "Linguistic Logic" of the Manuscript Space

Moving to the interior of the manuscript, we can see how the creation of the bounded manuscript space by the convention of incipit and explicit sets up a tension between the text and its material representation that cannot but affect our interaction with the manuscript. The manuscript creates expectations of annotation, not only by the incipit page, but by the folios immediately following. Were we to turn the incipit folios of M132 and M185, we would find a full spread across two pages of four columns with decorated initials, rubrics, and illuminations depicting Guillaume de Lorris's ecphrastic portraits of the noncourtly vices on the outside wall of Amor's Garden of Delight (figure 4).

The manuscript space can no longer be considered neutral, unexpressive. Any folio we confront represents a latent state of symbolic surplus. Consider a folio without formal annotation, like M132, folio 119v (figure 5). We cannot call the page neutral, but rather a folio in which the formal system has not been activated. But this page already poses questions. Why is it unannotated? Why unmarked? Why does this segment of the description of Nature's work go unremarked, even by decorated initials? Undoubtedly there are reasons, including economic ones. The point here is that the absence of annotation must be seen as intentional, as a decision not to emphasize this particular segment of discourse—a critical decision that betrays a tension between the text and the manuscript.

This becomes more apparent when one considers the way folio annotation can control readings of discourse passages. The vocabulary of rubrics is not uncalculated. Rubrics privilege certain terms denoting logical development: the rhetoric/dialectic and invention/judgment categories. We also find what amounts to an analysis of the discourse.

Folio 8 of M132 (figure 6) contains three different levels of narrative analytically demarcated by the rubrics: (1) "Ci parle Courtoisie a l'Amant"; (2) "Ci endroit parle l'Amant"; (3) "Ci deuise la facon de Deduire." (These appear somewhat faint in the reproduction, because the red of the rubric photographs as a lighter gray than the darker ink of the text.) The first rubric calls attention to the speech of the one of the allegorical figures within the dream. The second identifies the lover/narrator, also a character within the fictional framework. The diegetic value of the two characters within the work is not the same, since the lower participates in both the diegetic and extradiegetic economy, but the rubrication correctly distinguishes between the lover/actor of the second rubric and the lover/narrator of the third: "Ci deuise la facon de Deduire." The rubrics establish a reader's perspective by utilizing the present tense, the tense of reading/interacting with the text, as opposed to the perfect tense of the narrative.

The third rubric shifts its main verb from *parler* to *deviser*, "describe." *Deviser* indicates the special kind of ecphrastic description, imaging, that marks Guillaume's narrative, and it is the body of Delight (*Deduire*) that is going to be imaged. Speaking and description are the main narrative motors of Guillaume's work, which has a completely different dialectical economy from Jean's.

Folio 36 (figure 7) illustrates that difference clearly. It is a page recounting a heated moment in the long dialogue between Lady Reason and the lover in Jean de Meun's continuation. Space constraints do not permit a close analysis of how folio 36 presents this critical moment in the debate. Suffice it to say that Jean gives a greater dialectical weighting to discourse than Guillaume does. Folio 36 has exactly the same combination of rubric elements as folio 8 (figure 6): discourse identifiers and a rubric announcing the description of a character.

Whereas in folio 8 we have only two discourse identifiers and an ecphrastic marker, here we have three different groups, with three different kinds of discursive identity. The first group is the rapid-fire marking of stichomythic exchange between Reason and the lover. It consists of seven names: *L'Amant/Raison/L'Amant/Raison/L'Amant/Raison/L'Amant.* Rapid fire exchanges do not occur in Guillaume's poem. By repeating the names in rapid succession (thus actually interfering with the flow of the narrative), rubrication makes the differences between Guillaume de Lorris's dialogues and those of Jean de Meun. We also see the asymmetry behind the supposed symmetry of dialogue. One of the interlocutors will always have the last word.

The second group introduces more developed discourse, the *responsio.* Again, there is unbalancing of the dialogue by three rubrics: *Raison respont*; *L'Amant Respont*; *Raison parle.* Analytically, we move from dialogue, an exchange of responses, to exposition qua instruction, relayed by the final rubric: *La description d'amours.* The shift from the term "devise" to "description" signals a move from the imaging of ecphrastic rhetoric to the conceptual representation of scholastic dialectic, Lady Reason's preferred mode.

All this suggests that rubrication, like scholastic discourse itself, seeks to channel our reading into preset rhetorical and dialectical categories. Indeed, in a longer version of this, I have correlated the rubrication (vocabularly and mode of exchange between text and rubric) with rhetorical categories from the *Poetria Nova* of Geoffrey of Vinsauf. The comparison suggests that the rubrics correlate with poetic theories of the period to bring the practical and theoretical together in a manner allowing rubrication to impose a creative grid of its own on the text. This is not to be thought of as a writing over the text in the manner of a palimpsest, but a writing on the work itself. We should make no mistake as to the transgressive nature of this endeavor, even when, as here, it appears simply analytical.

The Transgressive Rubric

Morgan 132, folio 127 (figure 8) illustrates one of the most curious folios of the whole manuscript. The second column contains a normal decorated initial, a double rubric, and a second decorated initial twice as large as normal. The whole system frames a passage that contains two anecdotes. The first concerns Empedocles, who threw himself into the crater of Mount Etna; it includes a marginal correction "en Etna," replacing the "ou milieu" of the text. The second recounts how Origen, the early Christian Father, avoided sexual harassment charges as a young assistant professor by castrating himself: "Origenes qui les coillons/Se coupa . . ./Pour seruir en deuotion/Les dames de religion/Si que nuls souspcon n'eust/ Que gesir auec euls peust."

Before pursuing the implications of Empedocles' self-immolation and Origen's radical self-abuse in a work in which *couilles* in any form, diminutive or otherwise, constitutes a symbolically energized sign, we might grasp the interest of the rubrication system itself. The visual system contains a literal, twofold augmentation effect: twice the size and then the doubling of the colors. In short, this is the visual equivalent of what in rhetoric we recognize as *amplificatio*.

Indeed, the rubric itself falls doubly under the sign of *amplificatio*. Not only is the rubrication for the passage introduced by the augmented initial, but the rubrication itself is augmented. Two-line rubrics permitted a specular mimesis of the basic narrative unit of poetry, the rhymed couplet. Here we have a triple expansion of that system into a six-line rubric that becomes a homily or example in its own right (M132, folio 127b):

Ici dit nature sanz faille
Que dieulx a nul homme ne baille
Destinee. Mais franc voloir
De bien eslire a son voloir
Et aussi de mal s'il le veult
Mais du mal en la fin se deult.

[Here Nature tells without equivocation
That God gives Destiny to none,
But only Free Will
To choose according to his will
And that includes evil as well if he wishes
But in the end with evil he winds up sorrowing.

One could go on to refine the various kinds of "flowers" of augmentative rhetoric this rubric illustrates. Hypotyposis, hyperbaton, paronomasia—the categories are numerous, and the rubric with its wordplay, and self-reflexive rhyme scheme moving from rich rhyme to sufficient rhyme to the stark *veult/deult* (or *le veult/se deult*, if one prefers) that sets off the punch line—"Mais du mal en la fin se deult"—would do honor to the examples composed by Geoffrey of Vinsauf in his *Poetria Nova.*

It's not simply a matter of the rhetorical categories the rubric falls into, but of the double nature of its identity. Integrated within the narrative flow of the textual space, it is a rhetorical flower—and a red one at that—of real virtuosity. But annotation has a double nature. It seeks to integrate itself as writing by emulating the language of the text. Here, for example, the rhyme scheme of the annotation comes back to approximate in its punch line the textual rhyme—*n'eust/peust*—immediately preceding the intervention. At the same time it announces its status outside the text by graphic presentation and by the subject matter. For this is not narrative, but description—an ecphrasis, a verbal picture (with the colors of the visual image)—of the narrative. It is a "devise," to use the *Roman de la Rose*'s own favorite word for ecphrasis.

And like the visual illustrations in the miniatures that punctuate the manuscript space, this rubric is not an *amplificatio* or *expatiation* of the text, but an *abbreviatio*, a *compression* of it. The rubric is set up to be read by itself; it can be detached from the page by the eye and scanned independently of the narrative. As such it encapsulates a much longer narrative, digests and comments it. Responding to the self-mirroring that we have already begun to associate with the genre, the rubric contains the same mechanism for compression within its own economy that it manifests toward the text as a whole. We need only read the rhyme words, which detach themselves from the column more vividly than the sepia rhyme words of the narrative text, to read a compressed message that is, *in nuce*, the substance of the rubric: "without equivocation, bestow, free will, his will, wishes, sorrows" (*sanz faille*, *baille*, *franc voloir*, *voloir*, *le veult*, *se deult*).

Coupled with the final line, itself a compressed aphorism–"mais du mal en la fin se deult"—these succinct didactic sentiments have the force of moral law, the law that Nature enunciates in the narrative and that the rubric underlines with its first words: "Ici dit nature sanz faille" (Here Nature tells without equivocation). In effect the rubric begins to allegorize its presence in the textual space and its relationship to the narrative. Red lettering is not simply a graphic enhancement, but possesses cultural significance: *rubrica*, the Latin word for "rubric," originally meant red ocher or chalk, then came the denote the title of a law, its rubric, because written in red during the empire. In Quintilian, *rubrica* has come, by extension, to designate a law itself.[16]

More important, the cultural evolution of the term parallels closely that of *annotatio* discussed earlier; both are post-Augustan, and both have the sense of commentary with moral or legal implications imposed on a preexisting text. That early legal connection does not seem entirely lost when, in the twelfth and thirteenth centuries, the two terms came to be essential elements of philosophical discourse.

If we turn now to the question of Empedocles and Origen in this passage, we can begin to understand just how radically annotation can open texts to a hermeneutic that unseals social, philosophical,

16. Quintilian. *Institutionis oratoriae libri duodecim* recognovit brevique adnotatione critica instruxit M. Winterbottom (Oxford: Clarendon Press, 1970): 12:3:11. "Verum ea quae de moribus excolendis studioque iuris praecipimus ne quis eo credat reprendenda quod multos cognouimus qui, taedio laboris quem ferre tendentibus ad eloquentiam necesse est, confugerint ad haec deuerticula desidiae: quorum alii se ad album ac rubricas transtulerunt et formularii uel, ut Cicero ait, legulei quidam esse maluerunt, tamquam utiliora eligentes ea quorum solam facilitatem sequebantur. . . ."

and political concerns. The annotated text itself in its workings is at issue on this folio. The annotation that sets off the Emedocles/Origen exempla reminds us that rubrication and illumination mirror the text, calling attention to its materiality, the corporeality of language: its rhetorical imaging.

Empedocles and Origen have in common their efforts to do violence to their bodies, to destroy or dismember themselves as a result of too literal a reading or interpretation. Their efforts to rid themselves of their bodies, to become pure rationality, pure meaning, fail. Indeed, each becomes a symbol for the impossibility of eliding the body, and a particularly vivid image of corporeality. In trying to avoid glossing, in trying to reduce themselves to an essential meaning, they prove the impossibility of radical literality.

"Origen's Resolute Act" is the title of chapter 8, book 6, of Eusebius's *Ecclesiastical History*, the principal gloss on Origen's autocastration for the Middle Ages. In reading the following translation of Eusebius's brief account of this action, note how naturally he substitutes failed hermeneutics for castration. Emasculation was only the effect, the image of the failure of reading, but the periphrasis "Resolute Act," referring to both, tells us how closely rhetoric and the body were linked for Eusebius, bishop of Caesaria, and Jean de Meun.

> Whilst at this time Origen was performing the office of an elementary instructor at Alexandria, he also carried a deed into effect which would seem to proceed rather from a youthful understanding not yet matured; at the same time however exhibiting the strongest proof of his faith and continence. For understanding this expression, "There are eunuchs who have made themselves such (who have acted the eunuch) for the sake of the kingdom of heaven," in too literal and puerile a sense, and at the same time thinking he would fulfill the words of our Saviour, whilst he also wished to preclude the unbelievers from all occasions of foul slander, it being necessary for him, young as he was, to converse on divine truth not only with men but with females also, he was led to fulfill the words of our Saviour by his deeds, expecting that it would not be known to the most of his friends. But it was impossible for him, much as he wished it, to conceal such an act.[17]

17. *The Ecclesiastical History of Eusebius Pamphilus.* Trans. by C. F. Cruse (Grand Rapids, Mich: Baker Book House, 1962), p. 226.

Parenthetically we might note how Eusebius's observation, "it was impossible for him . . . to conceal such an act," shows how narrative takes over the role of extending meaning through dilation or textual self-glossing. It invites dilation or annotation as reflections on its reason, purpose, or meaning. As the Middle Ages knew perfectly well, narrative does not simply describe events; it implicitly postulates a double perspective of description and reflection corresponding to the double time of the narrative: the past of the event and the narrative present, the time of telling or "viewing," as it were. Time figures then as referent and as consciousness; language becomes its own consciousness. Eusebius's account glosses its own narrative-as-event in a way that makes a useful distinction between textual dilation or self-glossing—such as Guillaume de Lorris and Jean de Meun incorporate within their narratives—and editorial annotations of the kind the manuscripts demonstrate. Annotation belongs to the same reflective register as dilation, but at a remove from the originary act of composition. Annotation, the work of posterior consciousness, shows how medieval text production continues as a vital activity long after the work's composition.

Aristotle considered Empedocles to be the father of rhetoric. Origen, emasculated by radical literality in his youth, went on to become, among the early Fathers, an important source for a method of exegesis centered on allegorical troping that led to a reaction by the twelfth century, particularly in Hugh of St. Victor, that argued for a return to literal reading. Empedocles and Origen serve as cultural markers linking language and sexuality, rhetoric and the body. The issues they raise concern the role played by annotation as a rhetorical gaze, a specular reflection that reconstitutes the presence of the body in language.

What has annotation got to do with reconstituting the presence of the body in this passage? Many manuscripts do not rubricate this particular section of Nature's confession, apparently with justification. Nature is not talking about the body here, indeed she is not talking about Empedocles or Origen. They serve as seemingly offhand examples of the human penchant for behaving contrary to rational self-interest. Nature's topic is the cosmic harmony of the great chain of being, where the simplest to the grandest elements of the universe accord with the providential design entrusted to her supervision. Of all created beings, only humans accidentally or willfully depart from Nature's plans by harming themselves or taking their own lives. She cites quite a catalogue of the accidents and illnesses that lead to premature death. Insufficient will to guard themselves "des oultrages et des folies" (folio 127a) finally are what shorten their lives. Empedocles and Origin are the examples she cites in passing, before moving on to a discussion of free will.

The annotation calls attention to a deflection, if not an outright repression, of the body throughout Nature's speech. Evoked only obliquely at the end in the vague general expression "des oultrages et des folies," the body as the transgressive agent disrupting Nature's rational paradigm does not appear. This is so to the extent that Empedocles and Origen appear as illogical or tangential examples for the passage they are meant to illustrate. Or, rather, they seem to be rather superficial examples: Empedocles imprudently threw himself into Etna, and Origen castrated himself. It is the annotation that makes one pause to look more closely. Then one notices that by equating the elision of the body with castration, the text here takes a strong stand in favor of imaging in language by introjecting the term *couilles*, so dialectically overdetermined within the context of Jean de Meun's work.

It was that term that triggered the debate over literal versus figurative meaning in the argument between Lady Reason and the lover:

> Justice qui jadis regnoit
> Au temps que Saturnus vivoit
> Cui Jupiter copa les coilles
> Son fis, cum ce fussent andoilles,
> Puis les geta dedans la mer,
> Mout ot ci dur fiz et amer
> Dont Venus la deesse issi
> Car li livres le dit issi.[18]

> Certes, Dame . . .
> Mes or vous oï nomer ci,

18. "Justice who reigned formerly in Saturn's time—Saturn whose balls his hard and bitter son Jupiter cut off as though they were sausages and then threw into the sea, from which Venus was born just as the book tells it."

Si cum me semble, une parole
Si esbaulevree et si fole
Que qui vodroit, ce croi, muser
A vous emprendre a escuser,
L'en n'i porroit trover desfences.[19,20]

Jean de Meun is almost certainly invoking Peter Abelard's *Historia Calamitatum* and the other letters to Heloise in these passages and in the later one that the annotation of M132, folio 127, draws attention to. In one of his letters to Heloise, Abelard, touching upon his castration, compares himself to the Christian philosopher Origen. From the standpoint of Jean de Meun's emphasis on naming *couilles, couillons* directly, using the familiar vernacular term rather than a pariphrasis, one senses a reference to the following passage from Abelard that itself refers directly to Eusebius's account quoted earlier:

> So when divine grace cleansed rather than deprived me of those vile members which from their practice *of utmost indecency are called "the parts of shame" and have no proper name of their own*, what else did it do but remove a foul imperfection in order to preserve perfect purity. Such purity, as we have heard, certain sages have desired so eagerly that they have mutilated themselves, so as to remove entirely the shame of desire. The Apostle too is recorded as having besought the Lord to rid him of this thorn in the flesh, but was not heard. The great Christian philosopher Origen provides an example, for he was not afraid to mutilate himself in order to quench completely this fire within him, as if he understood literally the words that those men were truly blessed who castrated themselves for the Kingdom of Heaven's sake, and believed them to be truly carrying out the bidding of the Lord about offending members, that we should cut them off and throw them away; and as if he interpreted as historic fact, not as hidden symbol, that prophecy of Isaiah in which the Lord prefers eunuchs to the rest of the faithful.[21]

19. Certainly, my Lady. . . . But now I have heard you name here, or so it seems, a word so shameless and so crazy that whoever wished to find a way to undertake to excuse you, I believe, would never be able to find a defense."

20. Guillaume de Lorris et Jean de Meun, *Le Roman de la Rose*. Texte établi par Daniel Poirion (Paris: Garnier-Flammarion, 1974).

21. *The Letters of Abelard and Heloise*. Translated by Betty Radice (Harmondsworth, England: Penguin, 1985), p. 148. Emphasis mine.

Wryly, Jean de Meun seems to be pointing to the difference between Latin and the vernacular here: if the "parts of shame" have no name in Abelard's Latin, they do in Jean's Old French. At the same time, he enters into dialogue with Abelard on the relative powers of the word and the act. Implicitly Abelard acknowledges the power of naming by calling the members of which he has been deprived "nameless." Testicles obviously could be named in Latin. Neither in Abelard, nor in Eusebius, nor in the scriptures that constitute subtexts for both of them (e.g., 2 Cor. 12:7–8; Matt. 19:12; Matt. 18:8; Isaiah 56:4–5), are testicles named; they are always referred to periphrastically, Abelard calls his own "those amputated parts of my body with which I had committed that of which they complained" (eis videlicet corporis mei partibus amputatis quibus id quod plangebant commiseram."[22]

The refusal to name is clearly a sociological, not a linguistic, convention. More precisely, the convention amounts to a linguistic castration—the cutting off of the name from the object—in texts that do not shy away from discussing the act. These works recognize the power of the name by their refusal to invoke it, and thus the power of sexuality, the power of the body. Indeed Abelard, by condemning Origen as a murderer—"and the charge of homicide can be proved against him for his self-mutilation"—makes explicit this power, even when, as in the state of clerkly chastity, it was meant to remain virtual rather than, as in Abelard's own case or Augustine's before him, real.

Jean de Meun breaks the taboo against naming explicitly the generative organs as part of his liberation of the vernacular on the one hand, and his dialectic with overly spiritualized monasticism on the other. In Abelard's own vein of skeptical inquiry, Jean exposes the logical inconsistencies of linguistic castration as a means of controlling the power of the word. No less than Origen, Abelard may be charged, if not with linguistic homicide, then certainly with hypocrisy. The suppression of the name by Abelard reaffirms a theology of presence under a pretext of pretending absence. Jean rejects this casuistry by facing the issue of sexual power and linguis-

22. Abelard. *Historia Calamitatum*. Publié par J. Monfrin (Paris: Vrin, 1978), ll. 586–87.

tic desire directly. The force of Jean's work arises from its vigorous critique, its dialectical interrogation of the tradition on which it founds itself differentially.

Returning to Dame Nature's discourse, we see how she underlines the intratextual reference to the earlier passages when she adds *poi me reprisa* ("I don't apologize") after using the term the lover had found so offensive: "Origenes qui les coillons/se copa . poi me reprisa." Lady Reason first used the term when explaining how Jupiter had castrated his father Saturn to seize his power. Castration here signals the conjunction of power and sexuality. We now understand the differences between the Origen and Jupiter stories: Jupiter did not castrate himself, but took his father's genitals, thereby doubling his masculinity—like the doubling of the rubric and the doubling of the decorated initial *S* in our folio. The acquisition of power is thus the same kind of *amplificatio* as the annotation. Logically, the removal of the genitals is a diminution, like the diminutive *coillons* by which Dame Nature refers to Origen's genitals. The difference between the two is conveyed linguistically by the vernacular distinction between *couilles* and *couillon*. The latter connotes a diminished intellectual prowess—*couillon* has had the sense of "imbecile" from an early period—as well as diminished social status. Both Eusebius and Abelard questioned Origen's intelligence in castrating himself.

Power lies with accretion, with glossing, with annotation, in short with the control of text production here conceived in terms of sexual generation. At some level, annotation is thus appropriation of the text for new meanings. That's exactly what has gone on here. The framing of the annotative system on this folio sets off the Empedocles/Origen passage, isolating it from the rest of the text to give it the status of a gloss. The mirroring or framing of the annotation is the reverse of castration: it subtly augments the corporeality of the poetic text, that is, its rhetorical power, to make it yield the meanings that we have witnessed. Yet without the transgressive mirroring by the annotative frame, this brief passage would not have realized that rhetorical power. The passage would have been castrated, to use the text's own metaphor.

Now if we return to Hugh of St. Victor's paradigm for analytical reading, which earlier seemed so appealing as a schema for explaining the function of the rubric, it now appears as a rationale for literal reading, in fact, a reenactment of Origen's "resolute act." Hugh defines grammar as "the knowledge of how to speak without error"; dialectic as "clear-sighted argument which separates the true from the false"; and rhetoric as "the discipline of persuading to every suitable thing" (*Didasc.* 2.30). In short, thought proceeding not from phantasm, memory, or imagination, but from judgment: "the theory of argument is concerned with the conceptual content of words," as he says (2.28). Hugh does not go from the word to the body, but just the reverse: "The word 'gloss' is Greek, and it means tongue (*lingua*), because, in a way, it bespeaks (*loquitur*) the meaning of the word under it. Philosophers call this an *adverbium* (upon the word), because with one single word it explains that word concerning the meaning of which there is question" (*Didasc.*, 4.16).

Hugh's theory of analytic conceptualization suppresses the role of image, of phantasm in cognition, by substituting judgment and invention narrowly defined for memory and imagination, the principal motors of imaging as the Middle Ages understood them from Aristotle's *De Anima* and Plato's *Philebus*. In suppressing the image, Hugh's theory of literal reading cut off the interaction between mind and body, bodily pleasure and mental desire, that motivated the theory of cognitive fantasy. For Aristotle, fantasy became the principle of intelligence: "the objects of thought are in the forms that are perceived."[23] Both fantasy and imagination privileged vision. As Aristotle noted in *De Anima*: "since sight

23. Aristotle's *De Anima*, Books II and III. Trans. by D. W. Hamlyn (Oxford: Clarendon Press, 1974): 3:8 (432^{a}3). "Since there is no actual thing which has separate existence, apart from, as it seems, magnitudes which are objects of perception, the objects of thought are included among the forms which are objects of perception, both those that are spoken of as in abstraction and those which are dispositions and affections of objects of perception. And for this reason unless one perceived things one would not learn or understand anything, and when one contemplates one must simultaneously contemplate an image; for images are like sense-perceptions [*aisthēmata*], except that they are without matter. But imagination [*phantasia*] is different from assertion and denial; for truth and falsity involve a combination of thoughts. But what distinguishes the first [primary] thoughts from images? Surely neither these nor any other thoughts will be images, but they will not exist without images."

is sense-perception par excellence, the name for imagination [*phantasia*] is taken from light [*phaos*] because without light it is not possible to see."[24]

Origen's castration and Empedocles' suicide become symbols of the cost of confusing art with logical reasoning, or religion with socialization. As Leo Lowenthal has said: "The artist is no Cartesian but a dialectician focusing on the idiosyncratic, on that which does not fit into the system.[25] Literal reading is a philosophy of language that seeks to oppose contradictions, to limit the indeterminate interplay of memory and imagination through the intervention of the body. In short, it distrusts cognitive imaging.

Hugh's grid implements a reading theory for which Origen's "resolute act" might be taken as the reductive symbol, the ultimate in literal mimesis, as it were. Origen castrated himself as a radical solution to the mind–body problem. For Eusebius, it was a youthful act of overzealous literacy, corrected by maturer reflection. Abelard, while condemning the radical gesture, nevertheless repeatedly refers to Origen as the "great Christian philosopher," while Hugh of St. Victor himself cites Origen approvingly. For Abelard, both Origen and himself have become greater philosophers and scriptural interpreters as a result of their castration.

Abelard attributes his success as a philosopher and hermeneut to the extinction of "the fire within." Abelard is no literalist, but he and Hugh do share a skepticim regarding the body—a point that divides him from Heloise. Heloise repeatedly reminds him of the role of the body in monastic socialization, whereas he exhorts her to rise above her condition as a woman and "turn the Curse of Eve

24. *De Anima*, 3:3 (428^b30). The whole passage is instructive on the linking of imagination, sense-perception, and irrationality underlying the persistent iconophobia of Western rationalism. "[. . .] imagination will be a movement taking place as a result of actual sense-perception. And since sight is sense-perception par excellence, the name for imagination (*phantasia*) is taken from light (*phaos*), because without light it is not possible to see. And because imaginations persist and are similar to perceptions, animals do many things in accordance with them, some because they lack reason, viz. beasts, and others because their reason is sometimes obscured by passion, disease, or sleep, viz. men."

25. Leo Lowenthal, "The Sociology of Literature," *Critical Inquiry* 14 (1987), p. 7.

into the blessing of Mary." Like Jean de Meun, who translated their letters, Heloise insists on Abelard's addressing the presence of the body and of the *phantasmata* arising from mind–body intercourse.

Heloise underscores the fallacy in the Origenian model of suppressing the body: "Now particularly you should fear," she writes to Abelard," now when I no longer have in you an outlet for my incontinence." In cutting himself off from the body—the "homicide" Abelard accuses him of—Origen cut himself off from art; he ceased to be an artist. Art teaches the socialization process, "the development of human consciousness and self-consciousness essential for the individual's relationship to the world as experience," as Leo Lowenthal has written.[26]

Conclusion

The annotation on M132, folio 127, joins the debate begun by Abelard and Heloise and continued by their translator, Jean de Meun, in order to point to the fundamental difference between art and philosophy. Hugh of Saint Victor sought to privilege consistency and identity over contradiction by using literal reading to minimize art's mechanism for skewed vision—the gaze that equates rhetoric and corporeality.

In offering an allegory of castration and generation on folio 127, M132 engages a debate of the utmost importance for medieval culture, the battle for or against thinking in images. The rubricator responsible for highlighting the rhetorical power of Nature's speech clearly wished to leave no doubt of the importance of the *Roman de la Rose* as a document exploring the poles of idolatry and iconoclasm, the contradictory impulses that the Middle Ages seemed capable of nurturing simultaneously and that fuel the fascination of its cultural artifacts.

This passage, perhaps better than any other, shows that the role of annotation lay at the center of this contradiction, inspired at once by the radical literalism of Hugh of St. Victor's "logical linguistics"—a medieval precursor to twentieth-century logical

26. *Critical Inquiry* 14 (1987):5.

positivism—and yet equally illustrative of the linkage between rhetoric and the body. If annotation evolved beyond its imperial trope of origin, it nevertheless retained its powers of intervention and appropriation, its arbitrary and capricious authority to decide in favor of—contradiction, the precarious balance of opposing doctrines.[27]

27. I would like to thank Prof. Michael Riffaterre and the participants at the School of Criticism and Theory in 1989 for constructive comments that guided me in revising this article.

3

Dry-Point Annotations in Early English Manuscripts: Understanding Texts and Establishing Contexts

Thomas E. Toon

Annotations in modern books are literally marginalized by the text or, perhaps it is more accurate to say, by the editors of the text. They seem somehow outside the text, that is, other than (or different from) the text. For a linguist, things are (exist for us and are recognizable to us) largely because they are different in some significant way from every other meaningful element in the system. Obviously, part of the nature of a modern, printed text is its function as the defining context of what is appended to it as annotations. Just as surely, I think, the annotations also define a text, especially the text as it extends to the relationships between an editor and readers. The papers in this volume deal with the many things that annotations do: establish, challenge, or modify the authority of the text; indicate involvement with or estrangement from the text; establish the authority of the editor. Annotations constitute additional seals of authority. Their relegation to margins of page bottoms or chapter ends is a convention of modern printing. This paper deals with a time when the conventions were very different, when the relationship between readers and their books was more interactive. Ancient manuscripts contain all sorts of records of those interactions, which include corrections, elaborations, scribbles, and even public and private notes about the contents of the books, the weather, or other readers. All this is to say that modern annotation has a long history in the tradition of Western books and that modern usage reflects only some of the uses to which earlier books were put. The data of this paper offer some one thousand years of historical context for the more modern kinds of annotation discussed in its companion pieces. In addition, I hope to give an account of little-known medieval practices and to suggest how this knowledge informs our study of medieval manuscripts and the texts (and annotations) that we produce from them.

The subject of annotation thus raises a particularly interesting set of problems for those of us whose scholarship deals with texts written long ago. One set of problems has to do with gaining perspective on what notions of "book" and "text" might have meant then. Part of that task is understanding what users of texts were up to when they themselves annotated the manuscripts before them. At another level, one must annotate modern editions of ancient texts in order to elucidate problems peculiar to them, hoping to make the texts accessible to modern readers. Yet another set of problems has to do with the efforts to establish as fully as possible the original state of a text that has undergone changes through centuries of manual copying. The texts with which I will deal here were written over a thousand years ago. That means they were written just when the Germanic inhabitants of what we now call England were learning to write. Latin was our first language of literacy, but our Anglo-Saxon forebears soon began to experiment in writing their own language, Old English. Most regularly this use of the vernacular was extratextual and consisted in additions to the Latin text. These earliest attestations of English evidence the transition from native orality to literacy, as well as the transition from text in Latin to text in Old English. They give valuable evidence about these early users and uses of books.

Many of our presuppositions and prejudices about texts come from the privileged place that written texts have in our society. As writers of books, commentators on books, or annotators of books, we scholars deal primarily with written texts (or written versions of oral texts), and we most generally experience these written texts in some sort of printed form (or computer-generated graphics that resemble printed books). The formal annotations we encounter or produce, then, are footnotes or endnotes, supplementary material that is not integral to the text, that is intended to exist outside the main body of the text. Oral texts may have digression or asides, but they are necessarily embedded within the text itself. The printed book is a world apart from us. If we make private marginal or interlinear notations, we do not assume that those notations intrude into the life of the text we have so annotated. Only authorial revision and later editions can actually change the text. We have only written and formal means to enter the text's realm of discourse—published reviews or annotations to our own work. As modern authors, we usually annotate only our own written discourse, and do so to honor debts, to quibble, or to add what would otherwise be intrusive elaboration. In our society handwritten additions signal that we are treating the book before us as if we owned it. Only if correcting typographical or superficial errors would we think that we were modifying the author's text, and then we would assume that we were bringing it into line with his or her original intent. All this discussion recognizes a kind of tyranny the modern printed page has over our conception of text, and I belabor the obvious because it has become second nature to the producers and users of printed books and hence potentially obscures our appreciation of the relationships between medieval authors and scribes and their texts.

The early medieval experience of text was radically different. Medieval scribes would not understand our sense of the inviolability of the written page. Any ancient text that was well used shows ample evidence of that use. Only the most depraved of us think it appropriate to extend the rights of private ownership to public property, but medieval scribes felt no such compunction. Further, in making corrections or in adding material, they actually modified the text itself. Their annotations became part of the text and were regularly incorporated into the transmission of the text.

This paper aims to develop three central themes. The first is to give some texture to my increasingly strong impressions of the ways in which working with an ancient text in manuscript is different from working with a text in a modern printed edition, even a good facsimile edition. Second, imbedded in that concern is the whole complex of issues surrounding what any of us might mean by a "text"; what we mean when we talk of its residing in a manuscript or a modern edition (or anywhere); and the relationship of the text to a reading of it, or to readers of it. Finally, I hope to consider questions of authority—the relationships among a text's author(s), scribe(s), editor(s), lector(s), especially as evidenced in the habits and traditions of annotation. I shall approach these questions by discussing early medieval manuscript production and transmission in general and by drawing concrete illustrations from the manuscripts of Bede's *Ecclesiastical History of the English People*.

The manuscripts we will look at all belong to the century or so after A.D. 725, a period in which two important events occurred. The first of these is the political consolidation of the southern English under the Mercian overlords Æthelbald and Offa the Great. Early England was tribal in cultural and political organization, and the Mercian kings were able to establish hegemony over rival tribal chieftains, the West Saxons, the South Saxons, the East Saxons, the East Anglians, and the Kentish. In their charters, Æthelbald and Offa were the first to style themselves as kings "not only of the Mercians but also of all the provinces which are called by the general name 'South English.'"[1] This period also witnessed the success of early experiments in writing the English language. Before that the English had only been literate in Latin. The first examples of English were personal and place names in Latin histories and charters. Later occasional Old English glosses began to appear interlinearly in Latin manuscripts, which already often contained interlinear Latin glosses to difficult or troublesome words. Often these glosses were collected into glossaries. For students of the history of English, a family of early glossaries are important because they include a number of Old English interpretations and form our first substantial witnesses of early English. They are the Epinal Glossary (early to mid-eighth century), the Erfurt Glossary (a later continental copy), and most important, the Corpus Glossary (end of the eighth century). I have argued elsewhere (see Toon in References) that the coalition between church and state in manuscript production was genuinely synergistic in that it produced

1. Æthelbald thus refers to himself in an original charter confirming privileges to the Kentish churches, *Ms. B. L. Cotton Augustus ii.3*, translated by Dorothy Whitelock, p. 453.

written documentation of its effects. Kings would grant land and privileges for the establishment of religious houses that nurtured literacy; religious could record and witness the acts of kings. Working cooperatively, both parties could produce a written document, a charter or a history manifesting elements of authority, which neither party could effect independently. Overlords and their scribes made charters and wrote histories, and these written records made kings and kingship official in a dramatically new way. They constituted, in the substance of written words, concrete and permanent evidence of political structures.

The Irish and Anglo-Saxons perfected many of the arts of manuscript production and decoration. Insular membranes (usually called vellum even if made from calf hides) were distinctive because they took illuminations so well. The production of manuscripts was a difficult, slow, expensive process during this period in which mere survival was hard. For a Bible of standard format, the hides of 210 to 225 sheep would need to be cleaned, scraped, and preserved. In the final stages, whole hides would be divided into ten-inch-wide strips and then cut into pieces about twenty to twenty-two inches long. For a folio book the pieces would be folded once, producing two pages; a second fold would produce the four pages of a quarto; a further folding, an octavo. After folding, the leaves would be gathered in quires containing from four to twelve leaves. At this stage of preparation, the worker generally used a sharp instrument (a point, knife, or the like) and pricked the vellum with holes that served to define the margins of the text. Using the pricks as a guide, lines were ruled onto the vellum with a stylus (in the twelfth century a pencil, later a pen). The leaves of the quire might be drawn together with the hair side of the hide facing the hair side or flesh side (the sides are often nearly indistinguishable for membranes prepared in the insular manner, but more obvious for continental manuscripts). The sheet might be pricked and ruled before folding or folded first. The details of these methods of preparation become important data and the basis of establishing the peculiarities of various scriptoria and thus the provenience of manuscripts. From time to time scribes also used the dry-point stylus to doodle, make corrections, mark insertions, make reminders, or add glosses.

St. Bede was one of the most prolific writers of the Middle Ages.

He worked in and helped stock one of the finest libraries of his time. He and his extended community used that library as the basis of monumental intellectual achievements: the development of the genre of history based on carefully collected written resources; the preservation of the vulgate tradition of the Bible (through the Codex Amiatinus, now in Florence); and in the century after Bede, providing the manpower and resources (through Alcuin) for Charlemagne to establish his justly famous school and educational reforms. If all that weren't enough, one might choose Bede as an example solely for the role he played in establishing the status of written English. Bede's history replaced oral traditions with a written record that regularly codified English names for Celtic and Roman places. Bede himself pioneered the translation into English of important texts and urged that the clergy be able to teach the rudiment of Christian doctrine in English. We know from Cuthbert's eyewitness account that Bede spent his waning energies dictating from his deathbed a translation of John's Gospel, "which he was turning into our mother tongue to the great profit of the Church."[2] Such a fact helps account for why a word-for-word interlinear gloss might be considered a further adornment to a magnificently executed Gospel book, such as the gloss Aldred added to the Lindisfarne Gospels, another local product. Bede's students preserved in his *History* the poem he composed in English that we call Bede's Death Song. "And in our own language—for he was familiar with English poetry—speaking of the soul's dread departure from the body, he would repeat: . . ."[3] King Alfred affirmed Bede's role at the time (c. 875) when he attempted his own educational reform. He ordered, some think personally supervised, the translation into Old English of this book. Perhaps more striking is the way its popularity is still attested in modern libraries. For a book finished in A.D. 731, the modern reader can own or borrow any one of an impressive array of versions—paperback and inexpensive hardcover editions of modern translations, Colgrave and Mynors' authoritative Latin edition with translation, or Miller's

2. From Cuthbert's letter to Cuthwine on the death of Bede, *Ms. Hauge, Koningklijke Bibliotheek, 70 H 7.*

3. Ibid.

edition of King Alfred's Old English translation with its own modernization into nineteenth-century English (see References).

The *Ecclesiastical History* (BEH) was among the most popular works of the Middle Ages and survives in well over 150 manuscript copies—an unusually large number. Most of these manuscripts are post-ninth-century continental productions; their interrelatedness presents a complicated puzzle of textual transmission, typical of widely distributed texts. BEH is unusual, however, in having a large number of witnesses who are nearly contemporary with its composition. In fact, the scribes of our two oldest manuscripts were members of Bede's own community. Six manuscripts can be dated to within fifty years of his death in 735:

(1). M = Cambridge, *University Library Kk. 5.16*. This, the Moore Bede (named for the bishop of Ely, who owned it before George I gave it to Cambridge in 1715), was written before 737. It is not a deluxe book but a beautifully economical, fluid contemporary copy. It contains a large number of superficial mistakes, which suggests that the copy was made quickly either in Northumbria or by a scribe trained there. It was among the books taken to Europe presumably (on the basis of later French additions) for Charles the Great.

(2) L = Leningrad, *Public Library Lat. Q. v. I. 18*. This is an elaborate, beautifully adorned Northumbrian (probably Wearmouth or Jarrow) book, made no later than 747. The text of L is very close to that of M but is more accurate, so not likely a copy of it. L was also an early export, but before it left, A was probably copied directly from it.

(3) A = London, *B. L. Cotton Tiberius A. xiv*. This was copied in the mid-eighth century. It was superbly executed and illuminated. There is no internal evidence that it traveled outside England. A very important text in ancient time, it is understudied in the modern era because it was badly damaged in the fire of 1731 (although the damage has been greatly exaggerated).

(4) C = London, (B. L. Cotton Tiberius C. ii). This is a product of the middle or second half of the eighth century (contemporary with Æthelbald and Offa of Mercia). It is also written in an expert Anglo-Saxon minuscule with especially handsome initials. It is the

only clearly southern manuscript of this set. Some Old English glosses were added to it in the ninth century.

(5) K = Kasell, *Landesbibliothek 4º MS theol. 2*. An accurate, easily portable book, this manuscript was written in small Northumbrian hand of the late eighth century. Very early it became part of the collection at Fulda.

(6) U = Wolfenbuettel, *Herzog-August Bibliothek Weissenburg 34*. This is a late-eighth-century continental (Carolingian) copy of a Northumbrian exemplar with illuminations in the insular style.

These manuscripts represent the two rather distinct threads of manuscript tradition for this text. In general, the Northumbrian manuscripts (of which M, L, and A are most typical) became the basis of the later continental manuscript traditions of BEH, while English manuscripts tend to be of the tradition of which C is a part. For example, perpetuation of M's rather distinctive and minor errors mark no less than seven surviving ninth-century Carolingian manuscripts as direct descendents of the Moore Bede. Because there are no surviving English-made manuscripts of BEH produced in the ninth and tenth centuries, the close relationship of later manuscripts to C is harder to unravel.

The level of accuracy and agreement among the first three of these is testimony to the text's importance and the high standard maintained in early Northumbria. Comparison of M, L, and A allows reconstruction of a text very close to what Bede himself must have produced, since M and L are likely direct or near copies from it. Most of the textual difficulties, places where modern editors would be tempted to emend (thus generating one sort of annotation), come from Bede's sources and speak to how scrupulously he kept to those sources. The textual purity then affords direct insight into Bede's own methods, as well as enabling the study of the work of later scribes, "correctors," annotators, editors, and revisers. Another rather different aspect of that textual purity is the relative ease with which we can establish the archetypal, abstracted text, the text that shares all the salient features of M, L, and A and not their incidental errors. That abstracted text we can then assume is very close, on a word-for-word basis, to the critical text that Colgrave and Mynors offer in their edition. Textual histories are usually more complicated, and individual texts far more divergent from archetypes than we see among M and its chronologically immediate continental relatives. That is, heavier annotation is required to relate a twelfth-century English text of BEH to the Colgrave and Mynors idealized text. Since we need little in terms of critical apparatus or annotations to get from the abstracted text to its contemporary individuals, we can even speculate on what that original manuscript might have been like. We might compare such facts as E. A. Lowe's *Codices Latini Antiquiores* gives us about M, C, and L and make some good guesses, as well as get some of the flavor of the individuality of these manuscripts.

M: 128 folios, 292 × 215 mm (11½" × 8½"). Each folio contains 31 to 33 long lines of Anglo-Saxon minuscule. The pages were ruled after folding, several leaves at a time: pricking guided the ruling; there are single bounding lines. The quires are signed (Q + roman numeral in the bottom margin of the last page). There are quires of tens; the outside of the quires shows flesh with flesh or hair within. We find colophons written in red in the same script as the text, but they include majuscule letters. Simple black initials are outlined in red, and words are barely separated. The ink is black, the vellum is thick and greasy. The text contains insular abbreviations, with free use of ligatures. A ninth- or tenth-century corrector expands unfamiliar insular abbreviations; runovers are set off by a single oblique line. Cædmon's hymn, written in Northumbrian Old English, was a contemporary addition in a script similar to that of the text. The list of Northumbrian kings on the last page goes down to Ceolwulf, who died in 737. (Lowe, *CLA*, vol. 2, no. 139)

A: 200 folios, 246 × 170 mm (10" × 7"; shrunk by the fire of 1731). The manuscript was written in two columns of 24 lines. We find pricking in both margins, with gatherings of eight, signed in the lower margin of the last page with a roman numeral. Incipits and explicits and some headings are in Rustic capitals in lines alternating red and black. There is a distinct Northumbrian uncial on folio 46^v. Quotations are marked as in M and L. A master scribe wrote simple but geometrically artistic black initials (filled with colored bands) and a calligraphic pointed Anglo-Saxon minuscule of the northern type. The membranes are vellum. (Lowe, *CLA Supp.*, no. 1703)

C: 155 folios, 280 × 220 mm (11" × 9"), two columns of 26 to 29 lines. The manuscript was ruled after folding, on both hair and flesh sides. Slits on the inner and outer margins guided ruling. We find double bounding lines, gatherings of four within the quire, run-overs set off by two parallel oblique lines, and occasional accents over monosyllables. The vellum in parts is thick and rough, but some membranes seem to be parchment. The writing is a distinct pointed minuscule and a good artificial majuscule at the beginning of books. Large illuminated, zoomorphic initials (typically southern) begin each book. Old English glosses were added in the ninth century, with stylus writing passim. (Lowe, *CLA*, vol. 2, no. 191)

Comparison suggests that the Bede's own text was a large, well-made book; the exemplar could hardly be less accurate than its descendents and probably favored A (which is much like L). The materials would typically be of fine quality, the workmanship careful and demonstrative of an intellectual center where book production was a major industry. The text would literally, letter-by-letter as scribes wrote, be Colgrave and Mynors' text, if we can disregard major differences in medium and accommodate such superficial modernizations as distinct word division, paragraphing, capitalization, and punctuation. Some major differences would pertain as well. While our reconstruction would be textually accurate, we would still be lacking context—most of what is important about how the texts fitted into contemporary political, social, and economic affairs. Any of us can hope to posses our own copy of Bede, but in early Anglo Saxon times private ownership of books was possible only for royal persons. Then a text was usually a community affair whose production, ownership, use, preservation, and dissemination required the efforts of all. For modern book owners, our individual possessions are copies: the original is the author's typescript or the publisher's plates. Medievals treated each faithful transmission of a text as a genuine original.

It is nearly impossible to compare modern and medieval costs. We can own a Bede for the equivalent of a few hours of minimum wage labor. The same time expended by a highly skilled scribe would yield only a portion of a page, and we would not take into account the scarcity and high cost of materials. Given those facts, we should pause for a moment to reflect on what was produced in the north of England in this period—three full copies of the Vulgate (of which Amiatinus survives), numerous gloriously illuminated Gospel books, and at least four copies of BEH, to mention only a few of the larger, more significant productions. In addition, we know that the libraries at Wearmouth and Jarrow doubled in size. Bede's personal output included some fifty books of biblical commentary, an extensive martyrology, BEH, homilies, letters, poems, school treatises (*De Arte Metrica*, *De Schematibus et Tropis*, *De Orthographia*), and scientific treatises (*De Natura Rerum*, *De Temporibus*, *De Temporum Ratione*). The written resources that lie behind such productivity and are referred to in it required constant mobility of manuscripts and substantial upkeep. Requests for the loan of books, hopes for production, and accounts of the difficulties in getting work done figure prominently in the correspondence of the day. It is easy to underestimate the economic base required. Since Bede begins his history with a dedication to the Northumbrian King Ceolwulf and acknowledges him as a reader and critic of earlier drafts, we can assume that a history of the English people was not without its political benefits. How might we annotate our editions of the text so as to also account for facts like these?

Manuscripts of this period typically have inked additions, regularly not a part of the text proper. These may include "pen trials" (perhaps by the scribes using or copying the present manuscript), alphabets, prayers, requests for prayers of the readers, popular verses, drawings, scribbles, and doodles. Name of bishops, kings, and local religious are common (often adding clues to when and where a book was made or used). Among other things, they give the strong impression that the books were well and variously used. Frequently one finds clearly later additions and infelicitous attempts at "correction." Items of this sort are recorded in outline by as careful a cataloguer as Lowe, but usually have no place in printed editions or their notes. Lowe sometimes also makes note of noninked additions made most probably with the metal stylus used in pricking and ruling. It is extremely difficult to read these dry-point annotations, since one must tilt the page until shadows fill the indentation. That activity requires lighting that few manuscript reading rooms provide even on the sunniest of days. As a result, the bulk of these dry-point annotations have gone unnoticed for centuries.

In the following discussion, I wish to examine another kind of difference for which I will employ a metaphor of layers of text. We can begin with M, which is, as we know, not far removed from Bede's own composition. It announces itself as an English product in its fluid, clearly Northumbrian minuscule and minimal word division. The script emphasizes utility, economy, and ease of transmission in its often cursive, unadorned manner. C is strikingly different. The script is distinctly non-Northumbrian, a fact corroborated by the style of illuminations common to other manuscripts of southern provenience. Close attention to the names in the text reveals linguistic dialectal forms that are systematically Midlands (Mercian) in flavor. This manuscript represents a southern view of its northern original, a layer of relations removed from it. Its expansive, more pretentious layout and artistic initials suggest that it is an important book for an important person. We are not surprised to learn, from a letter of Alcuin to the Mercian king Offa the Great, that the political consolidator of the Southumbrian kingdoms himself possessed such a book. A northern text of this importance has obvious political value, as it proclaims the following about Æthelbald, Offa's immediate predecessor, and *documents* his achievements: "All these kingdoms and the other southern kingdoms which reach right up to the Humber, together with their various kings, are subject to Æthelbald, king of Mercia" (BEH, p. 559).

C includes a further overlay of textuality by virtue of a series of Old English glosses added in blank spaces at the ends of several books at about the same time when Alfred commissioned BEH's translation into Old English. These are published in Sweet's *Oldest English Texts*. Yet another layer of text is attested by several hundred scratched or dry-point glosses printed in part by Meritt. My own work has yielded many more previously unknown glosses and raised some further complications. The dry-point glosses and annotations in this manuscript have apparently been put there by different scribes working in very different styles and possibly at different times. Although one rarely feels confident about distinguishing between the contributions of various scribes, this case presents glosses scratched in two quite easily identified manners. One set of glosses was added mostly in the top and bottom margins in a large, rough, roundish hand; another group are interlinear and written in a small, careful, pointed hand. They might have been written by the same scribe, but they are different enough in character that readers of the printed edition should have the difference indicated for them. That is especially true, as preliminary study of the glosses also hints at tantalizingly different dialectal varieties in the same text, as for example in their approach to the raising and rounding of Germanic *a before nasals (*man* vs. *mon*, *land* vs. *lond*) and the loss of /h/ in initial clusters, as in *hlaf* to *laf*, *hring* to *ring*, *hnutu* to *nut*. Before one can begin to sift out such strands of text, one must be alerted to the potential difference, which is masked in a printed text.

From the point of view of those who annotated C in ink and in dry point, the manuscript had potentially very different uses, and thus includes several obvious layers of text. A medieval reader consulting the manuscript could not help but be aware of these different layers. On the other hand, only a single perspective is available to modern students in any of the individually published accounts of the different texts with the Tiberius manuscript of BEH. In Colgrave and Mynors we find only the normalized Latin version. The text does not make us aware of the dialectal variants of the Old English personal and place names (such as the Mercian ones found in the Cotton Tiberius C ii manuscript). To find them, we need to check Sweet's *Oldest English Texts*, where variants are collated, as in the following example from book 2: "aedilbercto *et* saberto *regibus*—sabericto—aeðilberhto *et* saberhto—aedilberto *et* saberto." A modern reader might well be unaware of the existence of Old English inked glosses in C. Even if we do know of their existence, we need to look in another place in Sweet to find them. Very few readers of Colgrave and Mynors know of the scratched glosses in C. To find them we must make another trip to the library for Meritt's *Old English Glosses*, and find the glosses printed not as they appear in the manuscript but as if they occurred in the form of a Latin–Old English glossary. Only if we get as far as Meritt's notes to his edition do we discover that some of these glosses are found interlinearly (usually over, but sometimes under, and occasionally not even near the Latin lemma), or that they are found as marginal insertions. These are two very different kinds of scribal notation, for different purposes. Interlinear notes suggest that they were added by a reader of the text; marginal citations of Old English/ Latin lemma suggest that these glosses were being imported into this text from a glossary. Meritt's note to *atrocitate : reetnesse* also sends us to the appropriate passage in the Alfredian translation, for which we need to consult yet another book, Miller's edition of the Old English versions.

Because of difficulties like these, the study of glosses particularly emphasizes the striking differences between studying a text in manuscript and studying the same text in the printed sources that record the manuscript's contents. In publication, glosses are usually excerpted from a text and "reframed" into a glossarial context (as in Sweet and Meritt in the examples cited). The scribe who added the inked glosses to C had a glossary format in mind, but the scribes and users who added scattered interlinear glosses were clearly working according to different principles. Further, one wonders if the glosses added in the present text were unique additions to that text, or whether they belong to another text embedded in the exemplar host text. Were they scratched or inked there? Should they be seen as evidence of one scribe's attempt to understand a difficult text, or a potentially different scribe's attempt to represent what he or she saw or almost saw in the exemplar? The glossarial format unduly suggests a finished character to what on closer examination appears a jotting in progress, while that format also encourages the habit of thinking of these annotations only as fodder for primitive lexicographers. Glosses were often other sorts of notes as well: indications of word class, clues to syntax, word associations rather than meanings, reminders of other contexts within which a difficult word is also known to occur (perhaps in contrastive rather than synonymous meaning), case markings, not to mention a multitude of genuine mysteries. The printing of scratched glosses ripped from context introduces its own interesting variant of annotation. This text simply cannot be read meaningfully without its notes. In fact, the notes nearly become the text, to which the glosses are "notes." These differences are lost in the printed accounts of the text.

Some of the scratches of the sort exemplified were apparently read by those who compiled the sources for the early glossaries, which may themselves have contained scratched glosses (other sorts of scratched annotations are common in the Corpus glossary). The Erfurt glossary has a number of highly suggestive mistakes. In one case we find a garbled *fiidi* where we would expect *gearnwinde*. From a series of scratched or inked minims in, say, *uind-*, a scribe trying to make sense of the unfamiliar item might change the *u* to an *f*. In similar fashion, the Erfurt divergence of *foetribarn* from the parallel reading of *fosturbearn* in Epinal is easily explainable as stemming from a scratch containing only the consonants *ftrbrn*, as scratches often do. Spurious Latin words were often created out of unfamiliar Old English lemmata, while in some cases the Old English (or the *s* that denoted its Saxon origin) got entertainingly incorporated into the Latin lemma. One wonders how much Old English material might be mined out of ghost words in the Latin glossaries.

The printed page also obscures some major differences from the text as it exists in manuscript form. All printed texts have the uniform format we expect of books; texts in modern editions tend to appear much more alike than they were in manuscripts. The Cleopatra glossary, in edition, looks a lot like Epinal or Corpus. Corpus especially was a deluxe full-folio production (perhaps a royal book), while Cleopatra was a very plain quarto. If one worked only with printed editions, one wouldn't know that the early glossary tradition was dramatically different from the crabbed practice so typical of later glossaries. Printed texts largely ignore or obscure the facts of ornamentation like the rich initials of Corpus or drawings common in Aldhelm and Prudentius manuscripts. Such difference as between economical and uneconomical manuscript formats is not easily conveyed in printed books, but these differences may be indicative of respect or potential use. Some biblical texts with their ample margins and generous spacing between lines looks like they were made with the intention of containing glosses, as is the case in several later manuscripts of Aldhelm's *De Laudibus Virginitatis* (London, B. L. Royal 5. E. xi, for example). Since nineteen out of twenty-one Aldhelm manuscripts contain glosses, we can understand that this material began to be thought of as part of the text rather than a mere addition to it.

Perhaps more serious, the glossary view of glosses limits us from a full view of the role of the writer of inked and scratched glosses. The evidence cited above strongly suggests that glossators were not always only mere copyists. The work of annotation shows them to be users as well as producers of texts. Careful examination of their notes can lead to speculation about what manuscript resources were available in a medieval library and even the uses to which those libraries were put. Glossators were perhaps collectors, perhaps teachers, in some cases clearly naive readers, maybe students. All this leads away from a single-framed vision of their work to raise questions of how these scribes worked, under what conditions, and to what ends. In other words, the study of "occasional glosses" and related items can be approached from so many different perspectives that we must express surprise at how fully the lexicographical perspective has dominated, even obscured, our approach to this material. Through frequent and exclusive usage, the glossary becomes the single frame of perspective into which we slip all too easily. Our focus is unnecessarily limited to individual words in the context only of other individual words.

Editions make a series of claims well worth reconsidering. The printed text of scratches allows us to forget how different scratches are from an inked gloss. Inked glosses are more clearly a public record, while scratches might more reasonably have been a private note. The printed edition of the Latin text is one thing (and so is edited separately); the inked (and perhaps scratched) glosses are then treated as a separate subject, ignoring potentials of intertexuality. In a curious way the Old English text is parasitic, being of interest only because it can be anchored from point to point by direct lexical contact to the Latin. In the manuscripts, glosses occur in the context of sentences and discourses, not single words. The fragmentation of the text leads to a simple-minded sense of completeness; having lined up glosses, what more is there to do than record them in our dictionaries?

Another example will demonstrate the kind of help these studies might be to historical linguists. The analysis of the linguistically heterogeneous data of the early glosses and glossaries is a multiply vexed issue. The interpretation of some of those difficult issues can be informed by establishing close ties between batches of glosses and individual aspects of the very complicated transmission of glossary materials. The heavy influence of Aldhelmian material in Epinal–Erfurt has been taken to suggest that Aldhelm might have compiled (or at least used) an archetype of that glossary. I am among those scholars who have argued that many of the features of the language of Epinal can be explained when viewed as a very early variety of Mercian Old English. Since the provenance of Epinal is uncertain, we need circumstantial secondary evidence of connections between Epinal and Mercia—or active intellectual centers during the period of Mercian political and cultural domination (see Toon). Mercia in fact dominated Kent just during the period in which there must have been active transmission of Aldhelm's works there. Vivien Law, in her perceptive analysis of the glosses to the *ars Tatuini*, makes a solid connection between the glosses—Latin, Old English, and Old English retranslated into Latin—and the continental Leiden and Erfurt glossaries.[4] She carefully demonstrates how archaic linguistic forms were fossilized, as scribes became less and less familiar with the Old English words they were copying. The grammatical text, she establishes, was written by the Mercian Tatwine before he received the pallium at Canterbury in his old age. It was glossed by students in his native Breedon or in Canterbury. Such explicit connections between Mercian features are very important elements in our understanding of the linguistic complexities of this period and its texts.

Much dry-point material is very hard to represent in a printed text. How, for example, does one convey the effect of sitting in front of a very boring Latin sermon and suddenly becoming aware of faces and animals scratched into the margins and facing in all directions? Those doodles have nothing much to do with the text as written, but are probably an easily interpreted comment of the text as received by a bored audience. The doodles further suggest that the manuscript was laid out on a table with pupils, scribes, or colleagues gathered round. Either several individuals were similarly bored on the same day, or the same or a like-minded scribe found himself in the same situation on several occasions. Even apparently

4. Vivien Law, "The Latin and Old English Glosses in the *ars Tatuini*," in Peter Clemoes, ed., *Anglo-Saxon England 6* (Cambridge, England: Cambridge University Press, 1977), pp. 77–90.

whimsical doodles and scribbles can be informative. Some dry-point annotations to the Cotton Vespasian A.1 provide examples of yet another kind. The magnificent Vespasian Psalter was produced in the south of England, probably Canterbury, in the eighth century and contains a continuous interlinear gloss (in Mercian Old English) added in the ninth century. I puzzled for several years over the individual letters scratched through the early folios. Strong internal evidence suggests that the marks were added before the leaves were gathered into quires:

12^{r}	c ψ	19^{r}	m
13^{r}	e	19^{v}	n
14^{r}	f	20^{r}	o
14^{v}	g	20^{v}	p
15^{v}	h	22^{r}	r
16^{r}	i	24^{v}	s
18^{r}	k	25^{v}	t
18^{v}	l	26^{r}	u

I noticed that they corresponded roughly (within a half page or so) to the beginning of psalms, but for a long time I could make little sense of the runelike symbol next to the "c" on folio 12^{r}. It is now clear to me that it is not a rune but a Greek letter and a fairly standard abbreviation for "psalm." The marks then take on meaning as notes made before the text was written and that helped a scribe lay out a plan for having the book copied, as he or she guessed how much space was needed for the text of the psalms. Such information can add insight into the processes of manuscript production and be very useful in attempting to demonstrate that the present text was a lineal descendent of a known text whose spacing better matches up with the scratches.

Bede's history provides another sort of challenge to those who hope adequately to represent a multilayered text in edition. Alfred the Great commissioned (and may have helped in the work on) an Old English translation of Bede, so that it could be more widely read and understood. In the succeeding centuries the Latin text and the Old English text would provide context for each other. A famous passage from Bede's *Ecclesiastical History* illustrates the dimensions of the problem. It relates one of the most poignant of Old English metaphors: the present transitory life is likened to a brief moment of temporary comfort in the flight of a sparrow that goes quickly from a storm though the temporary shelter of a mead hall back into the storm. Bede recorded the story in Latin, but the text was so popular and so obviously Germanic in its origins that it must have had an oral vernacular source. One can hardly imagine Edwin's heathen counselors conducting their debate in Latin. The spirit and vitality of the Old English even shines through the modernization and contrasts sharply with the syle and tone of the Latin. So Alfred's Old English "translation" was a retranslation of Latin that had been translated from an English model.

This paper has suggested several of many perspectives that can be taken on a "text" like BEH. It and its manuscripts have been studied by art historians, political historians, paleographers, Latinists, Anglo-Saxonists, linguists. Deciding what's in a text—even deciding the seemingly more pedestrian question, what's in a manuscript—becomes one of perspective. Those perspectives determine what is in an edition proper and what gets relegated to the apparatus or ignored entirely. The question of what isn't in a text looms as large as the question of what is, since it includes what might or ought to be. Very regularly our decisions about what is in the texts we choose to see is determined by what we do with the texts. Unfortunately, that all too often inhibits our ability to see clearly what the original makers and subsequent users of a text did with it. Returning to the original manuscripts with fresh perspectives holds the promise of producing more productive accounts of ancient texts, accounts that enable us to view the texts through a wide range of past, present, and possible frames of reference.

References

Colgrave, Bertram, and Roger A. B. Mynors, eds. *Bede's Ecclesiastical History of the English People.* Oxford: Oxford University Press, 1969.

Lowe, Elias Avery. *Codices Latini Antiquiores.* Vol. 2. Oxford: Oxford University Press, 1971.

Meritt, Herbert Dean, ed. *Old English Glosses.* London: Oxford University Press, 1945.

Miller, Thomas, ed. *The Old English Version of Bede's Ecclesiastical History of the English People.* Oxford: Oxford University Press, 1890.

Napier, Arthur Sampson. *Old English Glosses.* Oxford: Clarendon Press, 1900.

Sweet, Henry. *The Oldest English Texts.* Oxford: Oxford University Press, 1885.

Toon, Thomas Edward. *The Politics of Early Old English Sound Change.* New York: Academic Press, 1983.

4

Medieval Annotation: The Example of the Commentaries on Walter Map's DISSUASIO VALERII

Traugott Lawler

I have been working (along with Ralph Hanna) on Walter Map's *Dissuasio Valerii ad Ruffinum ne ducat uxorem*, a satire of the twelfth century, and commentaries on it, all probably of the fourteenth century. What I would like to do here is first describe the *Dissuasio* and comment on its curious blend of self-annotation on the one hand and opaque allusiveness on the other, and then discuss some of the commentaries.

Map says he wrote the *Dissuasio* to "a friend of philosophic life" who was about to abandon that life to get married. It consists chiefly of anecdotes, most of them very briefly and allusively told, of men and gods whose women caused them trouble. There are also a number of anecdotes and epigrams that bear on the rhetorical situation, that is, on offering advice to someone who doesn't want to hear it. Throughout, the strongest emphasis is not so much on blackening marriage as on celebrating the life of the mind, which is of course celibate. The style is quite playful and witty. I shall quote a brief portion in English, with a bit of the Latin original, just to give a taste of it, and also to provide a basis for my discussion of the commentaries. It opens by focusing immediately on Valerius, the adviser:

> I am forbidden to speak and cannot be silent. I hate cranes and the voice of the screech-owl, the horned owl, and other birds that wail dismally of muddy winter's heaviness; and you mock my prophecies of losses to come—true prophecies, if you persevere in your course. Therefore I am forbidden to speak, I the prophet of truth and not of will.
>
> (Loqui prohibeor et tacere non possum. Grues odi et vocem ulule, bubonem et aves ceteras que lutose hiemis gravitatem luctuose preululant; et tu subsannas venturi vaticinia dispendii—vera, si perseveras. Ideo loqui prohibeor, veritatis augur, non voluntatis.)
>
> I love the nightingale and the blackbird, which herald the joy of the soft wind in calm harmony, and especially Philomena, who, when summer actually comes with its longed-for happiness, brings the full measure of delight—nor am I deceived. You love parasites and girls from comic plays, who whisper of sweet enticements to come, and especially Circe, who will pour you out joys full of the scent of sighed-for sweetness, so that you may be deceived. Lest you become a pig or an ass, I cannot be silent.
>
> The ministers of Babel are offering you honeyed poison; it enters you sweetly and pleases you, and draws along with it the force of your spirit. Therefore I am forbidden to speak. I know that at the last it will bite like a serpent and will inflict a wound beyond any healing serum. You have many advocates of your desire, most eloquent against your life; and you have me, the lone, tongueless herald of the bitter truth that disgusts you. Therefore I am forbidden to speak.[1]

1. The Latin text quoted is that of the critical edition in preparation by Ralph Hanna and me; the translations of that text are ours. Our edition is based on collation of all twenty-one surviving manuscripts written before 1300, including London, British Library Additional 34749, ff. 75–83, to which reference is made here; this passage is on f. 75a. Our book (which will also present editions and translations of the commentaries discussed in this paper) is tentatively called *Jankyn's Book of Wikked Wyves*; it is intended as a volume of background material for Chaucer's *Wife of Bath's Prologue*, and is tentatively scheduled for publication in The Chaucer Library. Since Map added the *Dissuasio* to his *De nugis curialium* (4.3–5), it can of course be consulted in editions of that work, of which the most recent is C. N. L. Brooke's and R. A. B. Mynors's revision of Montague Rhodes James's edition (Oxford: Clarendon Press, 1914): *Walter Map De Nugis Curialium* (Oxford: Clarendon Press, 1983). A text also appears in J.-P. Migne, ed., *Patrologia Latina*, 30:254–61 among the spurious letters of St. Jerome.

Before I go to the commentaries, I want to speak of three intrinsic relations the *Dissuasio* has to annotation: it expects annotation; it uses the tradition of annotation; and it annotates itself. First, then, Map surely expected annotation and fits that expectation to his purpose. In the very first paragraph he mentions six birds. True, he explains them: the crane, the screech owl, and the horned owl all "wail dismally of muddy winter's heaviness," while the nightingale (lucinia), the blackbird, and Philomena all herald spring. But Map knew that Isidore of Seville was ready to hand with the traits of each species—or most—and knew especially that Philomena was not just the name of a bird but the name of a character in a classical myth whose story was relevant to his general subject. So too was Circe, and when he says "lest you become a pig or an ass," he is surely aware that only some of his readers will know that Circe turned Odysseus's men into pigs and asses, and that those readers will feel obliged to point that out to others. And above all, he knows that such readers are the very people he is out to hook: if you take the bait and annotate his text, he has secured you for scholarship.

Second, Map can use annotation itself for his purpose: "You poor man, you don't understand that it is a chimera that you pursue; however, you are devoting yourself to learning that that three-shaped monster is adorned with the face of a noble lion, besmirched with the belly of a stinking goat, armed with the tail of a poisonous viper." This is a standard gloss of the word "chimera": the chimera is a monster with the face of a lion, the belly of a goat, and the tail of a viper. Ruffinus will learn that gloss, but not from books, not even from this book: he will learn it by experience, and learn also the underlying assertion that woman is the chimera. I think this remarkably witty. On the surface, glossing words like "chimera" is the essence of pedantry, is just the kind of trivial, bookish, useless knowledge that Ruffinus is gladly junking, to replace it with flesh and blood. Not so, says Map: your experience itself will be annotated, as it were, it will bear on your pulses a footnote of painful learning as to what the chimera is. (There are other examples of similar toying with the tradition of annotation.)

Third, Map annotates himself. About a third of the way into the *Dissuasio*, he begs Ruffinus to give him his ear patiently *dum evolvam quod implicui*, "until I can unravel what I have tangled up." This seems to mean that from this point forward, what he writes will constitute a gloss on the "tangled" meanings his allusive style has so far embedded. And indeed, after one more example of a bad listener, everything that follows is examples of men who were hurt by women—examples that, to be sure, still need annotation, but that are clearer than the murky epigrams that have gone before. So he annotates himself; the last two-thirds of the text is a gloss on the first third. But here's a footnote, a further twist of annotation: even this signpost, this *evolvam quod implicui*, even this announcement that the latter part of the text is a kind of gloss on the first part, is itself buried in allusive rhetoric, so that I find myself obligated to point it out, and certainly will do so in our annotations to the *Dissuasio*. What this suggests is what has oppressed me from the beginning about this project: the endless nature of annotation. I hate the thought of annotating the commentaries, of producing a commentary on commentary, yet I feel I have to; and here too, at this passage on unraveling what is tangled up, we will be, in effect, annotating Map's attempt to annotate himself. I feel, however, a big difference between "structural" annotation of this sort, when by thinking and thinking I have come, or think I have come, to a new understanding of the structure of the letter, and the incidental annotation of identifying quotations or giving full background to allusions to people and stories. I confess to a special pride, whenever I have annotated a text, in writing notes that clarify its structure.

Perhaps the central question to ask, before we start annotating a text, is whether the text itself embodies an attitude to annotation. It isn't always opposition. Certainly poets regularly make fun of pedants, yet there is clearly also a close alliance. One thinks of Pope, annotating his *Dunciad* to make fun of Theobald and Bentley, but clearly also enjoying the process, and annotating his other poems, too; or of Chaucer, poking fun at pedants and yet himself a bookish man, and therefore poking fun at himself for his bookishness. I think it would be safe to say that every poet and indeed every writer is assailed by contradictory impulses, both to say and to leave unsaid. "I am forbidden to speak and cannot be silent," as it were. When they follow the impulse to say, they annotate themselves; when they follow the impulse to leave unsaid, they give others the opportunity to annotate them. Thus Map on the one hand constructs his text as self-annotation, and on the other fills it with unexplained allusions. And both impulses validate annotation, the first directly by actually annotating, the second by leaving a void that must be filled.

To summarize what I have been saying about the *Dissuasio* itself and annotation: it invites, even expects, annotation; it uses the tradition of annotation; it annotates itself. And thinking about annotating this text causes me to distinguish between two kinds of notes, structural and incidental. Let me pass on now to the medieval commentaries on Map's *Dissuasio*.

I have in mind a group of seven commentaries that I have been working on. (We actually have nine, but there are two rather special ones, one in Bodleian Library University 61 and the other in Lambeth Palace 330, that I am not yet competent to address.[2]) In a report I gave at the New Chaucer Society meeting in York in 1984, I divided them into five "humanistic" and two "Catholic" commentaries. Those I called humanistic all seem meant for boys or young men learning Latin: their chief interest is in explaining the allusions to history and mythology, identifying Map's sources, glossing hard words, and even analyzing the syntax; they take seriously, as it were, the nature of the *Dissuasio* as an invitation to scholarship, and constitute an exercise in the literary life that it fosters. The two "Catholic" commentaries concentrate rather on moral issues, one on various things the text touches on rather slightly, and one on marriage itself. Thus, of the seven, only one takes up the subject the *Dissuasio* is most obviously about. But that may very well be the nature of annotation: to stick to incidentals. The author has presumably said what needs to be said on his subject. It would be arrogant of the annotator to add to that. His job is precisely to concentrate on the obiter dicta, on what the author's concentration on the main subject has caused him to toss off without explanation.

2. Oxford, Bodleian Library University 61, ff. 2–21, Incipit "Sciendum quod tres fuerunt Valerii." This is Nicholas Trivet's commentary (discussed later) with someone else's additions, mostly additional authorities. London, Lambeth Palace Library 330, ff. 1–114, Incipit "Amicus fidelis protectio fortis, Ecclesiastici 6." This is an original commentary, though heavily based on Thomas of Ireland's *Manipulus florum*. Ralph Hanna is editing excerpts from it for our book. Lambeth 330 clearly belongs in the category of "Catholic" commentaries (to be discussed), and has some interesting things to say in defense of marriage and women.

Thus I am not sure that the two moral commentaries fit properly under the rubric of annotation; they are, rather, new treatises. At York I argued that these two, which actually take up the moral issues, and one of which constitutes a vigorous denunciation of Valerius's antifeminist and antimatrimonial stance, were the most interesting. And they are, from any ordinary, sane point of view. But from the rather mad slant that a conference on annotation gives you, it is the five school commentaries, since they are genuine commentaries and not new treatises, that command attention.

Three are relatively short and simple, and I am going to treat only one of them, *Grues ut dicit Isidorus*, as representative of the group.[3] Its author glosses most of the unusual words and most proper names and not much else; there is no attempt to unravel difficult syntax or paraphrase statements. The unit annotated is always a single word, usually a noun. There is an interesting distinction between his explanations of animals and those of human or divine characters. Characters he almost always connects to a story, and the story he tells is usually to the point, that is, it makes Map's point clear and concentrates on that point without giving superfluous details. Animals, on the other hand, are likely to have attached to them virtually anything the glossator knows about them or, better, can find in Isidore of Seville. The very first note, for instance, gives a series of facts from Isidore about cranes (*grues*)—the name is taken from their call, they fly in single file and very high so as to see far ahead, they take turns on watch at night, they get black as they age—but not the only relevant fact, that they fly south in the fall and so are a harbinger of winter. I suppose this weight of information about animals is a kind of cultural baggage the Middle Ages carried around with them. A lot of facts were available in books about animals, and an annotator like the one we are considering trots them all out.

The notes are rigorously factual; even when they stick to Map's point, they never mention that point: they just give the facts. I am reminded of our notes to the *Riverside Chaucer*,[4] where we distin-

3. All commentaries are cited from our critical text and translation; see note 1 above. *Grues* is in five manuscripts, including Oxford, Bodleian Library Additional A. 365, ff. 3v–6, which is cited here.

4. Larry D. Benson, ed. (Boston: Houghton Mifflin, 1987).

guished between "page-glosses," notes at the foot of the text, and "commentary," notes in the back. In page glosses we confined ourselves to facts: definitions of words and identification of proper names; but in the commentary we commented on rhetorical and structural matters, gave illustrative examples, sources, and so on. The author of *Grues* writes page glosses only. The one other kind he allows himself is quotations of verse, especially from Ovid and the *Ecloga Theoduli*. He also makes remarks on the length of syllables, quite rightly supposing that if his readers don't know what a word means, they probably don't know how to pronounce it. If modern annotation is any guide, this is a sure sign that the intended audience is students. The poetry too seems quoted not so much out of general belletrism but rather either as a pedantic reminder of something the students should recall, or as a device for committing the information to memory. His urge to annotate is so great that several times he annotates his illustrative verses. We don't know his name, and we shouldn't.

John Ridewall's commentary is much more satisfying.[5] He was an Oxford Franciscan of the first half of the fourteenth century, one of the "classicizing friars" Beryl Smalley features in her *English Friars and Antiquity in the Early Fourteenth Century*.[6] Ridewall has an eye not so much for nouns as for sentences and paragraphs: he elucidates Valerius's arguments. Indeed, his commentary shows, on a far deeper level than *Grues*, that devotion to the literary and intellectual life that the *Dissuasio* is designed to foster. He seems to me to be not just interpreting this text but teaching his students a method of very close reading, of accounting in interpretation for every detail. Let me show you what he does with the sentence about Ruffinus's flatterers, "The ministers of Babel are offering you honeyed poison." *Grues* and those like it simply tell you that "honeyed poison is poison coated with honey" and that "Babel means confusion." Ridewall says that Valerius is alluding to the story Peter Comestor tells of King Zedekiah, who was imprisoned by the king of Babylon, and one day brought before the Babylonian court and given "a delicious but laxative drink. He drank it and right away his

5. Incipit "Hec epistola continet principaliter tria." In twelve manuscripts, including Oxford, Bodleian Library Digby 147, ff. 183–204, which is cited here.

6. Oxford: Blackwell, 1960.

bowels were loosened shamefully in front of everyone. After that public humiliation he was led back to prison, where he died of shame a few days later." The key step Ridewall takes is to join the phrase "the ministers of Babel," taking it as the king and court of Babylon, to the phrase "honeyed poison," taking it equally specifically as the delicious but laxative drink. In the process he uncovers a far more specific allusion than the average reader—including me, I'm afraid—would be inclined to see. It's such a clever reading that it seems to me that here Ridewall is doing just what Valerius does, "privileging," as we say, the delights of the mind, here the delights of witty textual interpretation, over lesser delights such as marriage. Ridewall is in tune with Map, enticing his students into scholarship, offering them what Valerius offers Ruffinus, a babbling, a rhetoric, that is all honey and no poison, that offers power rather than a shameful and suicidal loss of control over the self.

By far the most ambitious and complex of the commentaries is that by Nicholas Trivet, that prolific Dominican who also flourished at Oxford in the first half of the fourteenth century. In the first place, although he will go on to pay close attention to the letter of the text, Trivet insists that his purpose is moral:

> It is clear what this letter [the *Dissuasio*] intends on the literal level; yet everything said in it can serve very aptly on the moral level, and it is in fact for that purpose that this entire commentary has been undertaken. Know, then, that woman stands for sensuality and the weaknesses and temptations of the flesh, and man stands for reason and strong resolve. . . . And so everything that is written in this letter can and should be applied to morals. . . . Dissuasion from marriage may be taken as a call to resist temptation to sin. The reproval of flatterers who urge marriage may be applied to the devil and the world, who by false promises incite us to sin.[7]

And so on. This is a level of insight—or perhaps sophistry—that none of the other commentaries approaches. In fact, however, Trivet rarely moves explicitly to the moral level, but contents himself with making the argument very clear.

7. Incipit "Mulier, si primatum teneat, contraria est viro suo, Ecclesiastici 25." In ten manuscripts, including Cambridge, Clare College Library 14, ff. 62v–78r. This passage is on folio 62v.

The fineness of his perception is immediately evident. Map opens by five times repeating that paradox, "I am forbidden to speak, and cannot be silent." It becomes clear, of course, that the urge to speak is after all greater than the prohibition against speaking. Nevertheless, a proper annotator ought to attend to this paradox, and no one but Trivet does. He points out in each of the five cases how finally what he calls the "spur" or *ratio movens* is slightly more powerful than the "check," or *ratio retrahens*. For example, this is how he sums up his discussion of the opening passage: "And so the first checking argument goes like this: I should not lose you who are my friend, but by speaking the truth I *will* lose you my friend, that is, your friendship. And the opposite argument goes likewise: I should not lose you who are my friend, but if by keeping quiet I allow you to marry, I will lose you, because marriage will turn you into a beast. And notice that this rejoinder tips the balance a little, because in the first loss only friendship is lost, in the second both friendship and Ruffinus's very humanity." And so on: in each of the five parts he makes a careful analysis that ends up showing that the reason to speak outweighs the reason to keep silent. No other annotator offers anything remotely approaching the sensitivity of that. Trivet is far more attuned to Map even than Ridewall.

Furthermore, he is learned and sure of his learning. He almost never quotes his dozens of authorities at greater length than he needs to, or quotes verse other than aptly. Here is a nice example of his sure learning. I had trouble distinguishing clearly between two of the birds that herald spring, lucinia and philomena, and the other commentaries were of little help. Here is Trivet:

> According to Isidore . . . the lucinia is so called because it sings at daybreak, as if it were the "way to light" [*luci via*]. Papias says it is the same bird as the philomena, and Ambrose seems to mean that too when he says, "Lucinia, the wakeful guard, soothes the sleepless toil of the long night with her sweet song, which enables it, I think, to animate the eggs it is hatching as much by its sweet rhythms as by the warmth of its body." Thus Ambrose. But what Ambrose says is the nature of the lucinia is clearly the nature of the philomena, so it appears plainly that both Ambrose and Papias consider philomena and lucinia the same bird. But that is not Isidore's opinion—and it is not Valerius's either. For the nature of the lucinia as Isidore gives it is not the nature of the philomena. Nothing, in fact, about the philo-

> mena is to be found in Isidore, and Valerius here obviously distinguishes between the two. Therefore, following the intention of this author, which I think is right, I say that lucinia is the bird that we call the goldfinch, since both its name and the etymology of its name fit the goldfinch better; and the philomena is the bird we call the nightingale. (folio 63ʳ)

I love that note for the range of its learning; for the confidence both of its negative statement—nothing about the philomena is to be found in Isidore—and of its willingness to dismiss Ambrose and Papias; and above all for its resourcefulness and common sense in resorting to the English words and the personal experience they imply. This isn't just a matter of giving the vernacular translation instead of a Latin synonym, as the other annotators occasionally do: you know that Trivet has been in the fields, and knows a hawk from a handsaw.

Let me compare *Grues*, Ridewall, and Trivet on a sample passage. One of Map's more teasing sentences goes like this (it just means "you're not listening to me"): "you bend your ear to me the way the asp listens to the snakecharmer; you pay attention as the boar does to the dogs' barking; you are soothed like the dipsas upon whom the sun beat down in Cancer" (folio 78ʳ). *Grues* dutifully explains all three images from Isidore: the asp stops its ears, one with its tail, the other with the ground, in order not to hear the snakecharmer; the boar trusts its tusks to ward off the dogs, and so ignores their barking when he hears it far off; the dipsas is a snake whose poison kills you before you feel it (folio 5ᵛ). Yet here, I think, we have a little trap laid by Map. He knew that readers would fly to their Isidore, and Isidore indeed comes through with the explanation of the first two. But nothing he says about the dipsas makes it clear how Ruffinus is soothed like it. Not by Isidore alone does a man annotate Walter Map. Our *Grues* annotator is not fazed, however: he has found a statement in Isidore about the dipsas and blandly quotes it. He doesn't even know that Isidore speaks of the dipsas in another place: "The dipsas is a kind of asp which in Latin is called situla because one bitten by it dies of thirst."[8] Since it

8. "Dipsas genus aspidis, qui Latine situla dicitur, quia quem momorderit siti perit." Isidore of Seville, *Etymologiarum sive originum libri xx*, W. W. Lindsay, ed. (Oxford: Clarendon Press, 1911), 12.iv.13.

seems sure that Map expected his text to be annotated, I think you can say that here he tests the annotator's skill: the pedantic annotator, the one who is merely looking for something to say to fill up the space, he sets up for exposure. And the *Grues* annotator is exposed.

Ridewall does better with the dipsas:

> Here Valerius compares Ruffinus to the snake *dipsas*, a kind of asp, and implies that just as one who has been bitten by this snake is always thirsty—the thirst kindled in him lasts until he dies—so Ruffinus is not held back from marrying by any dissuasion of Valerius's, but rather spurred on to marry like a man bitten and poisoned by the dipsas: a drink of water intensifies his thirst, not eases it, as the poet says, "And while Narcissus seeks to ease his thirst, another thirst grows" (*Met.* 3.415); "The more the waters are drunk, the more they are thirsted after" (*Fasti* 1.216). Note he mentiones the poison of the dipsas when the sun is in the sign of Cancer, for in that season the poison of that snake is stronger. (folio 196r)

This is better, and yet Ridewall is really to be faulted here. In the first place, the urge that they all show to quote Ovid whenever they can is here: the line about Narcissus is not about dipsas-thirst at all, but about his thirst for union with the image in the pool, and the line from *Fasti* is about someone with dropsy. Furthermore, Ridewall is attending to the larger rhetorical situation rather than to the logic of the particular passage, and he makes an unwarranted leap. The issue at the moment is not marriage but Ruffinus's refusal to listen to counseling; Valerius says that he "*is soothed* like the dipsas." Ridewall suddenly changes from comparing Ruffinus to the snake, as Valerius does, to comparing him to someone bitten by the snake: "just as one who has been bitten by this snake is always thirsty." Though he doesn't quote Isidore, he is actually forcing Isidore's statement about the thirst the dipsas induces into the passage: he too, for all his greater attention, is ultimately here the victim of cultural baggage.

Only Trivet has it right:

> "*You are soothed like the dipsas*," that is, you lay aside your anger the way the dipsas does: it kills instantly, without taking thought. This is how we speak of a resentful man: we say sarcastically that he is as kind as a snake. He does well to add, the dipsas *whom the sun has warmed in Cancer*, since the dipsas's—or any snake's—poison is

> at its most potent then . . . ; so he says sarcastically, you are soothed like the dipsas when it hurts most. The dipsas is also called situla, because it kills its victims by thirst. (folio 70ʳ)

In the last sentence we see even Trivet heaping on a needless fact because he knows it; still, he is the only one of the commentators who has figured out a plausible explanation of the passage, and the only one to notice the sarcastic tone that is the key to it.

Though he is good at avoiding superfluities, Trivet is at times almost infuriatingly complete. In speaking of Circe's turning Odysseus's men into beasts, he cites various stories of similar transformations, then gives us a long philosophical and theological discussion of just what such transformation can be. When Valerius mentions three winds, Trivet gives you all twelve, with their properties. When Valerius says that overcoming the wiles of Deianira was Hercules' thirteenth labor, at which he failed, Trivet gives you all twelve successful labors in detail. And yet each of these seems to me to work, and to bear out an important implicit level of Trivet's purpose, which is not merely to explicate Map but to promote his message. He concludes his inquiry into transformation with the opinion that accidental as opposed to essential change, or the deceitful appearance of change, is possible, and that the story of Circe is true. The effect of that is to force you to take Valerius seriously, to grant the danger of incipient beastliness at the hands of his Circe that Ruffinus is facing. Likewise the long yet swift recital of Hercules' labors gives a rhetorical power to the statement about the thirteenth that Map's two sentences don't quite have. Map says: "Duodecim inhumanos labores consummavit Alcides: a tertiodecimo, qui omnem inhumanitatem excessit, consumptus est. Sic fortissimus hominum, eque gemendus ut gemebundus, occubuit, qui celi arcem humeris sine gemitu sustinuerat" (folio 81ᵛ). (Hercules did twelve superhuman labors; by the thirteenth, which exceeded all superhuman labor, he was undone. Thus the bravest of men, who had held up the vault of heaven on his shoulders without a groan, died both groaning and to be groaned for.) Map compresses his point into the puns on *consummavit* and *consumptus est*, and *gemendus*, *gemebundus*, *gemitu*. Trivet, as it were, complements the power of this compression with the power of accumulation, reciting all the labors and concluding: "And when he had completed these twelve labors successfully, he was overcome at last by a thirteenth labor, the labor which is the subject here, in which he fought against a woman and lost." He then paraphrases the second sentence and adds: "From which it is evident that it is easier to bear the whole sky than the harm that is brought about by a wife" (folio 75ᵛ). At moments like this I feel that Trivet's commentary has become so eloquent that it amounts virtually to a continuation or imitation, a kind of "Son of Valerius" competing for equal status, rather than a commentary. The sensitivity, the being in tune, has gone too far: you long for a refreshing skepticism to go alongside it.

Trivet ends in a way that makes this rivalry for equal status with Valerius seem very open. Map ends abruptly with these words: "Sed ne Horestem scripsisse videar, vale" (folio 83ʳ; But lest I appear to have written an Orestes, farewell). Trivet explains the reference to a line of Juvenal's about a long, boring book on Orestes, then says:

> Jerome ends similarly in a letter in which he argues against marriage and urges virginity, and I can speak these words myself about my own work. "I know that I," he says, "I have spoken much more amply, and said more things by far in this catalogue of women than the custom of using examples allows, and that I may justly be blamed for that by a learned reader." But whenever I have said too much or too little, the fault and ignorance are mine; if I have said just enough, it is the gift and grace of God, to whom be honor and glory forever. (folio 78ʳ)

"I can speak these words myself about my own work"—Map's words (which are Juvenal's), Jerome's words, and my own words are similar. This seems to me, in its small way, to amount to a claim that Trivet belongs in the company of the great writers of antimatrimonial tracts: Juvenal, Jerome, and Valerius. It reminds me of Chaucer listing the epic poets at the end of *Troilus*. Trivet is kissing their steps, of course, with proper humility, and yet also associating himself with them. The collocation is brave—and, I think, earned. I don't suppose many annotators can aspire to creating the equivalent in the world of annotation to the original works they leech off, and I don't know if it is at all proper that they should. Some people say nowadays that criticism can reach that level, and so maybe annotation can, too; in any case I consider this commentary a rare example of annotation that rivals the original.

Let me sum up the chief points of interest, for this gathering, in these commentaries. They span a gamut, and in this respect are probably representative of medieval commentaries in general. At one end, the simpler commentaries focus on individual words and tend to offer "cultural baggage" rather than illumination, although they are sufficiently pointed on people and characters. They show a liking for quoting verse, often rather irrelevantly. Ridewall's commentary is of a higher order because it attends to arguments, not just words, though cultural baggage, including verse, is still there. Trivet's I count superior because it tackles subtler matters and in general follows Map's meanings more sensitively. Indeed, it is so in tune with the argument, and so original in the range of materials it brings to bear, that it constitutes a kind of rival treatise to the original. All these points of difference represent choices that I take to be still relevant for annotators today.

5

Discitur ut agatur: *How Gabriel Harvey Read His Livy*[1]

Anthony Grafton

How did they understand Livy my grandfather my great grandfather—[2]

Zbigniew Herbert's question provokes and puzzles the historian of early modern culture as well as the reader of modern poetry. No Latin prose author stimulated more scholarly interpretations or artistic representations than Livy did between 1450 and 1650. His vast though incomplete epic of Roman history was thronged with exemplary heroes and heroines, terrifying villains, precedents for modern customs, and policies for modern rulers. His many dramatic incidents were not so much stable, classic emblems as fluid Rorschach blots into which artists and writers, politicians and schoolboys could read any emotion or experience that suited their immediate needs. The rape of Lucretia, for example, could stand for anything from the political lesson about the loss of Florentine liberty taught by Botticelli to the erotic drama of helplessness and

1. This paper offers a first, informal report on my contribution to a collaborative enterprise: a study of Gabriel Harvey and other late Renaissance readers, to be written by me and Lisa Jardine. It owes a considerable debt to Professor Jardine's counsel and criticism.

2. Zbigniew Herbert, "Transformations of Livy," tr. J. Carpenter and B. Carpenter, *The New York Review of Books*, November 6, 1986.

compulsion imagined by Tiepolo. The smooth and eloquent lines of Livy's text were disfigured by commentaries that clung and spread like barnacles. The most eminent and passionate intellectuals—notably Machiavelli and Guicciardini—debated his relevance to modern conditions. No historian of early modern culture can avoid trying to explain why what now seems a swollen, bland, and artificial exposition of events and their morals served three hundred years ago as a lightning rod that drew down sharp and brilliant interpretations from the most diverse sectors of the intellectual firmament.

Herbert's poem is provocative in another, deeper way as well. In answer to his own question, he vividly reconstructs the physical and moral circumstances in which his grandfather and great-grandfather actually read:

> certainly they read him in high school
> at the not very propitious time of the year
> when a chestnut stands in the windows—fervent candelabras of blooms—
> all the thoughts of grandfather and great grandfather running breathless to Mizia
> who sings in the garden shows her décolleté
> also her heavenly legs up to the knees
> of Gabi from the Vienna opera with ringlets like a cherub . . .[3]

Through the eyes of Middle European schoolboys in the age of *Spring's Awakening*, he makes us see the text of Livy as a splendid but alien tissue of social prejudices and densely ornate language. Any modern reader must sympathize with the alienation and daydreams Herbert evokes; we remember that in the 1920s, when the (false) news spread that an Italian scholar had discovered the lost books of Livy, A. P. Herbert protested in *Punch* on behalf of the Amalgamated Society of Schoolboys, Past, Present, and Future that there was too much Livy already. But we are also amazed by the engagement the grandfather and great-grandfather eventually feel with Livy's Roman values and Latin style. And the historian must feel that even profounder emotion, envy. For the image of the Gymnasium classroom that Herbert calls so deftly back to life, with

3. Ibid.

its shabby, frock-coated master, portrait of the emperor, and pervasive smell of chalk and disinfectant, is the modern artist's counterpart of one of the scenes of early modern life that cultural historians would now most like to reconstruct. We know that the first modern intellectuals, from Petrarch to Montaigne, read seminal texts like Livy's in profoundly novel ways, that these new readings were in themselves the beginnings of the intellectual revolution of modernity. But we know almost nothing of the concrete circumstances in which readers encountered texts. Where did they read? With whom? How did the physical form of the text they read hinder or promote the reader's engagement with it? How can we locate this activity in the larger constellation of intellectual experiences and social rituals it formed part of?

To be sure, scholars of several kinds have recently focused their attention on reading and its history. Intellectual historians have argued that the Renaissance brought about a transformation in the lens through which Western readers inspected classic texts. The humanists saw the classics not as permanent, impersonal *auctoritates* but as historical, contingent works by individuals working in specific circumstances, addressing specific audiences that were clearly different—and distant—from themselves. The great Greek and Roman writers came to be seen as pagans whose assumptions no Christian could fully accept. And the modern scholar learned to pick and choose his ancient authorities, concentrating on texts produced in historical circumstances sufficiently like their own to be relevant. Thus Muret and Lipsius discovered that the histories of Tacitus, the product of an age of tyranny, offered lessons clearly germane to their own late-sixteenth-century age of tyranny. Literary critics, concentrating on the readings of the classics embodied in early modern literary works, have paid less attention to historical insight than to allegorical imagination. They stress the novel willingness of Petrarch or Montaigne to transform even the stateliest of their readings by self-consciously aggressive interpretation. Thus Erasmus forced an exemplary allegory of Platonic love on the most unwilling of recipients, the first line of Virgil's second *Eclogue*: "Corydon the shepherd was hot for pretty Alexis."

Historians of mentalities have worked out in rich case studies how a single imaginative reader could transform the most banal and traditional of texts into the most powerful—and heretical—of speculations or representations. Thus Carlo Ginzburg, in a dazzling piece of detective work, has shown that Titian rediscovered the erotic element in Ovid not by confronting the original Latin of the text or the humanist commentaries that had grown up around it, which he could not read, but by poring over the crude verse *rifacimenti*, prose allegories and woodcuts of the popular vernacular printed Ovids that he did know.[4] Historians of the book, finally, have worked out how classical and other texts were selected, edited, printed, and stored—and often reshaped or radically distorted in the process. All historians of early modern culture now acknowledge that early modern readers did not passively receive but actively reinterpreted their texts.

Yet all this intense specialized activity has led as yet to few powerful general results. In the first place, scholars have made far too little effort to combine forces. Practitioners of straight intellectual history still assume, in defiance of the critics, that the classics had a single, unequivocal sense that ignorant medieval readers distorted and that intelligent humanists finally recaptured. Literary critics still assume that the practice of a single exemplary writer—above all, his statements about his sources and his readers—can tell them everything they need to know about reading in a given century. Historians of the book embrace in their interdisciplinary enterprise economic history, social history, and the history of domestic furniture, but ignore the history of education and scholarship, as if educated men read books without employing any of the sharp intellectual tools they had spent their childhood learning to use. All students of reading have concentrated heavily on those acts that yielded emotional, personal, vivid responses to texts, as if the cooler searches for moral lessons and political axioms conducted by early modern readers from Machiavelli to Hobbes were insignificant because less appealing. And all students of reading have tried much too hard to find simple formulas that describe the reading practices of whole periods, and sharp moments of transition when one set of practices yields to another: when reading passes from

4. See in general A. Grafton, "Renaissance Readers and Ancient Texts: Comments on Some Commentaries," *Renaissance Quarterly*, 38 (1985): 615–49; for Ovid see C. Ginzburg, "Tiziano, Ovidio e i codici della figurazione erotica nel Cinquecento," in *Miti emblemi spie* (Turin: Einaudi, 1986).

speech to silence, from public to private settings, from intensive to extensive or passive to active.

This search for neat and dramatic periodizations merely distorts a complex and multivalent past. In any given period and milieu, many styles of reading coexisted and competed. John Lyly complained in 1578 that most texts were hardly read at all before they were recycled for wrapping paper: "Gentlemen use books as gentlewomen handle their flowers, who in the morning stick them in their heads, and at night straw them at their heels."[5] Thomas Nashe complained twenty years later that a "legion of mice-eyed decipherers and calculators" combed every word in print for possibilities of subversion, and "commacerated" their ruler with constant discoveries of unintended sedition.[6] Between the use of most texts to wrap fish and the McCarthyite combing of all texts word by word stretches a spectrum of ways of reading. Its varieties and modalities await—and often invite—exploration.

I will use a single case study—a single early modern intellectual making meaning in Livy—to suggest some of the ways in which older and newer intellectual, critical, and social forms of analysis should be combined, if we hope ever to take "second steps in the history of reading." My reader is a familiar figure, Gabriel Harvey (1550–1630), an ambitious Cambridge man from Saffron Walden, still remembered for his friendship with Edmund Spenser, his ambitions for high political office, and above all the magnificent quarrel with Thomas Nashe that led to the publication of Nashe's pamphlet *Have with You to Saffron-Walden* (1596). Here Harvey became the victim of one of the most dramatic muggings in literary history. Nashe produced a masterpiece of invective against the upstart he called Gurmo Hidruntum, Dagobert Copenhagen, Wrinkle de Crinkledum and, "our Talatamtana or Dr Hum." Harvey appears as a simpering fool who thrusts himself on pretty women and well-born men:

> He is beyond all reason or God's forbode distractedly enamoured of his own beauty, spending a whole forenoon every day in sponging and licking himself by the glass: and useth every night after supper to

5. J. Lyly, *The Anatomy of Wyt*, 1578, in *Life in Shakespeare's England*, ed. J. Dover Wilson (Cambridge: Cambridge University Press, 1913), p. 150.

6. T. Nashe, *Lenten Stuffe*, 1599, in *Life in Shakespeare's England*, pp. 148–49.

> walk on the Market Hill to show himself, holding his gown up to his middle that the wenches may see what a fine leg and dainty foot he hath in pumps and pantofles.

Harvey's social pretensions, foolish mannerisms, and elaborate handwriting are withered in turn by the blast of Nashe's abuse. Harvey himself is burned on our memory as a figure as corrupt and ridiculous as the dying Falstaff, "so lean and so meagre that you would think like the Turks he observed four Lents a year."[7]

What we are less apt to remember about Harvey is that he was not only one of the great victims but also one of the great readers of all time. He bought, borrowed, and was given many books, classical and modern, Latin and vernacular. He read and annotated them with single-minded energy; the margins and blank leaves of any book he owned are adorned with symbols, exclamations, and whole paragraphs of comment, all painstakingly and elaborately entered in what Nashe memorably called his "flourishing flantitanting [flaunting] gouty omega first." Often he secreted not one but several layers of notes, the result of repeated reading and meditation, that intricately intertwine in every space left vacant by the printer. More than fifty of his annotated books have been located; many of his notes have been painstakingly transcribed by Moore Smith and Colman. This corpus of printed books and manuscripts notes may be the richest set of materials we dispose of for reconstructing how our academic ancestors read.

Harvey's Livy—now deposited in the Firestone Library at Princeton—offers an especially rich lode of material to the historian's pick and shovel. It is a grand, heavy folio in sixes, printed in Basel in 1555. The text of Livy appears flanked by numerous critics and supporters. Two elaborate commentaries, one by Ioannes Velcurio and one by Henricus Glareanus, follow the text and explicate it, often phrase by phrase. Instructions for reading history precede it. Lorenzo Valla's iconoclastic demonstration that Livy had committed a genealogical error also appears, lest the reader feel even more reverence than a Roman classic properly demands. The entire book is heavily annotated by Harvey.

7. T. Nashe, "The Life of Gabriel Harvey," in Nashe, *Selected Writings* (Cambridge, Mass.: Harvard University Press, 1965), pp. 281–316.

We may begin with the occasions of reading. Harvey's elaborate, dated notes reveal much about the times, places, and purposes of his several discrete assaults on this rich and polysemous mountain of text. He bought the book in 1568. In 1570–71 he entered in it a record of a Livian debate that he had witnessed:

> Thomas Smith junior and Sir Humphrey Gilbert debated on behalf of Marcellus, Thomas Smith senior and Doctor Walter Haddon on behalf of Fabius Maximus, before an audience at Hill Hall consisting of me, John Wood, and several others of noble birth. At length the son and Sir Humphrey yielded to the distinguished Secretary.[8]

Other notes show that this debate was connected with at least one intense Livian experience. Harvey and Thomas Smith, Jr., read through the third decade, the story of Hannibal, in one week in 1570–71. Smith would shortly afterward die in the first colonization of the Ards, his father's Irish enterprise. Harvey records that they read along with Livy the military authors Vegetius and Frontinus, and that they did so critically: "We chose not always to agree with Hannibal, or Marcellus, or Fabius Maximus, or even with Scipio himself" (p. 518). Evidently, then, the reading was military in orientation, as its timing clearly suggests.

In 1576–77, just before Philip Sidney went on his mission to the Emperor Rudolph II in Prague, he and Harvey read books 1–3 of the first decade, which embrace the early history of Rome and its passage from monarchy to republic. The approach they took, Harvey says, was "as political as possible," as befitted an ambitious courtier like Sidney. They paid no attention to scholarly questions and dismissed the humanist commentators: "De Glareani aliorumque annotationibus parum curabamus" (p. 93). But as we will see, they did use other secondary sources.

8. *T. Livii Patavini, Romanae historiae principis, Decades tres cum dimidia* (Basel: Hervagius, 1555); Wilmerding Deposit, Department of Special Collections, Princeton University Library, p. 428. Here and below translations are my own. Passages by Harvey in Elizabethan English are the original texts; those in modern English, like this one, are translated from his Latin. For Harvey's library see V. Stern, *Gabriel Harvey* (Oxford: Clarendon, 1979); for his marginalia see the specimens edited by G. C. Moore Smith, *Gabriel Harvey's Marginalia* (Stratford-upon-Avon: Shakespeare Head Press, 1913); a much fuller edition is being prepared by W. Colman.

In 1584, back in Cambridge, Harvey read Livy again with Thomas Preston, master of Trinity Hall. They read Machiavelli's *Discorsi* at the same time, seeking to find the true political marrow hidden in the Latin text's dry bones. Indeed, Machiavelli's "method" and "politique positions" occupied them as intensively as Livy himself. They read several other up-to-date works on pragmatic politics as well, notably Jean Bodin's *Methodus* and *Republic*.

In 1590, finally, Harvey read Livy from still another point of view. "I haue seene," he wrote,

> few, or none fitter obseruations, or pithier discourses upon diuers notable particulars in Liuie, then sum special chapters in Augustines excellent bookes De Ciuitate Dei. Where he examines, & resolues manie famous actions of the Romans, with as sharp witt, deep iudgment, & pregnant application, as anie of those politicians, discoursers, or other notaries, which I haue read vpon Livie. (sig. Z5 recto)

Harvey read the *City of God* not on its own but together with its almost equally vast Renaissance companion, the commentary by Juan Luis Vives, famous for its vast learning, penetrating inquiries into Augustine's lost sources, and exuberant excursuses on such indelicate matters as farting. Here Harvey often found that subjects touched on by Augustine had been studied "*paulo exactius*" by the modern scholar.

Harvey's Livy bears in its margins, then, the bright stones and strange creatures he fished up in at least four separate trawls through the text, the first three carried out in company and the fourth in that solitude into which he fell in later life. The social, public character of the first three readings cannot be emphasized enough. Reading for Harvey was a skill with social as well as intellectual value. It brought him into contact with the Smiths and Sidney, leaders of the expansionist war party that would soon succeed in tearing apart the loose but toughly woven fabric of Irish social life, but would largely fail to involve England and Elizabeth in a Europe-wide Protestant campaign against international Catholicism. Reading took Harvey into high company and great houses, much as the ability to provide astute financial advice might now pull its possessor up the social ladder.

But while Harvey's Livy affords us new insight into the concrete profits to be drawn from effective reading, its revelations do not stop there. Consider, for example, Harvey's numerous references to the other texts that he—and his fellow readers—consulted. He claimed to have embedded his Livy in a mesh of mutually reinforcing parallel texts: classical works with complementary information, modern commentaries with helpful interpretations, Augustine and Vives with their powerful points of view. These were not the empty professions of the modern critic who wordily proclaims his debt to unread classics, "to all the people who have made this article possible: Karl Marx, St. John of the Cross, Friedrich Nietzsche, Sacco and Vanzetti, Sigmund Freud, and C. G. Jung."[9] Harvey really did read everything he named. He says, for example, that when he and Sidney went through books 1–3, they compared them to Frontinus's *Stratagems* (first century A.D.). A copy of Frontinus that he owned survives in the Hougthon Library at Harvard, and its copious notes deal with exactly the same problems and historical figures that the Livian notes attack. Harvey refers often to the *Silva* of political aphorisms (1583) by Lambert Daneau—a now forgotten work by a Calvinist minister chiefly remembered for his unsuccessful efforts to impose a natural science based on the Bible on the Protestant curriculum, and a church order based on the "Genevan Inquisition" on the liberal citizens and professors of Leiden. Harvey's copy of Daneau has so far evaded discovery, but his references are so frequent and precise as to make it clear that they were not conventional. He read the work as soon as it appeared, excitedly referring to its newness, and often praised it as a source of pungent and precise political axioms. And as he worked through Livy, Daneau's aphorisms often led him to choose subjects for comment and lessons for emphasis. When Harvey noted how wise Romulus had been to use religion to civilize and ceremony to overawe his primitive subjects, he simply repeated Daneau's lapidary Livian axioms.

Harvey's reading of Livy, with all its careful collation and cross-checking, was not unusual for him. His corpus of rhetorical works, which included his Quintilian (now in the British Library), several works of Cicero, and Ramus's commentaries, was similarly unified and explicated. And he himself describes other late Renaissance readers as going through similar efforts to domesticate and retrieve

9. F. C. Crews, *The Pooh Perplex* (New York: Dutton, 1963), p. 41.

the vast quantitites of information and advice that the printing press had put at their disposal. Dr. Dale, for example, a lawyer and statesman to whom Harvey devoted an admiring note in his Livy, had had a code worked out with his secretaries for finding the desired text quickly. "*Da primum*" meant that Dale wanted his Justinian, "*Da secundum*" that he wanted his *Speculum iuris*, "*Da tertium*" that he wanted Livy. Meanwhile Dale's own "manuscript codex of secrets" preserved and ordered the chief results of his consultation of the ancients.

Any way of reading is at least in part a learned set of habits and techniques. In the late Renaissance, humanists, jurists, and theologians actively debated in glosses and treatises the best ways to read. A self-conscious reader like Harvey had his pick of sources from which a method could be drawn, and his Livy gives a number of indications about which of these meant the most to him. At the outset, commenting on a humanist's preface, Harvey remarks that he has developed his own "unique method" for reading all historians without confusing those of Roman and those of foreign affairs (sig. a 7 recto). At the other end of his book he thanks Sidney, Smith, and "Monsieur Bodin," who "wunne mie hart to Livie" (sig. P1 recto). And in a comment on the Roman chronology of Glareanus, also included in his text, he made clear that he had met Bodin when the latter came to England in 1582 to help in the negotiations for the Alençon marriage: "My conversation with two expert Frenchmen, Jean Bodin and Peter Baro, helped me greatly; they consider Glareanus, Funck, Mercator, Crusius more industrious and precise than any ancient chronologer" (sig. P verso).

These nods are as good as a wink to anyone moderately steeped in late-sixteenth-century scholarship. They mean that Harvey set out to adopt to his own ends the method for critical reading of historians that Bodin had described in his celebrated *Methodus ad facilem historiarum cognitionem* of 1566. This shapeless but fascinating book went through a number of editions and became the core of a well-known anthology, the *Artis historicae penus*. It urged that Western society—and the French monarchy above all—could be pacified and reformed only if intellectuals embarked on a critical study of all past organized societies. The student must read all past historians (helpfully assembled by Bodin in an impressive bibliography). He must extract all effective actions and sensible institutions, enter the passages describing these in a notebook, and evaluate them, using marginal symbols to indicate their import (CH meant *consilium honestum*; CTV meant *consilium turpe utile*). He must assemble all this material, however, not as a magpie makes a nest but as a beaver makes a dam: he must scrutinize the material before picking what was rewarding. He must learn to distinguish the critical historian from the incompetent, and the judicious historian from the biased. One who failed to make critical discriminations of this kind would be overwhelmed by the mass and number of texts he confronted. One who made them, by contrast, could know and understand the facts—could see how each society's institutions and deeds derived from the collective character imposed on it by geography and climate, and then see which of these might be adaptable to his own circumstances.

Bodin offered an exemplar theory of history, traditionally moralized and providential, but stripped of the unhistorical Golden Age at the start and freed from the eschatological straitjacket of the Four Monarchies. Any advanced Protestant reader—from the historian William Harrison to Harvey—had to find Bodin's book impressive, and to consider, if not accept, his offer of an Ariadne thread to lead through the labyrinth of histories. Harvey followed Bodin's advice, albeit in his own way. He certainly developed a code for annotating his histories. Astrological symbols were his favorite way to call attention to interesting historical lessons. The symbol of Mars, ♂ , indicated military matters; the symbol of Mercury, ☿ , indicated diplomacy. The symbol of an opposition (when two planets were 180° apart in the zodiac), ☍, indicated scenes of battle. Occasional Roman letters—like the ubiquitous **JC**, indicating legal information—filled in where the symbols gave out.

But as Harvey's use of astrological signs suggests, he always applied Bodin's instructions in his own way. Harvey claimed that Bodin won him to Livy. But in fact, Bodin had rated Livy fairly low as a historian. Livy was important and informative, but his work was marred by his "piety—or shall I say superstition—in which he surpassed everyone. Nothing is more common than cows speaking, the heads of the Scipios bursting into flame, statues sweating." And Bodin followed ancient precedent in pointing out that "Livy and Sallust went too far for historians in inserting direct and oblique speeches into their works. As Cicero says, nothing is sweeter in straight history than elegant brevity. But if you took the speeches out of Livy, only fragments would be left."[10] No wonder that Caligula, in an outbreak of good sense, had wanted to burn all copies of Livy's *Histories*. They were a derivative mass of tralatician facts and invented speeches.

Harvey's reading of Livy differed sharply from Bodin's. In 1.23, when the Romans and Albans are about to go to war, the Alban Mettius makes an elaborate speech to the Roman Tullus Hostilius. He points out with polish and *gravitas* that the Romans and Albans should not fight, since they were linked by their common descent from the Trojans and threatened by a common enemy, the Etruscans. Harvey commented:

> The Alban's speech to King Tullus is strong and prudent, at once just and temperate. Thus it seems rather a speech by Livy than by the Alban—or at least it is polished in the Roman style, like many barbarians' speeches later on. Let it be enough to have said this once: Livy is always Livy, whoever the speakers were. (p. 12)

Harvey is positive exactly where Bodin had been negative. The artificiality of Livy's speeches becomes their strong point. After all, Harvey and Sidney were looking for guidance in courtly behavior—or, to put it differently, in effectively artificial speech. Powerful orations were what Livy offered them in plenty; they used as one collateral text a collection of his *Conciones* in which the intervening—and interfering—tissue of narrative had simply been pared away. Speeches seemed to them not peripheral but central to the text, and their artificiality not a detriment to their credibility but an enhancement to their value as models for imitation. Harvey's method of reading for models of effective speech at court was a conscious and personal refinement of Bodin's—a commentary as much on the *Methodus* as on Livy.

It may be objected that Harvey could have misunderstood Bodin's precepts. But this is to underestimate both his capacity as a scholar and the vast extent of intellectuals' interest in Bodin. Nashe, recounting the prodigies that accompanied Harvey's birth (his mother had dreamed that "her womb was turned to such another

10. J. Bodin, *Methodus ad facilem historiarum cognitionem* (Paris: Juvenis, 1572), pp. 75–76, 73–74.

hollow vessel full of disquiet fiends as Solomon's brazen bowl wherein were shut so many thousands of devils"), claims to hold back to suppress some details, in order to appear a credible historian: "Should I reckon up but one half of the miracles of his conception that very substantially have been affirmed unto me, one or another like Bodin would start up and tax me for a miraclemonger as he taxed Livy" (pp. 285, 287). And Montaigne, who learned from Bodin to enter summary evaluations in the end papers of his copies of historians, also both applied Bodin's method and rejected some of the conclusions Bodin drew with it. Bodin had called Plutarch a fabulous writer because he told the story of the Spartan boy. Montaigne devoted a long section of his essay on Seneca and Plutarch (2.32) to refuting Bodin's criticism. He claimed to have seen simple peasants and hardheaded Gascon women endure worse torments than the boy did, and for no more obviously urgent reason. Harvey's use of Bodin emerges then as typical. The critical late-sixteenth-century reader often found his tools in the kit Bodin had assembled. But he felt as free to alter and improve them as he did to read new lessons into the texts they were meant to manipulate.

The best way to enhance our sense of how Harvey made Livy meaningful is to proceed from principles to applications. How did Livy's early Rome change contours, shadows, and colors as Harvey switched microscopic lenses and inspected it again and again? We cannot work through the whole corpus of his notes. But two studies in his ways of reading will establish the identity of the major hoops through which Harvey made his author jump.

Toward the middle of book 1 Livy tells the story of the Horatii and the Curiatii. Romans and Albans, both descendants of the Trojans, have both stolen one another's cattle, refused restitution, and leveled ultimatums. They confront one another in order of battle but decide, given the danger posed by the Etruscans to both parties, to avoid a full-scale combat and arrange a trial by battle in its place. Each army has a set of triplets, the Roman Horatii and the Alban Curiatii, that can represent it. A treaty is made and solemnized with elaborate ritual. The brothers fight. Two Romans fall, but the third, unhurt, runs away, separates the three Albans and kills them one by one. Horatius, returning in triumph to the city, meets his sister, who had been engaged to one of the Curiatii. She cries out with sorrow on learning of her lover's death. Horatius promptly kills her, is found guilty of treason, and is then freed because of his popularity and his sister's lack of patriotism. Peace is made; but it does not last long.

The story has everything. Livy gives the details of disagreements among ancient scholars (over which set of triplets had which family name). He lovingly describes Roman institutions, showing the "fetial" (priest) pluck and use the holy herb needed for making treaties, and describing how the king and duumvirs declared and staged a trial for treason. Horatius provides an example of courage, patriotism, and athletic prowess—but also of the errors to which too much zeal and courage can lead. Mettius the Alban provides an example of statesmanlike prudence and eloquent oratory. And Horatius's nameless sister makes a fine subject for a cautionary tale about the eternal female conflict between love and duty.

Harvey had ample exegetical resources on hand as he attacked this passage. The commentators in his Livy, Glareanus and Velcurio, both discussed book 1, and though Glareanus left the Horatii alone, Velcurio treated them at length, paraphrasing every phrase or sentence that could possibly pose a difficulty. After the first two Horatii die, Livy describes the situation of the third: "Forte is integer fuit, ut universis solus nequaquam par, sic adversus singulos ferox" (1.25.7; The young man, though alone, was unhurt. No match for his three opponents together, he was yet confident of his ability to face them singly). Velcurio found a surprising amount of grist for his mill here: "Is) scilicet Horatius. Integer) id est, non vulneratus. Vniversis) scilicet tribus coniunctim."[11] And he went into technical detail of a more refined sort as well when it came to the legal aspects of Horatius's murder case, explaining at length why the taking of private revenge amounted to treason as well as parricide: "He punished his sister by private vengeance, when she should have been punished by the magistrate" (sig. K1 recto).

Harvey's notes on the passage show no interest whatever either in elementary problems of construing or in deeper ones of law and antiquities. Instead, he draws a political lesson:

11. *Livii decades*, sign. K 1 recto.

> Monomachiae Exemplum nobile. sed decisio praeceps magis, quam politica. Nec vero Politicum est, rei universae summam committere tam paucorum Virtuti, aut Fortunae. Sed hic usus manavit a paucorum Antiquorum Heroica Virtute: qua omnia magna videbantur decernenda. (A splendid example of single combat. But this was a rash rather than a politically prudent way to reach a decision. It is in fact not politically prudent to entrust the general welfare to the virtue of fortune of a few. But this custom derived from the heroic virtue of a few of the ancients, by which, it seemed, all great questions should be decided.) (p. 13)

Harvey was hardly the first to suggest that this trial by combat had been imprudent and was not an example to emulate. Daneau had derived a similar axiom from the same passage: "It is always dangerous and often useless to entrust the general welfare (*summa rerum*) to a dual of two or more in a war. For the vanquished do not keep faith, and they do not suffer a great loss because of it."[12] And Machiavelli—who no doubt lurks, here as elsewhere, behind Daneau—had devoted three chapters of his *Discorsi sopra la prima deca di Tito Livio* to the story. He made it the pretext for a long and general argument that "one must never risk his entire fortune with part of his forces."[13] He drew from it the specific recommendation that one should not try to stop an enemy at one's border by confronting him with a small force (1.23). And he found in it food for reflection on the corruption of republics, arguing that while good citizens must be rewarded, it had been wrong simply to let Horatius go free after he had been fairly condemned for killing his sister (1.24).

Harvey begins from the prudential, "political" reading of Machiavelli. Like Machiavelli—and like his contemporaries Justus Lipsius, and Daneau, whom he much admired—he wanted to extract and shrink to durable, pill-like axiomatic form the pragmatic lessons of the text. But unlike them, he wanted to speculate about other matters as well. What captivated his imagination was less the imprudence of the custom Livy described than the reasons why it had been practiced. He locates these in the ancients' belief in

12. L. Daneau, *Politicorum aphorismorum silva* (Leiden: Maire, 1620), p. 124.

13. N. Machiavelli, *Discorsi sopra la prima Deca di T. Livio* (Rome: Blado, 1531), 1.22.

individual heroism, which made them think single combat an appropriate way to solve such problems. He may deplore the early Romans' heedlessness, but he applauds their chivalry. And his other notes show that what he—and perhaps Sidney—most appreciated in Livy was less the pragmatic maxims he could inspire than the heroic feats of arms that he so vividly described. Harvey's further notes on the passage include a Mars symbol; the exclamation *Vnicus Horatius*; and, most revealing of all, a reflection on the feigned flight by which Horatius tricked his opponents into separating: "strategematica fuga. ne Hercules quidem contra tres, aut duos selectissimos Pugiles" (p. 13).[14] Here we see Harvey making clear what Livy meant to him: a treasury of military devices to be imitated and heroic battles to be savored. This was what Harvey found in Roman history as he read about it elsewhere as well—for example, in his copy of Machiavelli's *Art of War*, also in Princeton, where one battle scene more than a page long is decorated with a mars symbol at the end of every line. Harvey read not simply to reflect, boil down, and imitate, but also to savor, speculate, and admire. No wonder that the pleasures of the naked text outweighed the more refined rewards of learned commentary, when he and Sidney did their reading.

Yet Harvey did not stop here. A further note on the slaying of Horatius's sister takes quite a different tack.

> De impietate belli, quod Albanis Romani intulerunt; et de victoria dominandi libidine adepta. August. l. 3. c. 14. de Civit, ubi de Horatiis, et Curiatijs scite. [In darker ink:] Ecce biblica Goliae, et Davidis monomachia. Heroica etiam Herculis, et Cygni apud Hesiodum: Achillis, et Hectoris apud Homerum: Æneae, et Turni apud Virgilium. (p.13)[15]

Here Harvey, probably reading by himself and later in life, refers to the eloquent chapter (3.14) of the *City of God* in which Augustine

14. A strategic flight. Not even Hercules could handle three, or two outstanding opponents in a fight.

15. See Augustine, *City of God* III.xiv, on the impiety of the war that the Romans waged against the Albans, and the victory that resulted from desire to rule; there he skilfully treats the Horatii and the Curiatii. [In darker ink:] Cf. the biblical duel of David and Goliath. Also the heroic ones of Hercules and Cycnus in Hesiod, Achilles and Hector in Homer, Aeneas and Turnus in Virgil.

ponders the Horatii and the Curiatii, condemns the murder of Horatius's sister, and insists that the war itself deserved not honor but condemnation, like a gladiatorial combat. Harvey knew that Augustine's account amounted to an attack on the whole Roman heroic scheme of values that he and Livy loved. "Ecce quoties et quomodo humanam Livij prudentiam, divina redarguit Augustini Sapientia" (p.6; See how, and how often, the divine wisdom of Augustine refutes the human prudence of Livy), he wrote early in book 1. He concluded that while each city had its virtues, the divine one was both *firmior* and *foelicior*. The application of Augustine in the 1590s seems to undermine the "heroic" reading of Livy with Sidney in the mid-1570s, as if the older and wiser Harvey—perhaps saddened by the death of Sidney and the downfall of the aggressive Protestantism Sidney symbolized—had repented. Yet this simple, sentimental account does violence to the form and content of Harvey's note. He does not stop with Augustine. His final lines on the passage list heroic duels from Hesiod, Homer, Virgil, and the Old Testament as well, offering David and Goliath, perhaps, as an example of a vivid heroism that even Augustine could not condemn.

How did Harvey read Livy? Clearly this simple question cannot be simply answered. Harvey's reading of Livy is not a single thing and never froze in a fixed form. It did not eventuate in a formal commentary, and probably was never meant to do so. More remarkably, it seems never to have established a single fixed method or point of view. Rather, it was centrifugal and mobile. Harvey proceeded from Livy to his friends, from life to Livy, from treatise to text and text to treatise, finding that each reflected light on the other. There was no point at which the investigation logically had to stop, for each deeper insight into a single passage could result in novel interpretations of the rest. And the whole game started anew every time a new event or text, a Sidney or a City of God, penetrated Harvey's consciousness and set it turning again. This centrifugal mode of reading—one in which the journey seems eternal and the arrival disappears from view—bears a strong resemblance to some contemporary ways of reading the sacred texts. And it helps, I think, to explain just how Livy's crisp, vital heroes and episodes could slip so easily as they did from meaning to meaning. What mattered, in the end, was less the power of the solution than the ingenuity with which it was proposed; the humanists, like participants in a perpetual Passover *seder*, seem drunk with the possibilities of interpretation afforded by an emblematic history.

Harvey's encounters with book 1 produced layers of interpretation that acted rather like polarized lenses. Each was clear enough in itself, but when superimposed, they tend to obscure rather than to magnify the text. But other encounters with other sections were more dramatic and direct. In his week-long collaborative reading of the third decade, the story of Hannibal, Harvey moved quickly (the text takes up four volumes of the modern Loeb edition). He read with only one end in view: to grasp and then to criticize the tactics of Hannibal and his Roman adversaries. Harvey represents himself and Smith, Jr., as two young military intellectuals on the make, learning through Livy how to think strategically for themselves: "We were freer and somewhat sharper judges of Carthaginians and Romans than was appropriate to men of our fortune, virtue, or indeed learning; at least we learned not to adulate anyone, ancient or modern" (p. 518).

Harvey's summary references through the decade to Hannibal and the Romans are single-minded in their concentration on leadership:

> Fabius Maximus bie Warie, & cautelous proceding, somewhat cooled his [Hannibal's] heate: but liker slie Saturne, then gallant Jupiter, or braue Mars. Onlie Marcellus, & Scipio beat him at handstrokes (22 *ad init.*)
>
> Braue & redowted young Scipio: full of mightie courage, & valour (22.53)
>
> Flauius, uersutus pragmaticus (25.16)
>
> Fabius, bello melior: Marcellus, praelio: Martius, facinore: Nero, itinere: Scipio omni bellica laude excellentissimus (25.20)
>
> Martius, a most braue & terrible knight, at a pinch. Which of the Heroical Worthyes could have dun more in the time? (25.37–39)
>
> [Scipio] As peerles fine, as matchles braue: a Mirrour of sweetest courtesie, & terriblest valour (29.18)

The purpose of these laundry lists of heroic virtue is plain. Harvey saw—and no doubt took part in—debates about Carthaginian and

Roman leaders. These lists of deeds and adjectives were the substantive preparation for such debate. Much as Erasmus compiled as his distinctive aid to eloquence a matchless list of 250 ways to say "Thank you for the letter" in classical Latin, so Harvey and Smith, Jr., devoted much of their private effort to assembling material to be used in public.

But the third decade has a strong narrative line as well as individual stories of heroism. At the outset Hannibal's march on Rome seems irresistible, his victory inevitable. By the end his army is in disarray and Hannibal himself in despair, while Scipio returns to Rome in triumph. Harvey's marginal notes show how eagerly he followed Hannibal's progress and appreciated the Carthaginian general's *industria, & uigiliantia horribilis*. Hannibal stalks onward like an ancient Clint Eastwood, implacable and unbeatable. Yet Harvey and Smith found more than virtue in Hannibal's feats of arms. They saw the seeds of his eventual failure planted early in his campaign. In book 22 he fails to take the opportunity afforded by Cannae and attack Rome at once; in book 23 he winters in Capua, letting his army lose cohesion and morale; in book 30 he has become pitiable. Harvey remorselessly tracks each error of judgment. At book 30 he reflects: "Hannibal was beaten first in spirit; it's no surprise, then, that he was immediately beaten in the flesh as well. One's fortune corresponds to one's strength of mind and body" (p. 510). Harvey finds a simple explanation for Hannibal's many related failures. He lacked the indomitable will needed to make the most of each opportunity as it occurred. "Occasion is only a point: now or never." "The sole essential for a great man is to seize the instant with great possibilities forcefully, with shocking power, and to play the powerful leader, when it is important to do so, with terrifying power" (p. 317). Indecision, Machiavelli had long ago shown, was the most destructive of all errors in a ruler. Now Harvey read indecision into Livy's Hannibal.

The motive for this reading is not far to seek—and need not be overdetermined, since it was inspired at least in part by Livy's own clues. Harvey read the Carthaginian and Roman past in terms of the English present. A rising member of the rising war party, he ached for action, like his patrons. By finding the reason for Hannibal's failure not in want of resources but in failure of will, he taught exactly the historical lesson that Walsingham and Leicester would have most liked Elizabeth to learn. The alchemy of present needs turned Hannibal from Fortinbras into Hamlet, in the margins if not in the text.

Harvey's transformation of Hannibal involved not only the explanation of a failure but the development of sympathy for it. Harvey seems, as the third decade proceeds, to feel sorrier and sorrier that Hannibal did not carry out his aims. If he had only acted when he should have . . . "Maharbal's consummate advice [to march on Rome immediately after Cannae] could have made Hannibal as great as Alexander. But Hannibal, intent on lesser goods, lost his one chance for the greatest success. Now or never" (p. 317). To find the moral he needed in decade 3, Harvey had to feel sympathy for the devil, had to find in Livy's glorification of Rome the possibility of a counterhistory that glorified Carthage. This he did with ease and dexterity that one might not expect from a humanist.

"Only my father and myself after him," writes Herbert,

> read Livy against Livy
> carefully examining what is underneath the fresco
> that is why the theatrical gesture of Scevola awoke no echo in us
>
> . . . .
>
> My father knew well and I also know
> that one day on a remote boundary
> a local conflagration will explode
>
> and the empire will fall.[16]

Harvey and Smith were certainly no Freuds; they did not identify themselves with Hannibal or their enterprise with subversion. Yet their margins swarm with enticing modernist possibilities that one would not expect from the tidy text imprisoned in its moralizing and critical humanist verities by its editors.

The lessons to be drawn from this rich material are themselves rich. First, it seems clear that the existing separation between intellectual history and history of the book is artificial, not natural. Harvey's case would resist any analysis that did not employ both sets of methods in complementary ways. Classicists have combined the two approaches since the eighteenth century; medievalists see

16. Herbert, "Transformations of Livy."

them as complementary. Early modernists could learn from their colleagues in this as in other respects. Second, it seems clear that Harvey's methods and experiences were not eccentric but normal. Collateral evidence shows that contemporaries of social standing as high as Harvey's, or higher, and intellectuals now far better known than he, shared his concerns, interests, and approaches. Third, Harvey's case establishes that reading in the Renaissance was above all a rhetorical enterprise. Like rhetoric, it was a public enterprise, aimed at an audience. Like rhetoric, it proceeded by well-defined rules. Like rhetoric, it sought not to attain deep truths but to advance convincing arguments. Like rhetoric, it aimed always at a defined and limited audience and a set occasion. Harvey and his contemporaries read for effect. Their interpretations—even when privately arrived at—were meant to serve as preparation for public performances. That explains why the reader in the margins of Harvey's Livy feels so evidently free to shift assumptions, styles, and points of view from decade to decade in Livy and in his own life. Reading was a tool, not an end.

Was Harvey deluded to think that flexible reading could take him to the top? Not necessarily. Another collateral document suggests how sharp his insight may have been. A memorandum prepared by Robert Beale for the private use of Edward Wotton, it explains in severely practical terms the "Office of a Councellor and Principall Secretarie to Her Majestie." It offers sage advice about how to define the Privy Council's agenda, avoid cabinet councils "which doe but cause iealousie and envie," and abbreviate the letters submitted to the council so that its members will at least have read a summary of the matters they must decide on. It also offers readings of many ancient historians: "Remember what Arrian sayeth in the life of Alexander. . . . So likewise towards your fellow Councellors behave yourselfe as Maecenas counselled Augustus. . . . Be dilligent. Remember the sayinge of Salust." Beale is quite unapologetic in his provision of these humanist axioms. Indeed, he emphasizes in his conclusion that a good principal secretary must be a good reader of the classics: "By the readinge of histories you may observe the examples of times past, judginge of their successe."[17]

17. C. Read, *Mr Secretary Walsingham and Queen Elizabeth*, 1 (Cambridge, Mass.: Harvard University Press, 1925), pp. 423–43.

I submit that Harvey hoped his skills could win him a position exactly like Beale's, as a valued political adviser who combined practical experience and legal expertise with detailed study of the ancients. Harvey's mode of reading, in fact, was precisely the sort of serious political discourse that his authoritative contemporaries esteemed. And I would suggest that, though Harvey did not succeed as wildly as he hoped—"hewed and slashed he had been as small as chippings if he had not played 'Duck, Friar' and hid himself eight weeks" from a peer he attacked, and landed in Newgate for a while and had in the end "to spur cut back again to Cambridge"—his humanism was not at fault. Harvey's ability to read was perhaps his one uncontested asset; it took him far and yielded fascinating and contradictory visions of the Roman past. Can we ask more of commentary?

6

Undermining the Text: Edward Gibbon, Alexander Pope, and the Anti-Authenticating Footnote

Peter W. Cosgrove

Among those components of textuality that have hitherto escaped the scrutiny of literary critics, one of the more obvious is the footnote. Perhaps this indicates a too-general acceptance of its claims to be regarded as an objective tool rather than a rhetorical device, claims that in almost every other literary or philosophical form arouse instant suspicion. Although the scarcity of comment means that examination of these claims could start from almost any conceivable point of departure, one of the more fruitful approaches seems to be the historical. This would entail not so much a narrative of the footnote's origins or genealogy as an investigation of its appearance in the period before it has fully stabilized into its present positivist form. By discussing two contrasting usages of the footnote in the eighteenth century—Pope's apparatus to the *Dunciad Variorum*, and Edward Gibbon's notes to the *Decline and Fall of the Roman Empire*—it becomes possible to demonstrate that the claims of scholarly apparatuses, the footnote among them, to participate in a "scientific" objectivity have not only been virulently contested in the early modern period, but that even eighteenth-century empiricism was content with weaker positions than those adopted by the triumphant positivists of the following age. While this demonstration would by no means be a definitive dismissal of later claims, the restoration of a history to the device of footnoting may point toward the larger failure of an "objective" discursive vehicle to escape an inherent instability between its rhetorical and its factual elements.

The idea of objectivity has a long and fascinating history that has not yet come to an end, but suffice it to say that among its origins was the desire during the Reformation to formulate an ideal of knowledge free from the influence of partisan religious struggles, or from the apriori syllogisms typical of medieval Aristotelianism. The idea very quickly became associated with mathematics and with experimental science, and it is in this sense that we regard it today as a way of thinking uncontaminated by prejudices personal, professional, national, or ideological, whose definitions still seem surprisingly close to the "idols" of one of its earliest proponents—Francis Bacon. Later, objectivity came to be defined against a wider range of distorting elements gathered together under the catch-all complex term "subjective," which ultimately seemed to refer to any human response whatsoever. We in literature stand of course on the wrong side of the objective/subjective division, but there is at least one aspect of our work that takes its cue from scientific method, namely, textual scholarship. Here we devote ourselves to something tangible—the real incarnate form of the text itself. We can examine different editions, compare them with surviving authorial manuscripts, and develop theories and methodologies for deciding questions of intentionality and determining textual priorities; above all, in the tangible texts we have means by which we can test the validity of these theories and methods. A humble subaltern in the ranks of the apparatus that textual scholarship has developed over the years is the footnote. Along with bibliographies, indexes, catalogues, reference books, and dictionaries, the footnote has become an indispensable if anonymous tool. Without it, the whole enterprise of the critical edition would become a nightmare, and the most soaring flights of speculative criticism would feel obliged to offer reassurance for the skeptical reader by providing a solid plinth of phlegmatic notes frequently tucked away at the end of the article or chapter.

Notational supplement brings something very interresting to light. A reader, it is implicitly acknowledged, is not to be convinced by rhetoric alone; like a good positivist, or a jury in a court of law, he or she demands that the manipulations of the text come equipped with an independent support system. As we follow the argument we wonder, "Where did this remark come from?" or "What facts or arguments back this up?" We turn to the back of the book or the bottom of the page for confirmation, reassurance, for titles of other works that will bear out sketchy ideas that our author has not had time to elaborate; in short, we look for hard evidence that the author's views, however brilliantly put forward, still depend upon verifiable objective fact. The author of a speculative work thus appears in two persons: first, as the interested pleader of the text who does not conceal his subjective interests as the proponent of a specific idea; and second, as the objective gatherer and presenter of evidence. This internal division in the author is communicated to the reader as division in the work. We turn from the text to the notes as a jury might turn from a trial attorney to the display table where the very unrhetorical discontinuity of the evidence is the guarantee of its disinterestedness. The discontinuity is emphasized further by the arbitrariness of the numerical reference system, whose mathematical connotations also reinforce the scientific objectivity of footnoting. We might even go so far as to say that the more successful as evidence the footnote is, the further it gets from any connection with the rhetorical. The connection, however, is repressed rather than annihilated, and there remain many and varied ways in which the footnote can be aligned under the rubric of textuality as much as any other component of the written page. In the eighteenth century the particular aspect that remains as a symptom of the footnote's literariness is the rhetorical form that I shall heuristically call "genre."

Without inquiring too deeply into the problematic nature of the relationship between the generic and the particular, I want to employ the term "genre" to indicate the possibility of discerning at any point in history the deliberate or de facto incorporation of a set of literary practices that writers may draw on in their work—in Hans Robert Jauss's terms, "'rules of the game' which as such can then be varied, extended corrected, but also transformed, crossed out or simply reproduced."[1] Such a set constitutes a problem for post-romantic literature insofar as it implies a series of constraints that curb and limit the originary expressive source. The curb of genre on the footnote, however, is not quite identical to that on the Romantic lyric, since the footnote could hardly be further in conception from the ideal of authorial voice. Its power depends to a large degree on its being perceived as the opposite of expression, on deriving, that is, from a language that stands outside the speaker, and is akin to the voiceless language of mathematics. In these two relations, then, genre shows a Janus face: one aspect threatens expression, and the other threatens objectivity; expression is diminished by being tainted with an origin external to the individual speaker, objectivity by being embedded in a literary form that draws it away from the impersonal to participate in the human. But, although the eventual source of the footnote's power comes from association with empirical claims for an objectively knowable reality, its own humble realm is that of the mere fact. The footnote as used today is hardly a scientific tool or even a mode of description; it is, however, a vehicle for evidence and, like all such vehicles, must remain uncontaminated if the evidence is to be considered sound. To consider it in any way generic is to deprive it of its independence, that position outside the text that ensures its freedom from contamination. Under genre, the privileged exteriority of the independent witness becomes part of the forms of persuasion, and in fact the most insidious of all the forms—that which disclaims any intention to persuade, in "the interests of a scrupulous attention to the facts however divisive they may be."[2]

Although I am quoting a phrase from Lee Patterson's essay on "The Logic of Textual Criticism," it could apply to the ideals of members of almost any discipline whose written communication employs footnotes—everything from biophysics to history: ideals

1. Hans Robert Jauss, "Theory of Genres and Medieval Literature," in *Toward an Aesthetic of Reception*, trans. Timothy Bahti (Minneapolis: University of Minnesota Press, 1982), p. 88.

2. Lee Patterson, "The Logic of Textual Criticism and the Way of Genius: The Kane-Donaldson *Piers Plowman* in Historical Perspective," in *Textual Criticism and Literary Interpretation*, ed. Jerome J. McGann (Chicago: University of Chicago Press, 1985), p. 86.

memorably catalogued by Nietzsche as the scholar's "bent to doubt, his bent to deny, his bent to suspend judgment (his 'ephectic' bent), his bent to analyze, his bent to investigate, seek, dare, his will to neutrality and objectivity, his will to every *sine ira et studio.*"[3] This scholarly will to objective truth comes into focus most particularly in the fifteenth century as the ancient texts begin to be recovered, assessed, and edited. From this point on, works that had hitherto been isolated in monasteries or been fondly regarded as upholding the religious and political order became subject to the investigations of scholars whose veneration for the texts did not obstruct their reduction to easily analyzable fragments. This fragmentation, however, this will to factuality, is countered by a will to power of the older forms of interpretation. Those forms of humanism that saw the past as glorious and fit for imitation resisted these developments, and in some cases scholarly apparatus became the locus of a contestation, not confined to the charge and countercharge of intellectual debate, but ramifying into satire and burlesque.

Resistance to fragmentation takes a number of forms, but the one I am most concerned with here is the battle that occurs in the eighteenth century over the footnote as one of the most despised scholarly intrusions into the holistic text. Alexander Pope in his poem *The Dunciad* and Edward Gibbon in *The History of the Decline and Fall of the Roman Empire* both use the footnote in ways that today even a quick glance would consider outside the norms of scholarly writing. But the differences between their usages are as instructive as their historical similarities, which are the result of a contemporary debate that thrusts questions about the nature of scholarly apparatus to the fore. In the second edition of *The Dunciad*, commonly known as the *Dunciad Variorum*, Pope provides an enormous apparatus of his own footnotes, many of which he attributes to a scribal persona, Martinus Scriblerus. The intention of Pope's notes is to supplement the thrust of the verse satire on Grub Street authors and poor pedants, and to incorporate the satire against scholarship in a parody of the structure of the footnote itself. That is, the footnotes to Pope's poem are written and appended by Pope not in order to clarify or authenticate, but in order

3. Friedrich Nietzsche, *On the Genealogy of Morals*, trans. Walter Kaufmann and R. J. Hollingdale (New York: Random House, 1967), p. 112.

to satirize the footnote as apparatus. In James McLaverty's words: "Pope intended his poem to be hemmed in by scholarship: the work was designed not only to refer to the dangerous plight of literature but to exemplify it as well."[4] Gibbon, who has all the attributes of a Popian pedant except dullness and obscurity, provides a similar enormous apparatus whose remarkable playfulness does not disguise the fact that he regarded it as a legitimate scholarly tool. As we shall see, however, this view may be too superficial, and Gibbon may turn out to be doing something very much like Pope, not to invalidate but to reformulate the basis of Pope's attack.

The debate in which the *Dunciad Variorum* is situated is the English side of the Quarrel of the Ancients and the Moderns—often called the Battle of the Books. For a time this resolved itself in England almost into an attack on one man—Richard Bentley. And as Bentley was one of the foremost textual scholars of the age, the choice of victim necessarily revealed itself as a thoroughly powerful attack by the supporters of the ancients on the idea of textual scholarship as such. This attack was the culminating point of a social struggle that had been waged since the invention of printing gave new impetus to the revival of learning—a struggle between the hierarchical domination of a relatively easily controlled body of literary and philosophical knowledge, and the erosion of that domination by a combination of the relaxing of ecclesiastical and civil control of the rate of literary diffusion and by increased investigation into the validity of the texts both sacred and secular that upheld the hierarchical social structure. In *The Printing Press as an Agent of Change*, Elizabeth Eisenstein points out the importance of the fact that "different texts, which had previously been dispersed and scattered were also being brought together for individual readers," with the effect that "the era of the glossator and commentator came to an end, and a new 'era of intense cross-referencing between one book and another' began."[5] Cross-referencing enabled scholars to do what the dispersal of documents in an age of slow communications had hitherto made prohibitively difficult. By comparing

4. James McLaverty, "The Mode of Existence of the Literary Work of Art: The Case of the *Dunciad Variorum*," in *Studies in Bibliography* 37 (1984): 82–105.

5. Elizabeth Eisenstein, *The Printing Press as an Agent of Change*, vol. 1 (New York: Cambridge University Press, 1979), p. 72.

texts they were able to make judgments on their origins and provenance, and therefore, at a time when authenticity was becoming an essential value, on their validity.

One of the most famous texts to fall victim to the comparative method was the *Donation of Constantine*, a presumptive deed of gift of Italy and the Roman provinces to the papacy by the first Christian emperor, which Lorenzo Valla demonstrated to be a forgery shortly before printing had made its presence fully felt. The methods he used—demonstration that the syntax and vocabulary were inconsistent with those of the supposed period of composition—were almost identical to the methods employed by Bentley to expose the *Epistles of Phalaris*, a second-century A.D. forgery whose attribution to the sixth century B.C. was uncritically accepted by Sir William Temple, the statesman and friend and counselor of Charles II and William III. And as the methods were similar, so the eventual results, more momentous in the case of Valla than of Bentley, had a similar impact. In the first case the hegemony of the church hierarchy, and in the second the claims to superiority by the elite politician, were shown to rest on an unsatisfactory textual basis. Such application of scholarship's will to objective truth undermined the textual basis for the existing social order for as long as both accepted the ideal of objectivity as transcending social forces—almost, that is, until our own day. But this is not to say that all scholars were deliberate iconoclasts. Bentley was a religious man, his Boyle lectures were essentially a refutation of Hobbes's materialism, and he was by no means a disloyal one; Valla, the client of Pope Leo X, was certainly no church reformer. What Nietszche calls the "unconditional will to truth" came into conflict with their other loyalties. Perhaps the remark of the nineteenth-century classicist F. A. Wolf, who came to the conclusion that the *Iliad* had neither form nor author, can stand for all scholars who set out to purify their texts and ended up fomenting, however indirectly, a revolution in values: "No one can be as angry with me," he exclaimed, "as I am with myself."[6]

6. McGann, ed., *Textual Criticism*, p. 77. Leslie Stephen makes a direct application of this notion to Gibbon, although perhaps in rather extreme terms: "Meanwhile the fat, phlegmatic little man polished his sarcasms, and sneered Christianity away with the most perfect unconsciousness that hot-blooded revolutionaries were drawing strange lessons from his pages." *The History of English Thought in the Eighteenth Century*, vol. 1 (New York: Harcourt, Brace and World, 1962), p. 379.

The defenders of the old order, however, were quick to see the dangers. The Renaissance consistory itself might have been cynical about the *Donation*, but when Ulrich von Hutten adopted Valla's findings in the cause of Protestantism, the papacy took another line. Later developments added other kinds of threats to the preservation of the various sacred texts of the Greco-Roman and the Hebraic past as iconic monuments of the canon. Among these threats was historicization. The persistence of the epics and the Bible as living exemplars depended to some degree on assuming a continuity between the time of their composition and the present. The speech of Sarpedon that Pope translated as a dry run before embarking on the complete *Iliad* still spoke to a warrior aristocracy: "Why boast we, Glaucus, our extended Reign,/ Where Xanthus' Streams enrich the Lycian Plain?/ . . . /Why on those Shores are we with Joy survey'd,/ Admir'd as heroes, and as Gods obey'd?/ Unless great Acts superior Merit prove,/ And vindicate the bounteous Pow'rs above?"[7] And until Richard Simon, in *A Critical History of the Old Testament*, demonstrated that Moses could not have written the Pentateuch, God spoke to us all in the interview on Mount Sinai.[8] But the same sense of historical periodization that permitted Valla and Bentley to locate the true date of the text's production also began to create an impassible barrier between the past and the present. Slowly, the sacred texts were pried loose from a continuous tradition and subjected to a system of analysis that investigated the historical period which produced them as an alien and, to the degree of difference, a nonexemplary *mentalité*. To some extent Pope is responding in the *Dunciad Variorum* to the threat posed to the literary classic by textual analysis as it asserted itself in Lewis Theobald's edition of Shakespeare, which was in essence the application of Bentley's conjectural criticism to a modern poet. In the subsequently added fourth book of the poem, Pope takes on the work of Bentley himself, partly as a justified protest against the scholar's editorial treatment of Milton, which Patterson characterizes as "the prime exhibit in a rogue's

7. Alexander Pope, "The Episode of Sarpedon," *The Poems of Alexander Pope*, ed. John Butt (New Haven: Yale University Press, 1963), p. 60, ll.27–36.

8. See Richard H. Popkin, *The History of Scepticism from Erasmus to Spinoza* (Berkeley and Los Angeles: University of California Press, 1979), pp. 221, 226.

gallery of editions conceived under the sign of genius,"[9] and partly as a little-deserved sneer at Bentley's great discovery of the digamma, the missing letter of Homeric Greek. McLaverty shows that the typographical format is similar in appearance to Bentley's edition of Horace, and almost identical to the 1716 Geneva edition of Boileau's works. "The knowledgeable reader approaching the *Variorum*," he points out, "would note the parallel with Bentley's Horace and the authorized edition of Boileau[,] alert to ridicule of editorial absurdities, and the ways in which they obstruct poetic meaning."[10]

Mistaken though Bentley's edition of *Paradise Lost* might have been, his Horace was a triumph for conjectural scholarship, and Theobald's work laid the path for many later editions of Shakespeare, including one by Pope's own literary executor, William Warburton. Pope's real intent may be seen, however, not as a defense of individual works but as a defense of poetry in general against textual criticism. He had just completed his own translation of Homer, in which he had firmly relegated a rather massive textual apparatus to the back of the book, where it could not interfere with the progress of the narrative. Furthermore, the source of many of his notes was the work of thirteenth-century Byzantine bishop, Eustathius, and the remarks were those of "glossators and commentators" rather than of the critical editor. Indeed, their purpose, besides pointing out and dilating upon the beauties of the text, was to ward off carping critics, Bentley among them, who were already at this period springing up from among the ranks of the moderns to hint that Homer was, if not a collection of unidentifiable minstrels, at best a ragged vagabond singing for his supper.[11]

Pope's commentary not only is not arranged in footnotes but has an entirely different intention from modern academic apparatus. In

9. Patterson, "Logic," p. 74.

10. McLaverty, "Mode of Existence," p. 104. He includes reproductions of pagespreads from three texts that very effectively underline his argument.

11. "Take my word for it," says Bentley, "poor Homer, in those circumstances and early times, had never such aspiring thoughts [as designing his poem for eternity]. He wrote a sequel of songs and rhapsodies, to be sung by himself for small earnings and good cheer, at festivals and other days of merriment; the *Ilias* he made for the men, and the *Odysseis* for the other sex." R. C. Jebb, *Bentley* (New York: Harper & Brothers, n.d.), p. 143.

the Middle Ages Eustathius's comments surrounded the text, top, sides, and bottom, flowing from it like the decorative acanthus that adorned monastery capitals and liturgical mosaics—a humble dependent whose function was to beautify and dignify. Similarly in Pope's Homer the commentary is an adornment; it points out the beauties of the text, and elaborates on it in ways designed to illuminate it and laud the merits of the author. "Indeed," Pope effuses over the description of Pallas donning her armor, "there is a Greatness and Sublimity in the whole Passage, which is astonishing and superior to any Imagination but that of *Homer*, nor is the there any that might better give occasion for that celebrated Saying, That *he was the only man who had seen the Forms of the Gods, or the only Man who had shewn them.*"[12] The footnote, however, is neither an adornment nor a humble dependent. It functions in ways that always constitute a threat. Whether its position at the bottom of the page is seen as a prop or a mine (and these are the same image reversed), it always poses the question: "Are you fair? Are you honest? Then let not your beauty admit any discourse to your honesty." In our own rhetorical texts—our suasive essays or our historical narratives—the footnote is there to guarantee, by supplementing our style with facts, that our beauty does not admit such discourse. In our critical editions it questions the text and forces it in the name of truth to give up its beauty secrets. But it always implicitly retains the power to undermine or to uphold. Far from being a humble dependent, it asserts itself as the true master, and does so by claiming to represent the truth that always stands outside the literary text and has the power of judgment over it. This claim makes it into strategic terrain whose occupation is essential for both the scholar and his opponents. As long as the footnote remains a textual Archimedean platform, the scholar is in an almost impregnable position. Nothing has more importance for the defenders of the sacred text than to demonstrate that the footnote has no such claim and that in fact it is just another special pleader, another rhetorical device deployed on behalf of what the eighteenth century would call "partial" interests.

12. Alexander Pope, "The Iliad of Homer, Books I–IX," in *The Poems of Alexander Pope*, vol. 7: *Translations of Homer*, ed. Maynard Mack (New Haven: Yale University Press, 1965), p. 309.

When Pope, then, on completion of the translation of the sacred epic text, turned to the mock epic attack on the enemies of poetry, he also appended to it a mock commentary—the footnote. Marshall McLuhan has noted approvingly Pope's criticism of the social effects of the printing press in which scholars and Grub Street hacks are savaged impartially under the common appellation of Dunces. The following quotations attack scholarship from two angles. The first criticizes the obscurity of the learning, and the second, through the device of adopting Theobald's own voice, the uses to which learning is put.

> But high above, more solid Learning shone,
> The Classicks of an Age that heard of none;
> There Caxton slept, with Wynkin at his side,
> One clasp'd in wood, and one in strong cow-hide.
> There sav'd by spice, like mummies, many a year,
> Old Bodies of Philosophy appear.
> De Lyra here a dreadful front extends,
> And there, the groaning shelves Philemon bends.
> . . . .
> There, thy good Scholiasts with unweary'd pains
> Make Horace flat, and humble Maro's strains;
> Here studious I unlucky moderns save,
> Nor sleeps one error in its father's grave,
> Old puns restore, lost blunders nicely seek,
> And crucify poor Shakespeare once a week.[13]

Here we can easily perceive the attack on historical scholarship. Theobald's library is the victim of Pope's scathing antiantiquarianism, which also includes some *ancienneté* in sneering at those books from the British past that to Pope's mind will never make it into the canon of great works. But it is precisely through the knowledge of these works that Theobald gained the acquaintance with the usages, the *mentalité*, of the past that enabled him to make substantial emendations to the corrupt Shakespearean texts. In the second quotation, the same *ancienneté* appears more clearly when Pope defends the great canon, with the charge that the depredations of

13. Alexander Pope, "Dunciad A," in *The Poems of Alexander Pope*, vol. 5: *The Dunciad*, ed. James Sutherland (New Haven: Yale University Press, 1965), pp. 82–83, ll.159–64.

scholarly emendation make Horace insipid and humble the imperial grandeur of the *Aeneid.*

So to this extent the text of the *Dunciad Variorum* bears out McLuhan's claims. But it is surprising that *The Gutenberg Galaxy*, a work emphasizing medium rather than content, should overlook entirely the extremely complex typographical format of the *Dunciad Variorum*—a format made possible only by the printing press. Pope's attack overlapped the familiar confines of the verse into prefaces, indexes, glossaries, and footnotes. In the 1729 edition, the contest for page space between the notes and the text is reminiscent of a Japanese board game: sometimes the neat decasyllabics press the notes all the way down to the bottom margin; sometimes the heterogeneous prose of the notes squeezes the verse superstructure up to a single couplet. The context between them, however, is not real; thematically, Pope's notes always supplement the verse. One note to the line "There Caxton slept, with Wynkin at his side" reads: "Caxton, A printer in the time of Edward IV. He translated into prose *Virgil's Aeneis* as a History: of which he speaks in his Proeme in a very singular manner, as of a book hardly known. Tibbald quotes a rare passage from him in *Mist's Journal*, concerning *a rare and marvellous beast called Sagittarye*, which he would have *Shakespear* to mean rather than Teucer, the Archer celebrated by Homer." Notice the ahistoricism or antihistoricism of the passage, in the contempt for Caxton for not knowing any better than to think the *Aeneid* was a history. And in Pope's resentment of this idea we can suppose his dislike, first, of the historicization of poetry in general, and then for simply not being from the right historical period. Pope is not able to divest himself sufficiently of the prejudices of his age to evaluate the contribution of someone so far removed in time; whether he was aware that Caxton was the first English printer, I do not know, but since his theme is the pernicious multiplication of useless books, the information would probably not have mollified him. Subsequently this antihistoricism appears in the principle he seems to establish for scholarly procedure, that great minds speak to each other over the eons, which leads him to adopt the remotest similarities between Homer and Shakespeare as a firm basis for textual emendation. In fact, Pope vastly overreached himself in this note, since Theobald's delving into "all such reading as was never read" yielded the fact that in the word "sagittarye" Shakespeare was indeed referring to the "marvellous beast" in *Troilus and Cressida*, and not to the Homeric archer.[14]

This kind of supplement is not only untrustworthy in its information but furthermore does not maintain the necessary structural barrier between the text and the apparatus that allows the footnote to function as testimony to the truthfulness of the text. Just as the text attacks the dusty antiquarianism of the scholars, so the footnote, instead of providing the facts whose objective aloofness should support the claims of the text by countering its reckless rhetoric, joins in the assault. It brings suspicion on itself as gleeful participant in the realm of satirical baiting, and straddles the threshold of the rhetorical and the factual, destroying the distinction that enables their interdependence to work. With the collapse of this difference, the footnote begins in Pope's hands to fall from its privileged position of disinterested guarantor outside the persuasive text into the thick of the fray.

But if the two sorts of text seem to have a complex typographical relationship in the original *Dunciad Variorum*, even this appears simple compared to the complexity of the current standard edition. There the board game has a third participant in the form of the explanatory and elucidating footnotes that modern editors have added to Pope's work, now in its turn become the object of the textual criticism he mocked. And their eminently professional endeavors provide the perfect foil for Pope's antiprofessional badinage. Where he is intemperate, they are grave; where he is accusatory, they exonerate. At times they even take it upon themselves to gently rebuke his derisory inaccuracies. At the verse, "Earless on high, stood unabash'd Defoe," they tell us, "Pope must have known that Defoe did not lose his ears" (*Poems*, ed. Sutherland, p. 117). But as in the game of Go, there comes a point when it must be decided who has surrounded whom. Does the editor's temperateness rebuke Pope, or does Pope's derision point to the fallacy of the editorial aloofness? Because eventually the effect of Pope's procedure is not merely to demote temporarily the individual objective footnote to the level of participant; it brings the footnote's objectivity itself altogether into question. Unlike the mock epic, the mock footnote does not imply that the form it parodies remains un-

14. *Poems*, ed. Sutherland, n. 1. p. 213.

scathed. In this there is a formal distinction between the top and the bottom parts, we might say, of the *Dunciad Variorum*; the verse defends the epic forms that it traces, as it were, in negative. The notes, on the other hand, insinuate themselves under the skin of the form and transform it into something different. They assist in its mutation from a series of autonomous facts that measure the text against some implied reality into a partisan of a world view (in Pope's eyes a less attractive one) antagonistic to the values of the text it pretends to evaluate. Thus, by repeating the structure parodically, Pope brings down the footnote from its aloof objective status into the arena on which it presumes to sit in judgment.

By now it is obvious that the specific mode of the footnote that opens the possibility of genre is a collaboration that collapses the tension between the authenticating function on which its efficacity depends and the polemic function of the text. And although Pope's attack on the footnote may have successfully (or not, depending on your point of view) demonstrated its bad faith by exposing its rhetorical aspects, this does not make it a genre. Where are the examples of its extension and transformation that would fulfill Jauss's definition? The *Dunciad Variorum*, however, was by no means the inaugural of, or even the only moment in, this adaptation of scholarly apparatus. Already in the Battle of the Books, Atterbury had mocked Bentley in the third edition of *Boyle's Examination* by appending an index that had only one entry—Bentley—and whose subheads consisted of personal attacks on the scholar. In the *Tale of a Tub*, Swift had incorporated his opponent Wotton's notes in a gesture of mockery and disdain. Moreover, strange to say, the very *Dunciad* notes we have been considering became a small industry in themselves even after Pope's death, when Warburton made his "unauthorized" additions to them to revenge himself on his own enemies. At this point it is advantageous to turn to Edward Gibbon both because, like the *Dunciad Variorum*, his work stands high in the eighteenth-century canon, and because the extensive footnotes have long been considered a remarkable aspect of *The Decline and Fall of the Roman Empire*. For one thing they take up, by David Jordan's count, almost a quarter of the work.[15] And

15. David P. Jordan, *Gibbon and His Roman Empire* (Urbana: University of Illinois Press, 1971), p. 41.

again, like the notes to the *Dunciad*, they go beyond any authenticating function to set up a variety of interactions with the text. In Gibbon's case this takes such forms as extended quotations from Dryden and the French dramatists; presentation of facts whose function of modifying the text renders it incomplete without the notes; and commentary that is unabashed opinion and hearsay rather than scholarly precision: "I have somewhere heard or read," he casually remarks in one note to his discussion of the rise of monasticism, "the frank confession of a Benedictine abbot: 'My vow of poverty has given me an hundred thousand crowns a year; my vow of obedience has raised me to the rank of a sovereign prince.' . . .—I forget," Gibbon slyly concludes, "the consequences of his vow of chastity."[16]

The majority of Gibbon's notes, however, are perfectly respectable examples of serious scholarly annotation similar to that of the victims of Pope's satire. Although Gibbon is not primarily a textual critic like Bentley and Theobald, he practices a historical comparatism of the kind burlesqued by Pope when, in the "Testimonies of Authors," Pope makes Martinus Scriblerus say, "but we shall likewise with incredible labour seek out for divers others, which, but for this our diligence, could never at the distance of a few months, appear to the eye of the most curious. Hereby thou may'st not only receive the delectation of Variety, but also arrive at a more certain judgment, by a grave and circumspect comparison of the Witnesses with each other, or of each with himself."[17] Fifty years earlier, Gibbon's scholarly ideals, if not his stylistic elegance, would have been a prime target for Pope's assaults on the pretensions of scholarship to objectivity. There was no greater exponent in the eighteenth century of the Tacitean *sine ira et studio* which Nietszche alludes to in his exemplification of the scholarly ideal. Yet no one more completely demonstrates how scholarship can live up to an ideal of impartial assessment of sources while maintaining a brilliant and subtle rhetorical offensive. And Gibbon's offensive was directed against many of the things which Pope stood for, religion

16. Edward Gibbon, *The History of the Decline and Fall of the Roman Empire*, ed. J. B. Bury (London: Methuen & Co., 1912), ch. 37, p. 76. (All subsequent references will be given parenthetically in the text.)

17. *Poems*, ed. Sutherland, p. 23.

being among the foremost of these targets. No one can be unaware of the corrosive effects of the irony in Gibbon's "candid enquiry" into the origins and growth of primitive Christianity. But perhaps more important from the point of view of incompatibility of the ideals of these writers is the whole complex thrust of the *Decline and Fall* against fiction and poetry.

This complexity is due to the problem confronting the Enlightenment historian of what Hayden White calls "the crucial opposition between 'truth' and 'error,' with it being understood that many kinds of truth, even in history, could be presented to the reader only by means of fictional techniques of representation." These techniques White characterizes further as "rhetorical devices, tropes, figures and schemata of words and thoughts, which, as described by classical and Renaissance rhetoricians, were identical with poetry in general."[18] But the unspoken history behind White's remarks is that which we have already presented as the struggle between those for whom the literary text was a model for emulation and those to whom it was an object of knowledge. This brief definition hardly conveys the difficulty of discussing a conflict that could sometimes be waged in the mind of a single person, yet could be projected onto the social stage. Edward Gibbon was himself such a man. Although his narrative contains many elements of the romance and the epic, his scholarly sympathies lie with Valla and Bentley, and indeed in him the demystifying effect of their procedures is intensified by his Enlightenment skepticism. In particular he distrusts many of the discursive vehicles that are available to him from the past. The Enlightenment historian did not think the genres of the epic, the oration, and the encomium to be capable of delivering the truth without distortion, if at all. They spring from primitive conditions, or from superstitious mythmaking, priestly mystifications, and the lies of "venal orators" whose livelihood depended on the approval of their masters. Gibbon constantly laments the various forms that this distortion takes. Sometimes it is the actual structure of a trope, as when he charges that in the remark of one author, "there is an air of rhetoric, and perhaps of falsehood, in this antithesis" (Bury, 3:31.344). Sometimes it is the false priorities of his source: "How

18. Hayden White, *Tropics of Discourse: Essays in Cultural Criticism*, (Baltimore: The Johns Hopkins University Press, 1978), p. 123.

many interesting facts," he complains, "might have Orosius inserted in the vacant space which is devoted to pious nonsense" (Bury, 3:30.280). And in a footnote on the lost works of Claudian, of all the poets to appear in the *Decline and Fall* the one most favored by Gibbon, he makes the general comment that "[i]t is more easy to supply the loss of good poetry than of authentic history" (Bury, 3:30.300). His problem, however, as White pointed out, is that he is obliged to use narrative structures in many ways similar to those of the fiction he is condemning. It is at this point that we may observe another transformation of the footnote genre—one which, although it is used to the opposite effect of Pope's, nevertheless builds on the freedom for rhetorical play with which Pope had saddled it.

Much of the *Decline and Fall* is in narrative form, although it has been disputed whether this form is epic, oratorical, "structural," or all three. And one could easily add "romance" to the list of models that Gibbon draws on. The narrative is in tandem, however, with a system of footnotes that not only incorporates authorities, facts, and details that would impede the narrative process, but that also contradicts and counteracts aspects of the narrative that in themselves would be distortions of the facts available to the scholarship of the time. The footnote thus becomes the means by which Gibbon enters into a context with his own text both thematically and structurally, and this he does through the process of authentication itself. Where Pope undermines the disinterestedness of the fact by making the reader uncertain whether he can trust it or not, Gibbon does so by using the unimpeachable fact either against the assertions of the text or against its form. The kind of information Gibbon sets forth in the footnote ranges from mere reference to what are almost minidissertations, complete with scholarly methods of ascertaining probability, weighing dependability of sources, assessing rival interpretations, and offering controlled speculation. In a footnote to a mention in the text of "the small island of the lake of Bolsena, where after a short confinement [Amalasuntha] was strangled in her bath," Gibbon provides the following:

> The lake, from the neighbouring towns of Etruria, was styled either Vulsiniensis (now of Bolsena) or Tarquiniensis. It is surrounded with white rocks, and stored with fish and wild-fowl. The younger Pliny

> (Epist.ii.96) celebrates two woody islands that floated on its waters: if a fable, how credulous the ancients! if a fact, how careless the moderns! Yet, since Pliny, the island may have been fixed by new and gradual accessions. (Bury, 4:41.324)

This note is by no means one of the most striking in the work; I have chosen it by reason of its typicalness. In the midst of a tragic narrative drawn from an old chronicle, the author is enticed into a judicious digression on the possible name of the place where the action occurs, is led to a lyrical description, and thence to a question of the trustworthiness of an ancient source, which besides providing a sense of depth about the ancient world (Pliny lived some three hundred years before the period under discussion) permits a speculation on natural history couched in an elegant antithesis. As a digression it is singular enough. But if we examine it in relation to the narrative in progress, we shall see that it can be considered as more than a digression: it can also be seen as an example of what I am calling structural contestation.

The note just cited is not in thematic opposition to the tale of the fate of Amalasuntha; if anything, the fish, fowl, and white rocks provide a lyric complement to the story of secret assassination. But the tone of detached speculation on the possible name and nature of the locale has a pronounced effect on the tragic climax of a narrative whose traditional nature may be indicated by the conventional opening statement of the protagonist's pedigree some pages earlier: "The birth of Amalasuntha, the regent and queen of Italy, united the two most illustrious families of the Barbarians" (Bury, 4:41.321). This effect is one of extreme bathos, created by the intervention of cold fact at the moment when our sensibilities are most aroused. Here is the culminating sentence, at the conclusion of a story of a strong woman thwarted of her desire to attain absolute power by having her son forced on her as coregent:

> The letters of congratulation [on her elevation to the throne beside her son Theodatus] were scarcely dispatched, before the queen of Italy was imprisoned in a small island of the lake of Bolsena,[*note*] where, after a short confinement, she was strangled in the bath, by the order, or with the connivance, of the new king, who instructed his turbulent subjects to shed the blood of their sovereigns. (Bury 4:41.324)

Overly concise, perhaps, but note the narrative pathos of the ironic juxtaposition of the crime and the letters of congratulation. And the other themes, so reminiscent of the Tacitean account of the reign of Nero, give a Gothic flavor to the condensed drama: the horrors of matricide, the taint of lewdness in the murder in the bath (or is it merely a contrast to the death of Seneca the Stoic?), and, to round off the tale, a standard moral that could be described as a narrative reflex, since Gibbon elsewhere does not hold tyranny in high esteem. But in the middle of all this, stop at "the lake of Bolsena" and read the note that cautiously speculates on its name. In the midst of such a charged narrative, the concentration of scholarly attention on this detail has a disenchanting effect on the reader; it distracts us from the story, it dispels the illusion. Gibbon, in one of his many scattered remarks on epic, commented unfavorably on this intrusion into an affecting story of details in the form of catalogues of ships and generals: "Ils refroidissent l'interêt, ils ralentissent l'action au moment que l'attention est la plus attachée." In a history, he goes on to say, one forgives the same thing because it is necessary: "c'est ordinairement le nombre et la qualité des troupes, qui donne la victorie."[19] We could say, then, that insofar as in the text he is writing a narrative, he wishes to preserve it from chilling detail; but insofar as he is a scholar, he slackens the action with the intrusion from below. The reader, however, does not escape the contradictory effect. What occurs in this contrast can hardly be seen as anything other than scholarly subversion of the very structure of the narrative text through the disenchantment of disassociated factuality in the footnote apparatus.

The footnote, then, maintains in this form a double existence. It stands outside the text to impart information, but it enters the text to interfere with its narrative function. In this particular example the aloofness of the footnote predominates, since the details that it gives us bear only the slightest connection to the events recounted. In my next example, however, the footnote opposes the text both structurally and by directly contradicting its contents. Gibbon tells a tale from the fourth century that explains why part of France is called Brittany. Maximus, a British claimant to the imperial throne

19. Edward Gibbon, *Miscellaneous Works*, vol. 4, ed. John Lord Sheffield (Basel: J. J. Tourneisen, 1796), p. 1.

> boldly and wisely resolved to prevent the designs of Gratian [the incumbent emperor]; the youth of the island crowded to his standard, and he invaded Gaul with a fleet and army, which were long afterwards remembered as the emigration of a considerable part of the British nation.*note* The emperor in his peaceful residence at Paris was alarmed by their hostile approach. (Bury, 3:27.145)

But the text does not do justice to Gibbon's doubts about the authenticity of this emigration, which, although it is not mentioned again directly, is implicitly referred to in a later note to the effect that "the loose declamation of Gildas [a chronicler of the Anglo-Saxon invasion] . . . may countenance an emigration as early as the middle of the fifth century. Beyond that aera, the Britons of Armorica can be found only in romance" (Bury, 4:38.161). But since this note does not occur for another eleven chapters, it does not form part of a coherent collection of adjacent reflections on the subject. Thus the following footnote to the phrase "British nation" is the only clue the reader has that the discursive text describing Maximus's invasion is completely misleading:

> Archbishop Usher (Antiquitat. Britain. Eccles. p. 107, 108) has diligently collected the legends of the island and the continent. The whole emigration consisted of 30,000 soldiers, and 100,000 peasants, who settled in Bretagne. Their distined brides, St. Ursula with 11,000 noble, and 60,000 plebeian, virgins, mistook their way; landed at Cologne, and were all most cruelly murdered by the Huns. But the plebeian sisters have been defrauded of their equal honours; and, what is still harder, John Trithemius presumes to mention the children of these British virgins. (Bury, 3:27.145).

In this doubling of narrative and apparatus, factuality is represented in the text and fable in the note, an inversion of Gibbon's normal use of genres. But read carefully: what the note does is to unravel the masquerade of fact in which the narrative travels; it exposes the power of narrative to mislead. If we had not turned to the note, or if, as Dugald Steward wished, it had been made more difficult of access by relegation to the back of the book, a casual reader would have assumed that in A.D. 383 there was a large emigration of Britons to Brittany.[20] As it is, we ourselves are

20. For Stewart's comments see Michael Bernays, *Schriften zur Kritik und Literaturgeschichte*, vol. 4 (Berlin: V. Vehr Verlag, 1903), pp. 313–14.

allowed in the note to exercise the historical methods of probability by which this kind of fraud can be uncovered. The sets of figures at first appear to be supplementary, but as the number of virgins accumulates we become suspicious of the figure's authenticity, and when the class distinctions in martyrdom are pointed out (leading us to suspect an aristocratic origin for the fable), we are prepared for the final fact, a contradiction in terms (virgins with children) overlooked by the source. This encourages us to suspect similar contradictions at every level. Turning back to the text, we find that, if we insert an active verb for the cunningly passive phrase "long afterwards remembered," and ask ourselves who was doing this remembering, the answer would not be annalists or historians, but rather fabulists, poets, legend mongers, and hagiographers. In the text, then, Gibbon provides a seamless narration in the form of "relation of fact," and in the note he evacuates it of meaning by scooping out its rotten interior. Finally, the thematic element in this footnote ought not to be neglected, since besides the structural intervention the content also has a polemic force, directed against the falsities of fable and the absurdities of hagiography. In Gibbon's passing demolition of the renowned fable of the martyrdom of St. Ursula and the 11,000 virgins, he is carrying out the Enlightenment program of sorting through the records of the past on the basis of a true/false formula, with the demystifying results that Pope deplored, at least when they affected poets.

Between the footnotes of Pope and Gibbon, then, we see a dynamic of transformation operating on the same field, with similar results for our understanding of the function of the note despite the quite different ideational contexts and even practices of the authors. Both authors expose the rhetorical elements of the note, but whereas the former does so as a direct attack on the note itself, the latter does so by employing it against the seductions of the narrative text. In each case the note is wrenched away from its objective aloofness and made to participate in the rhetorical process. Both procedures, furthermore, are inhabited by essential contradictions. While Pope's aim is to destroy the power of scholarly apparatus to attain exactitude by demonstrating its failures, by proclaiming its irrelevance and absurdity, and eventually by indicting its trustworthiness, the satire leads him into an absurdity of his own. As an author he is defending an ideological position at odds with his authorial interests. While he fears the disintegrating effects of textual criticism, the aim of this criticism is to establish a text that conforms to what can be known of the author's intentions. Authorial desire and the satire of exactitude are here suspended in an aporia that may indeed be the aporia of Pope's own life.

In Gibbon the aporia derives from the insistence on the opposite contention—that the note is capable of carrying truth. But Gibbon could be said to be an example of someone whose literary skills contest his scholarly method. Where it is to his advantage to maintain the note free from rhetorical elements, he succumbs to the temptation to supplement his skeptical polemic by adapting a form dislocated from its moorings by one of the more formidable opponents of his historiographical principles and his scholarly skepticism. His scrupulousness leads him to assess reliability of source material in front of the reader's eyes, if one should care to look at the bottom of the page. But concern for the truth is transcended in the higher goal of making the footnote argue against the false text by disagreeing with it and undermining the narrative it is ostensibly supporting. Hence the truth that is guaranteed by the medium's disinterestedness is betrayed by its interestedness on behalf of truth.

The culminating aporia, however, is that of the internal structure of the footnote itself. In these transformations we can see that the note does not merely undergo modifications making it more accessible to the reader or more convenient for the printer, but that under certain pressures its pose of disinterested attestation gives way to participation. In the process of temporarily becoming a definable genre in the eighteenth century, it allows us to see some of these pressures at work. And insofar as, during the transition from Pope to Gibbon, it fails to maintain its objectivity, it demonstrates the essential literary elements in those aspects of its form that claim to be superior to the dubious charms of rhetoric.

7

Who Was Benjamin Whichcote? or, The Myth of Annotation

Thomas McFarland

In a portmanteau discussion, in *The New York Review of Books* in March 1984, of fourteen studies on the eighteenth century, Lawrence Stone concluded with an annoyed statement about current trends in scholarly annotation:

> A final point concerns the ethics of publishing that affects scholarship in every field. The books of Porter (Penguin), Holmes (Allen and Unwin), and Corfield (Oxford) are packed with facts and quotations, many of them new even to experts in the field, but all three are entirely without footnotes. It was bad enough for publishers twenty years ago to begin to cut costs by stuffing footnotes into the back of the books; but it is intolerable to eliminate them altogether, leaving the author, like Professor Holmes, to publicize in his preface his willingness to answer personal inquiries about his sources. This is a trend in publishing that should be stopped in its tracks, before it becomes the norm.[1]

The present essay will attempt to use that statement as a doorway to larger issues involving the meaning and use of annotation. At the outset one notes a cultural anomaly in Stone's charge that "publish-

1. Lawrence Stone, "The New Eighteenth Century," *The New York Review of Books*, vol. 21, no. 35, March 29, 1984, p. 48.

ers twenty years ago"—it is actually longer than that—began "to cut costs by stuffing footnotes into the back of the books." For a moment's reflection makes clear that the footnotes either are or are not part of the text, that is to say, essential to the text or not essential. If they are part of the text, they should be presented as part of the text, that is, at the bottom of the page. Only if they are not considered part of the text, and therefore not essential, may they be relegated to the back of the book. But the question of location, which is so clearly bound up with the question of essence, is, as Stone's vexed comment indicates, not treated as one of essence but as one of economics.

To the extent that the placement of the annotation is merely a question of economics, or rather seems to be that, the author will not see fit to contest the relegating of footnotes to the back of the book. The fact that myriad books, perhaps even most, regularly appear with their notes at the back would seem to indicate that the majority of authors do not trouble themselves about the nature of annotation's relation to the text. But the matter is actually not so transparent. Many authors of the kind of books that require annotation are young scholars without previous occasion to meditate on the structure of annotation; many others do not realize that they might be able to control what the publishers do; still others have no idea, until the book has actually been designed and is in the preliminary stages of printed proof, that the notes will indeed go to the back. And some authors actually like to have the notes at the back, although, as seems evident, this is actually to conceive the relationship of note to text in a different way than if the annotations are at the bottom of the page.

But some authors—and I suspect that, in every case, these hold their opinions more emphatically than do those who are content to have the annotation at the back of the book—insist on annotation at the bottom of the page. Stone is certainly one of these. I myself have always made it a point of negotiation with publishers to insist on notes at the bottom of the page, and I have been uniformly successful in persuading them to agree. When my dealings with publishers involve not entire volumes of my own but chapters in a collection, I have not of course been able to control matters. Perhaps some instances will be instructive here. (I apologize for talking of my own work, which I shall do throughout this paper; my excuse is that I know this work and its circumstances better than any other work.) The first instance was one where I was asked to contribute to a memorial volume and did so with an article entitled "Romantic Imagination, Nature, and the Pastoral Ideal." I cite the title to indicate that the essay was full of quotations and references to literary and historical texts and might naturally seem to have required footnotes. I, however, not wishing to see notes relegated to the end of the volume, announced to the editors my intention of not having any annotation at all. To my surprise, they acquiesced, and printed my article first in the volume, all the others then being produced with their attendant footnotes duly relegated to the back.

Shortly after that volume appeared, I was asked to contribute to a collection called *The Age of William Wordsworth*. Flushed with my recent success, I again announced my intention of having no annotation. This time, however, the editors replied in agony that the press insisted on annotation in order to preserve the symmetry of the volume; the editors themselves supplied the annotation to my article, or attempted to do so, reassuring me that it was merely a matter of aesthetics and accordingly did not have to be very thorough. Naturally, I came back to the article myself and supplied what I thought was suitable documentation, which was then printed at the back of the book.

For still a third collection, I submitted a paper called "Coleridge and the Charge of Political Apostasy," again with the declaration that I would have no annotation. This time, without comment, the editor himself supplied some 125 notes, again necessitating my own return to the project to alter the documentation in ways that I myself would approve. The task now, however, in addition to causing guilt feelings in the author for having so imposed on the uncomplaining editor, became onerous in itself; for the annotated version of the paper evolved into something a bit different from the version without annotation, and in fact has still not been completed. The new notes are not restricted to identifying citations, but frequently become small essays that function as textual interventions. The essay is still incomplete, and everyone—author, editor, and printer—is annoyed.

I cite these three instances of the politics of annotation both to note their variation, and to suggest that the appeal for notes was presented either as a matter of aesthetics or as a matter of convention, but not as a matter of essence. My annoyance at the situation last described is largely occasioned by the fact that I intended to use the statement on Coleridge and political apostasy as part of a book that would have notes at the bottom, where they would plainly constitute a dialogue with the text.

When notes that constitute a dialogue with the text—we may henceforth call them dialogical notes—are combined with reference notes at the bottom of the page, the maximum harmony in annotation is achieved. When dialogical notes are combined with reference notes at the back of the book, the maximum disharmony obtains. For instance, a work that I have found almost unreadable, although I have tried to read it on a number of occasions, is Lawrence Thompson's biography of Frost, the first two volumes of which I own. The reason for my difficulty is the jarring cacophony of annotation. In the first volume, called *Robert Frost: The Early Years, 1874–1915*,[2] there are 477 pages of text, followed by 128 pages of notes and an index of 35 pages. The notes are preceded by a page called "Table of Contents for the Notes," where the introduction and the 34 chapters of the volume are listed with paginations for the relevant notes, preceded by an explanation: "In the Notes, whenever a last name or a short title is given as a reference, the Index will serve as a convenient guide to the first reference and the full citation." Turning to the index, one encounters what looks like another table of contents with the assurance that

> Names, Places, Dates are correlated with topics, interpretations, conclusions—all previously deployed on three separate levels: Introduction, Central Narrative, Notes. Because this Index thus makes available some outlines, configurations, summaries, which are not explicitly given elsewhere, it amounts to a fourth level of reading.
>
> Readers are particularly invited to browse through the Robert Frost entries under the forty-three topical subheads, which help to illuminate the complicated and contradictory responses of Frost as man and as artist. To expedite reference and cross-reference, the topical subheads are grouped here with page numbers. (Thompson, *Frost*, vol. 1, p. 607)

2. Lawrence Thompson, *Robert Frost: The Early Years, 1874–1915* (New York, Chicago, San Francisco: Holt, Rinehart and Winston, 1966).

The second volume, *Robert Frost: The Years of Triumph, 1915–1938*,[3] repeats the labyrinthine process, with 512 pages of text, 192 pages of notes with their own table of contents, and an index of 40 pages, this time with the reader being invited to browse through not 43 but 63 topical subheads. In either volume, when an actual process of reading is attempted, the reader's brain is embroiled in an "undescribable feud." Footnote signals constantly obtrude from the text, and the reader must decide whether to page back to the end of the volume and check the note or not. He or she is always asked to take it on faith that the note, if dialogical, will be worth interrupting the reading, or indeed even losing the train of argument, whereas in a dismaying number of instances the note will prove, after the reading process has been interrupted, to be merely a page number or a precise date. The effect in reading very long past the amassed footnote indicators in the text is something like driving over a road with innumerable potholes; for it does no good to decide to read straight on and not turn to the back of the volume. The constant note indicators jar one remorselessly with the thought that something important might be signaled by the little numbers.

Some works, to be sure, explicitly attempt to deal with the pothole effect of constant footnote indications to material at the back of the volume. Frequently footnote numbers are simply absent in the text, although a complete body of notes and citations occurs at the back, keyed in by phrases from the text. I have just finished a biography of Jean-Paul Sartre by Annie Cohen-Salal and, at least at the translation, this was the form of the annotative apparatus.

The two studies just randomly cited, of Frost on the one hand and of Sartre on the other, have in common their status as intellectual biographies. It might seem to follow that an apparatus of annotation, however organized, is a necessity for responsible biographical endeavor, and one suspects that at the present time there would be considerable pressure from any publisher to document a biography accepted for publication. Such, however, has not been the case in the past. The three greatest biographies in English are usually considered to be Boswell's *Life of Johnson*, Lockhart's *Life of Scott*, and Froude's *Life of Carlyle*. None has an apparatus of

3. Lawrence Thompson, *Robert Frost: The Years of Triumph, 1915–1938* (New York, Chicago, San Francisco: Holt, Rinehart and Winston, 1970).

annotation. Nor do less massive masterpieces such as Southey's *Life of Nelson*.

Indeed, Lawrence Stone's shock that three of the volumes he surveys are "entirely without footnotes," and his statement that, though it is "bad enough" for publishers to stuff footnotes into the back of the books, it is "intolerable to eliminate them altogether," are not justified by the history of publishing. Some of the finest works of intellectual history have in the past dispensed with annotation. Three with which I am intimately acquainted are De Quincey's long essay on Coleridge, originally published in installments in *Tait's Edinburgh Magazine* and now included in his *Recollections of the Lakes and the Lake Poets*; Leslie Stephen's essay on Coleridge, published in *Hours in a Library*; and G. M. Young's "Portrait of an Age," which was the final essay in the notable collection he edited called *Early Victorian England, 1830–1865*.

In these three essays the common factor seems to be an intensity of focus in which all materials are synthesized, smelted really, into a unity of the author's vision. Their relative brevity is essential to such synthesis, and documentation would tend to disperse their intensity. No other common factor seems to account for their structure. Two of them, indeed, are biographical, but the third, Young's essay on the spirit of early Victorianism, is not. One of them, De Quincey's, is written by a man who knew his subject personally, yet another, Stephen's, does not depend upon such a basis. The third, Young's, is written out of a nostalgic empathy with a period that obtained just before the horizon of the author's actual experience. Young does have a few notes, but they serve as repositories for telling anecdotes and other obiter dicta, not as an apparatus of annotation.

It might seem probable, however, that though the brevity of the three essays dictates the exclusion of annotation, longer ventures in intellectual history require extensive documentation. Still, the point of demarcation is not easy to ascertain. Burckhardt's *Civilization of the Renaissance in Italy* is rather long, very distinguished, and without annotation. On the other hand, P. M. Fraser's *Ptolemaic Alexandria* consists of three volumes, of which the first is text, and the second and third are footnotes, mostly in Greek, with maps and other apparatus. This vast annotative domain, however, has somewhat ambivalent borders drawn by the exigencies of printing. At breakfast with an Egyptologist named Grimm, I happened to mention Fraser's work, which my interlocutor knew so well that he corrected me: the work, as he said with confidence, was indeed in three volumes, but only the second volume contained notes. I remained silent under the rebuke, though I had just been handling all three volumes in a Cambridge bookshop. A week or so later, I saw Grimm again at breakfast and he apologized; it seems that the work was originally published in the manner he had described, but I had seen a reprinted version in which the notes were redistributed so as to occupy most of volumes 2 and 3, not simply volume 2.

I recite the anecdote to suggest that annotation in some instances can seem to have a life of its own. It can, in truth, be celebrational and monumental, not utilitarian. Even further, it can in this line become more important than the text, which serves merely as a rack of support for a monumental display. As a case in point, one should look at the Clarendon Press edition of the *Agamemnon* of Aeschylus by Eduard Fraenkel. It consists of three volumes, the first containing the Greek text with preliminary materials and an English translation, the second and third being line-by-line commentary that marshals the variorum opinions of scholars across the spectrum of European culture. The entire edition is as awesome as the pyramids, and perhaps ultimately of about the same utility. We might well wonder if another text of the *Agamemnon* were needed by the world of classical scholarship, let alone a less specialized intellectual audience. Certainly, we might wonder whether anyone sufficiently involved with Aeschylus to need Fraenkel's gigantically learned commentary would also need an English translation of the play itself. We might, in short, wonder why the three volumes were published at all.

But such ungenerous questions are justified only if we think the edition was really intended to have a use. Its subtext of justification has little to do with need or use. The edition is an offering to the memory of Fraenkel much more than it is a necessity for the intellectual world. As to why such an offering is appropriate, part of the answer is that Fraenkel, as a pharaoh of classical scholarship, might well be thought to deserve for his honored bones the labor of an age, if not in pilèd stones, in pilèd volumes. But the work, which, unlike Shakespeare's folio, will survive less as a book than as an edifice, does not merely honor Fraenkel. The dynamics of its publishing go deeper. Fraenkel was considered the prime classical scholar to be connected with the University of Oxford in this century. Furthermore, he was a German expatriate, a pupil of the great Wilamowitz, and his relocation in Oxford was considered as shifting the balance of classical scholarship from German to English preeminence. The great three-volume edition of the *Agamemnon*, produced under Oxford's own university imprint, emphasizes that shift in eminence. Indeed, the work was followed by a commentary on Horace, also proudly produced under the Oxford imprint and with a special note from the author testifying to how well he had been treated. The putting forward by the great Hellenist of a magisterial work in Latin studies was a further assertion of the unplumbed depths of his, and by extension the university's, scholarship. It is interesting to realize, however, that Fraenkel's cultural role is almost wholly defined as that of an annotator. He really did almost nothing else. The book on Horace, in fact, is one giant footnote of 460 pages, with footnotes to that footnote cascading magnificently down the bottoms of those pages.

I have spoken of Fraenkel's work at some length in order to illustrate a point. Annotation is not a simple manifestation, but rather a combination of six sources of authority and power: (1) the intention and need of the author; (2) the economic interests of the publisher; (3) the stylistic skills of the editor; (4) the aesthetic perceptions of the printer; (5) the expectations and needs of the reader; and (6) the conditioning sociology of the intellectual assembly of which the individual author is a part. Not all these sources are mobilized in every publishing decision about annotation, but all are potentially dynamic factors, and more than one, even if their effects are not immediately discernible, are always active.

To illustrate this contention, I shall once again advert to my own work, about whose publishing history and circumstances I can speak with a finer certainty than about other instances. Some years ago I brought out a long book called *Coleridge and the Pantheist Tradition*, which was unusual in the variety of its annotational forms. The volume contained notes at the bottom of the pages. It also contained at the end nineteen titled essays that I called Excursus Notes. The Excursus Notes were followed by another seventy-five small essays that the printer called End Notes. To add to the general effect of denseness, the Excursus Notes were printed in a smaller type than the text itself, and the End Notes in a type still smaller than the Excursus Notes. The effect of the whole volume was somewhat parallel to the paradox of Achilles and the tortoise. No matter how assiduously one read, one never seemed to be able to reach the end of the book; it was particularly dispiriting for the type continually to become smaller as one tried to hasten forward. Indeed, I have sometimes wondered whether anyone except me and my editor has ever actually been able to read the book through.

But the book's unusual structure was only in part the result of the author's decision and intent. Actually it was an effect of five of the six dynamic sources listed above, acting in combination. Curiously enough, the only possible source of annotational decision not activated in this instance was the one that most often prevails: the economic interests of the publisher. The book was published by the Clarendon Press in those halcyon days before it seemed aware of printing costs and economic interests, and from first to last I heard not one word of demur about rising costs.

All the other factors, however, were vibrantly active. The typescript, as I recall, came to more than eleven hundred pages, and I submitted it for consideration with only about half the notes completed. It was accepted in that form, and I then moved to London and Oxford to work with my editor on some five hundred additional but unwritten notes, which, under the circumstances of my leisure and my access to sources, became more luxuriant than might otherwise have been the case. The notes had initially been written as simple footnotes to be carried at the bottom of the page. It soon became apparent, however, that the text in this event would be an aesthetic monstrosity of the type of Mommsen's *Römisches Staatsrecht*, where bottom-of-page notes sometimes reach almost to the top, with only about one-eighth of the page devoted to text and the rest to notes. The Clarendon Press at that time was noted for the elegance of its printing and design, and the printer, Vivian Ridler, was an artist of print. I was urged by him, through my editor, to cut the annotation in the interests of the typographical aesthetics of the printed page. Having worked assiduously to assemble the notes, I was perhaps not unnaturally disinclined to jettison them. My editor then suggested that I might try combining some of them and placing them at the back of the book, in order to enhance the typographical elegance of the textual page. The suggestion seemed compelling, and after due meditation and joiner's work I produced nineteen essays that I somewhat redundantly called, following Ernst Robert Curtius's excursus in his *European Literature and the Latin Middle Ages*, Excursus Notes.

The Excursus Notes, one must stress, were not composed as essays; they rather were put together from cullings of reference and statement on various topics connected with the larger argument of the book. Thus they bore titles such as "Coleridge and Later Theological Thought," or "The Reaction Against Spinoza," or "Leibniz and Spinoza," or "The Personal Influence of Jacobi," or "Coleridge and Descartes." The End Notes differed from the Excursus Notes not so much in length, as in the fact that they were not composed as cullings but were from the outset notes, that is, individually dialogical essays on some particular point at issue. The completed three-tiered system of annotation was the result primarily of the aesthetic interests of the printer, secondly of the stylistic skills of the editor, and thirdly of the author's acquiescence in their expertise.

But the fact that there were notes at all engaged the author's intention and need more deeply, as well as engaging the fifth and sixth sources of authority listed above, that is, the expectations and needs of the reader, and the conditioning sociology of the intellectual assembly of which the individual author is a part. With regard to the expectations of the reader, the work without footnotes does not have the prestige of the annotated work. Indeed, the fact that a press at the present time will insist on annotation, whereas in the nineteenth century it would not, indicates how essential annotation has become simply as an offering to the reader's expectations. For instance, in the last century a polymath such as Ranke, who specialized in archival research, produced over sixty volumes of scholarship with only sporadic reliance on annotation. On the other hand, to revert to my own work as illustration, the Clarendon Press recently published another book of mine, designed to be of what I hoped was a telling brevity. I wrote it without annotation and submitted it in that form. The press received a favorable reading and in accepting the volume inquired when the footnotes would be coming. When I replied that I had not intended to have footnotes, the press promptly stipulated that acceptance depended upon my providing an apparatus of annotation. I decided to acquiesce, and that is the way the book was eventually published. Indeed, the fact noted above, that I doubt whether anyone except me and my editor has ever read all of *Coleridge and the Pantheist Tradition*, in itself shows to what an extent annotation functions as a symbol demanded but not used by the reader, rather than as a necessity for the text itself.

I shall have more to say about this curious shift whereby a body of annotation comes to function as a symbol of intellectual security. Here, however, it suffices merely to point out that annotation is required in order to conform to intellectual fashion. But that in itself is no light matter, for fashion is one of the most mysterious and ineluctable of all sociological phenomena. As we all know, even in such slight matters as length of hair or cut of trousers it is impossible to stand against fashion. If men's hair is being worn long, for instance, one can still wear a crew cut, but in that case the penalty will be stylistic ostracism. I well remember the football player George Sauer saying of the football player John Unitas, who still affected a crew cut well after its social message was no longer being heard, "He looks peculiar." Whether trousers are cut full with pleats or tight without will inundate any would-be Canute who thinks he can reverse the flow of their fashion; I remember the delight with which I greeted the fashion of bell-bottomed jeans in the late sixties, and the chagrin I felt when my liking for such jeans came up against the shift in fashion from bell-bottoms to stovepipes, and I, feeling very peculiar indeed in my own bell-bottoms, eventually gave them up. Fashion, in other words, though seemingly always manifested in trivial instances, shows by its ineluctability its deep roots in the human situation. What its factors are can only be glimpsed occasionally in the reality of the dispersal of human life in time, its confinement within existential boundaries, and the overwhelming human need for transcendence that arises from those conditions. That footnotes are now the fashion is, in short, a trivial matter that is also deep, as I shall presently try to indicate.

The needs and expectations of the reader are reciprocally validated by the conditioning sociology of the intellectual assembly of which the individual author is a part. To state this relationship in its starkest terms, it is solely the great engine of university functioning that powers the pistons of scholarly annotation. The reader in part expects footnotes because they make a work conform, in what David Riesman calls marginal differentiation, to other and prior works that present themselves as bearing and conferring prestige. But the repetitions that establish the grouping by which the work is identified are a result of the techniques taught by graduate education. I wrote footnotes because I was taught to write footnotes by the sociological group that produced me.

The graduate education I underwent, however, though accounting for the sixth source of authority that produced the footnotes for *Coleridge and the Pantheist Tradition*, does not wholly account for those footnotes. The reader has no doubt noticed a contradiction between my repeated bringing forward of examples where I did not have footnotes, or at least did not want them, and the example of my book with the three-tiered system of annotation. To try to analyze this opposition along the lines attempted for Fraenkel's edition of Aeschylus, one might say that three discrete authorial attitudes underlie the discrepant phenomena. One of those attitudes is characterized by an egotism of assertion—a kind of Stirnerian fantasy—whereby I seem to feel that the uniqueness of my statement is enhanced by the absence of footnotes. The second authorial attitude is one where I seem to be attempting some form of harmony between my own self-presentation and the other five sources of annotational authority: I have footnotes in order to mollify the press, along with its allied powers of printer and editor; to ingratiate myself with the reader, along with his symbolic representative, the critic; and lastly, to gain the protection of the sociological community of scholars of which I am both product and part.

This explication of the second authorial attitude leads to an understanding of the third, which can be indicated by a single word: anxiety. The three-tiered system of annotation in *Coleridge and the Pantheist Tradition* resembles nothing so much as an interconnected system of fortifications, and in this apprehension I myself appear as the Vauban who designed them. But what are they defending against, if not an anxiety on the part of the author? And what is the nature of this anxiety, or, to maintain the metaphor, what is the nature of the expected onslaught? When the question is put in those terms, the answer readily presents itself. As a student I was unusually erratic or, not to put too firm a point on it, decidedly neurotic. I would do things at the last moment, if at all, would read Milton when I was taking a course on Spinoza, and Spinoza when I was taking a course on Milton, would speculate boldly and sometimes wildly in speech and writing. In no very long run, I came to be regarded with a mixture of admiration and suspicion, along the classic lines of such judgments as "brilliant but unsound."

By the time I reached graduate school, my various neurotic excesses had resulted in a most uncomfortable sense of being pounded by the judgments of others, and when I issued forth as a journeyman into the academic profession I was very slow in publishing at all. I had discovered in graduate school that I had a knack for commenting on my own statements, and this had led to a few rather impressive moments of documentation in my papers, although most were written so hurriedly that only rarely was anything of that sort possible. When I began work on the book on Coleridge, therefore, I was feeling, had indeed long been feeling, defensive. In direct opposition to my previous facility for rapid writing, I took a long time writing the book; I built it, as I said in the preface, rather than wrote it. I generated the documentation defensively, much as a soldier at the front might throw up earthworks, my aim being nothing less than an impregnable fortification for my own argument. In due course there took shape the three-tiered system of fortification—or rather annotation—whose structure I have described.

But if my own anxiety as author might appear somewhat atypical in light of its neurotic origin, it is nonetheless anxiety—as I shall maintain as the ground tone of the remainder of this paper—that underlies the institution of annotation itself, at least in its modern currency. Such linking of the anxiety of the individual author to the social condition of intellectual endeavor justifies the subtitle of this paper, "The Myth of Annotation," because myth originates, as Durkheim was the first to show, in social need, and it binds social anxiety. In addition to that, the rubric of the myth of annotation implies a special relation of annotational practice to reality.

In order to do justice to the nuance of these claims, I shall proceed slowly and emphasize differing factors. As noted at the outset, footnotes themselves are of two kinds, reference notes and dialogical notes. And here one must interpose parenthetically that the inner dynamics of footnoting are entirely different, though the footnotes may look the same on the page, when annotation is supplied by editors of someone else's text, as opposed to the author's supplying it for his or her own text. It would be fascinating to pursue this fundamental difference, but here, alas, and for the remainder of the paper, I shall speak only of the relation of the author's annotation to his or her own text. With reference to this latter situation, it may be said that both of the footnoting forms, reference notes and dialogical notes, participate, though in diverging ways, in the structure of anxiety.

Dialogical notes are palpable in their anxiety. Whether at the bottom of the page or at the back of the book, they always recognize a limitation in the argument as presented in the text. All their usual functions—explaining, qualifying, adding, specifying, rebutting, bulwarking—are with regard to the text so many indications of a defensive anxiety. As Lawrence Lipking says, in an article in *Critical Inquiry* in 1977 called "The Marginal Gloss": "footnotes, as everyone knows, are defensive. They stand for a scholarly community, assembled by the author specifically so that he can join it."[4]

Actually, footnotes are both historically and structurally bound up with the marginal gloss summoned by Lipking's title. If one looks at a late-seventeenth-century text such as Richard Bentley's *Dissertation upon the Epistles of Phalaris*, one will see a wealth of citations, all carried in the margins of the book. As with all aspects of the annotational phenomenon, these early forms were involved with the economics and technology of printing. It was a printing trend, not an authorial trend, that began in the eighteenth century to move annotational reference from the margins to the bottom of the page. Lipking points out that this technological change effected a structural and qualitative change as well, for whereas the marginal gloss existed parallel to the text, and therefore indicated a voice on an equal footing with the textual voice, the relegation of annotation to the bottom of the page changed the notes to a subordinate status. Henceforth the text was the primary voice, and the notes—explaining, qualifying, adding, specifying, rebutting, bulwarking—were not only a subordinate voice, but by that very fact a condition of anxiety itself.

What had been the marginal gloss was replaced by a new form, marginalia. Of course marginal notations had occurred ever since the book as an entity existed, as we can see for example in Sears Jayne's edition of John Colet's marginalia to Ficino. But margin-

4. Lawrence Lipking, "The Marginal Gloss," *Critical Inquiry* 3 (1977): 639.

alia as a generic form did not emerge until the Romantic era. According to the *Oxford English Dictionary*, the first use of the word "marginalia" was by Coleridge in 1805, and it is fitting that the five huge volumes of Coleridge's marginalia now being printed in *The Collected Coleridge* are the largest and most varied representation of this genre.

It is of interest in studying the dynamics of the text taken in the largest sense, that the marginal space historically drained of annotational material was not left vacant, but in the adjoining and ensuing moment of cultural history was filled on the one hand by the raising of an author's jottings to the generic condition of marginalia, and on the other by the propagation of a new kind of gloss, a mock annotational form, so to speak. Here too the most pregnant example might be that of Coleridge, whose marginal gloss to "The Rime of the Ancient Mariner" introduces a new voice and a differing awareness of temporality into the poem. Indeed, as Kathleen Wheeler, Lipking, and others have shown, the gloss generates antithetical lines of force throughout the artifact. But the extension of the text as a deliberately fabricated glossing voice, no less than the actual generic form of the marginal notation, introduces and witnesses anxiety. As I have written in a recent paper on Blake's marginalia,

> marginalia always, whether in greater or less degree, invade their host text. In this sense, indeed, no form so fully participates in the literal significance of the word "intertextuality." If one were designing an abstract symbology for literary types, doubtless the best computer symbol for the marginal comment would be a spear-shaped wedge. For the marginal notation forces open the text, constitutes itself unavoidably as an intertext.[5]

That marginalia and the artistic gloss participate in the same antithetical structure is indicated by Valéry's later musings about Poe's marginalia and by his own experimental glosses to his writings on Leonardo da Vinci. And that these phenomena, the artistic gloss and marginalia as such, so clearly exert pressure on the stability of the textual material leads us to realize that the utterance

5. Thomas McFarland, "Synecdochic Structure in Blake's Marginalia," *European Romantic Review* 1 (Summer, 1990): 78.

subordinated at the bottom of the page, symbolically repressed into small print, is also potentially subversive. Like the Spartan helots, meek hewers of wood and drawers of water who nevertheless aroused so much anxiety in their ruling society that the strongest among them were periodically put to death, the small-print notes, however tidy they may look, always threaten the text; irreducibly they threaten to drain off the power and authority of the author's voice. Here, one can hardly doubt, is one part of the explanation for my own tendency, noted earlier, to wish to jettison footnotes in my writing.

It is the reference notes, more than the dialogical notes, that threaten this diminution of compositional authority. Indeed, although dialogical notes always seethe with testimony to textual limitation, they nevertheless retain something of the authentically personal textual voice; their charge of anxiety, though great, is not so vast as that in the seemingly innocuous reference notes. The anxiety in this latter case is of two distinct kinds and two distinct origins. In both instances the anxiety is denied by a lie against reality that constitutes a major part of the myth of annotation. The first lie against reality is that reference notes are necessary, so that the reader may have access to the context of the material being cited. The second lie against reality is that the reference notes connect the textual argument with other stanchions of culture, and thus allow the text to take its place in a network of cultural forms.

To attempt to illustrate the nature of the first lie against reality, I shall, with continuing apologies, again have recourse to my own work. In a large volume called *Romanticism and the Forms of Ruin*, I attempted to do in chapter organization what the ode did in Romantic poetry, that is, present a statement in heterogeneous and rough-hewn segments. To that end, among other anomalies, I composed the book with footnotes throughout, but dispensed with them in the first chapter, which was designated as an introduction and entitled "Fragmented Modalities and the Criteria of Romanticism." My editor, in this instance representing both publisher and printer, anxiously questioned the absence of notes in the chapter. I fended off the objection by saying that the examples and quotations in the chapters were illustrations meant to seem, as indeed had been their origin, to rise spontaneously to mind as the argument progressed, and that therefore the supplying of references would misrepresent their genesis as something more formal than it was.

Predictably, a certain number of the reviews the book was accorded complained about the absence of reference notes in the initial chapter. One reviewer complained of "innate defects" and of "erratic practices," and specified "the absence of references for the many quotations from the European Romantics in the introduction." The absence was made to seem more vexing by the reviewer's subsequent description of the book's "wide-ranging familiarity with the Romantic period, including . . . often striking knowledge of recondite primary material." In the word "recondite" we may perhaps focus both the reason for the reviewer's irritation and my own unacknowledged reason for not supplying references. Many of the quotations were outside the kind of familiar currency that is handed about from secondary work to secondary work, and I wanted, so to speak, to protect myself from claim jumpers. Another reviewer in fact cannily pointed to my protecting of my own authority as the reason I had not supplied references. "In an engagingly old-fashioned way," said this reviewer, "McFarland aggressively underannotates the chapter, so that nonadepts will be unable to steal fruit from this orchard without acknowledging its source."

In this awareness, the truth that one may point to as denied by the lie against reality is that references—never required by any so-called common reader, but only by other scholars, by competitors, that is, in the scholarly race—are demanded, not so as to have access to contexts, but precisely to obviate the need for searching those contexts. With regard to one of the footnoted chapters in *Romanticism and the Forms of Ruin* I remember encountering, in a book presented to me by a genial colleague, a long German passage translated into English, along with its citation to the best German text, both calmly offered as if rising from contexts of the author's learning. In fact, through the unmistakable marks of the translation, they had been removed from my volume like a cassette and reinserted in the author's discourse. This, the treating of quotations and citations as prepackaged cassettes rather than as ore from a mine actually worked by the author, is the true reason for one part of a scholar's demand for reference notes.

The matter is so undignified, both in my own proprietorial claims and in my ungenerous ascription of motives to others, that I must attempt to normalize it; dignity having been abandoned, I shall delve still further into the backgrounds of my own practice. One of the reasons Wordsworth did not allow *The Prelude* to be published in his lifetime was, as he said, that it was a thing unprecedented in literary history that a man should talk so much about himself. This paper may seem to be fast approaching the Wordsworthian imperative for silence and withdrawal. But, as I have been pleading, no other material is so accessible to me as my own annotative experience. With that renewed apology I shall now adduce some of the correspondence surrounding my own publication.

I referred earlier to a brief book of mine on the English Romantic essayists recently published by the Clarendon Press. I had composed the text without notes, but then supplied notes at the insistence of the press. The actual negotiations surrounding this issue will perhaps illustrate more richly the claims I have just been making. I submitted the manuscript without notes; but the reader's report sent me by the press concluded with the following words:

> My only *caveat* concerns the lack of annotation. It may well be that Professor McFarland plans to add these in any case, but it is certainly essential that they be included. This is a book which is clearly intended to encourage further reading in the authors which [*sic*] it discusses. Whereas some modern criticism is so mannered that it seems intended to be read as an end in itself, this is criticism which means to awaken interest; it would be disastrous if such interest were then to be immediately thwarted by a need to root through bibliographies and library catalogues in search of the works mentioned. This is a book which emphatically needs references.

One remarks about this statement that the anonymous reader can hardly be charged with an intent to lift out prepackaged cassette citations. The reader puts forward in impeccable good faith what I have called a lie against reality. His or her own integrity cannot be challenged; the lie against reality is a lie only in its epistemological structure, not in the intent of its invocation. On the contrary, the scholarly reader posited for any scholarly work is conditioned to expect annotation, and his or her initial welcoming of its presence has nothing to do with an intent to lift out prepackaged cassettes. The annotated text rather signals the reader that the work is indeed a scholarly contribution and so will repay the investment of attention. Inasmuch as they are justified by the fiction of access to contexts, reference citations as a source of prepackaged information never arise as an issue in theory; this use rather occurs as a seemingly sporadic and isolated event in practice. And I hasten to add, lest it should seem that I am exempting myself from such a situation, that I myself—and I am sure we all must concede as much—make use of encountered quotations and citations that pertain to what I need to say, and that I do so with a clear conscience. I try, as do we all, to ensure that my writing issues from authentic depths of my own lived experience and assiduous research, yet I pick up nuggets when I find them at my feet.

Still, despite all the good faith that surrounds the invocation of the lie against reality, it is nonetheless a lie. Perhaps my own aggressive letter to the editor in response to the reader's call for annotation will be instructive in this regard:

> What does seem to require comment is the reader's emphatic demand for footnotes. The main reason I do not have footnotes is to render homage to the mode the essayists themselves developed. None of them would have dreamed of presenting scholarly references, though they themselves knew many things and used many books. I find somewhat specious the reader's belief that footnotes would save my potential audience from the trouble of using a library, should they be inspired to read further. There is no secret about the standard editions of any of the writers I treat, nor are other secondary works at all hard to come by; in any event "to root through bibliographies and library catalogues" is synonymous with using a library on any level. To be quite cynical, I really see no other need for footnotes than to allow scholarly readers to purloin my citations without having to give *me* a reference. Certainly the average interested reader, who does not himself contemplate publishing on these topics, is pleased rather than put off by the absence of footnotes. It is only other scholars who cry for footnotes, for reasons that they would be hard put to defend.

I may in that statement sound unduly concerned with protecting my references from predatory readers, but even if we concede a certain paranoia in my attitude, the point remains inviolate. Reference notes always, in greater or less degree, oppose the text conceived as symbol of the author's authority. Reference notes, no less than dialogical notes, are irremediably in conflict with the text.

That these matters do not constitute inert quantities, however, but rather variable ratios, is witnessed by the subsequent paragraph of my letter to my editor:

> Nevertheless, I am not intractably opposed to references in this particular instance, however cynical I may be about their efficacy. What do you yourself think? Should you and your people want to make the addition of notes a condition of publication, my agreement would entail the counter-condition that the notes be carried at the bottoms of the pages rather than at the end of the book. It would make printing more expensive to have the apparatus; it would entail a certain amount of extra effort on my own part. But if you otherwise want the book and feel strongly about this one issue, I suppose I have no insuperable objection to providing footnote references.

To this the editor's letter in reply said that the delegates had voted to accept the book on condition that annotation be supplied, and that the annotation would be printed at the bottom of the page.

Interestingly enough, when I actually produced the apparatus of citations, by adding quite a few dialogical notes I came up with a book that I liked better than the version without the notes. Lest it should seem that this effect contravenes all I have been saying, however, I should stress that what actually occurred was an exchange of values: I gave up authority and originality by supplying notes, but I gained a better page both in terms of printing aesthetics and in the tensions that now existed between the dialogical notes and the text itself. I had designed the book to be brief; the notes in the event worked to justify the brevity by making the argument seem symbolic, still open, rather than conclusive and complete.

Before moving from the dynamics connected with the first lie against reality to those connected with the second, we might consider one further example. In a review of four books on Victor Hugo in the *Times Literary Supplement* for October 11, 1985, the reviewer is harsh throughout. The only book for which he concedes or rather grudgingly suggests much merit is Victor Brombert's *Victor Hugo and the Visionary Novel.* It is perhaps of interest, in view of the reviewer's uniform censoriousness, to know that he is a Cambridge don, and apparently one of no wide repute. I commented to Brombert himself about the tone of the review and said that I failed to recognize the reviewer's name. Brombert sharply replied that no one else recognizes it either.

The reviewer finds an aspect of one book, in his words, "simply irritating", and says of the next one, "A similar irritation is provoked even more intensely." He is annoyed rather than irritated by another, and his annoyance centers upon the book's lack of annotation. He writes:

> The centenary has been marked by a number of more or less fictionalized biographies, presumably destined for the bookshelf of the middle-class *honnête homme*. The most serious of them is the second volume of Hubert Juin's *Victor Hugo*, covering the vital years 1844–70 in meticulous detail. Juin's erudition is clearly enormous. But it is annoying that he refuses to share it with his readers by referring to his sources or even offering a bibliography. It is difficult to see whom the book is aimed at, for it would be an extremely dedicated general reader that could stick with it for the 2,000-odd pages which the three volumes will eventually comprise, and it is invalidated as an academic work by its lack of references.

If we analyze the reviewer's statement we shall find, I believe, a choice illustration of the tension between the first lie against reality, that annotation is necessary so that the reader may have access to the contexts from which citations are made, and the truth denied by that lie, that the reader really wants to have the use of prepackaged citations specifically disburdened of the need to investigate contexts. This tension underlies the palpable fact of the statement's turbulence and contradictoriness. The reviewer says that "it is difficult to see whom the book is aimed at," whereas three sentences before he has haughtily said that it is "presumably destined for the bookshelf of the middle-class *honnête homme*." Though he speculates that it "would be an extremely dedicated general reader that could stick with it for the 2,000-odd pages which the three volumes will eventually comprise," the inanity of the remark is revealed simply by considering that it would be an extremely dedicated scholarly reader as well.

The reviewer's conclusion that Juin's book "is invalidated as an academic work by its lack of references" is not only a choice example of *petitio principii*, but implies a most unguarded view of the reality of scholarly endeavor; for it clearly suggests that scholarly books are not produced for reading but for mining by other scholars. It is at this point that Brombert's comment upon the reviewer's lack of status in the world of Hugo scholarship takes on point. The reviewer throughout presents himself as superior in knowledge and judgment to the four authors; of one of them, Alain Decaux, he says that the author "has produced a *Victor Hugo* of over a thousand pages, which offers little that is new in terms of our knowledge of Hugo, and which acquires its momentum from the author's obvious fascination with his subject. It is a book of a kind which it is difficult to imagine being taken seriously in Britain."

But the reviewer cannot sustain this attitude of superiority with reference to Juin. "Juin's erudition," he admits, "is clearly enormous." It is immediately following that concession that he finds it "annoying" that Juin "refuses to share it with his readers by referring to his sources." Yet Juin is quite plainly sharing his erudition with his readers, if the three volumes are to comprise 2,000-odd pages. Furthermore, the reviewer's suggestion that the unannotated length of the three volumes will deprive them of an audience can hardly have much purchase, since the economics of publication are the province of the publisher, not of the reviewer, and the publisher, Flammarion, must be presumed to be comfortable about that aspect of the enterprise, or it would not have proceeded beyond the first volume. The reviewer is not able to suggest that Juin's work is inaccurate or fraudulent or lacking in authority. The only charge he can bring is that the author should make over to his readers the precise detail of his sources. And yet the despised general reader is not asking for such detail; only this remote and ineffectual Cambridge don stakes disgruntled claim to it. Its function, such is the naked truth, would be to expedite his own self-presentation to the scholarly world, a self-presentation based on Juin's erudition rather than on his own research.

So much for the first lie against reality encompassed by the myth of annotation. This paper will close with a truncated consideration of the second lie, that annotation is necessary to connect the textual argument with other stanchions of culture and thus allow the text to take its place in a network of cultural forms.

But at this juncture in cultural history, that network is sadly rent and hanging like dispersed cobwebs. In a recent book called *Shapes of Culture*, I argue that the forms of culture have been or are in the process of being overwhelmed by repetition and exponentially increasing commentary. As a result, I argue, what used to be forms definingly related to other forms, are now increasingly transformed to a congeries of unrelated and self-referential shapes. I shall spare my readers any quotation from that work; it exists and can be consulted by those interested in its examples. Here I should rather supply a few fresh and recent illustrations simply as they rise to mind.

I had occasion not too long ago to try to identify the three most learned figures now alive, and I came up with the names of Joseph Needham, René Wellek, and Albert Cook. I was fully aware of how ridiculous the situation was, most obviously in the assumption that I myself had enough knowledge to attempt such an adjudication. What is not perhaps so obvious is that any names suggested, either by me or by more likely nominators, were so pitifully limited in their knowledge as not really to deserve identification in such terms at all. Around the turn of the nineteenth century the philosopher Friedrich Jacobi used the phrase *radikale Unwissenheit*—radical unknowingness—to describe the state of our knowledge, and in that same era Hazlitt wrote a scintillating essay, "On the Ignorance of the Learned."

It had not always been that way. Aristotle's knowledge was more or less in touch with all cultural forms in his era, as supposedly was Varro's somewhat later. Various figures in the Renaissance and seventeenth century could aspire, like Bacon, to take all knowledge as their province. Yet though there have been people in all subsequent eras who have amassed facts and developed expertise, the growth of what there is to know or comprehend has so exponentially outstripped the possibilities of cognizing it, that one may say with some confidence that Leibniz was the last figure able to hold all or most of the cultural forms of his day in some degree of connection.

But Leibniz's generous bowlful of knowledge has proportionately shrunk in our own time to thimblefuls commanded by our most learned figures. Carlyle once remarked, with reference to the ancien régime, that it is astonishing how long the rotten will hold together, if only it is not roughly handled. The same comment holds true with our own claims to cultural comprehension. As long as we occupy our academic posts, read the *New York Review of Books* and the

Times Literary Supplement, talk to our fellows in ignorance, and attend mutually self-congratulatory conferences, we may feel somewhat comfortable in our illusions of cultural command. But take us out of our reassuring context, and the illusion dissipates. Only yesterday I saw the heartbreaking report of the great fire in the Leningrad Library. Among other portents of cultural horror was the notation that the library had contained 17,500,000 volumes. Yet it is by no means the largest library in the world.

Seventeen million five hundred thousand volumes. In a conscientious lifetime an active intellectual might scarcely comprehend 1750. Cultural data has expanded beyond all defining bound; cultural activity continues, but culture as an entity no longer exists. To dramatize the effects of the shrinking ratio of the actually comprehended to the potentially knowable, I shall conclude this paper by adducing four brief illustrative occasions. All are anecdotal but none is humorous, as they might on the surface seem to be, and as might reasonably seem to be the case with some of the examples one encounters with regard to the first annotational lie against reality. These examples, on the contrary, speak of the abyss.

The first occasion occurred on a train trip from Princeton to New York the other day. I happened to sit with one of my former students, who had just graduated last year as an economics major, and who had been a rather good student when I taught him in his freshman year. Somehow the conversation turned onto the question of what a university student might reasonably be expected to know. In a spirit of what I thought was playful exaggeration, I said, "I'm afraid the students now don't even know who Rousseau was." My student friend calmly responded, "Who *was* Rousseau?" I tried to hide my amazement and set out to explain that Rousseau might possibly have claim to be the most important intellectual of the past two and a half centuries. The student exhibited neither interest nor defensiveness at the news, and it was not until I began to talk of some of the more disreputable episodes of the *Confessions* that there was any glimmer in his response. Yet I have come to realize that the student's ignorance is not his fault, nor is it the university's fault; it is rather a portent of the momentous cultural transformation of which I speak.

The second occasion sets the stakes a little higher. Frank Kermode recently commented to me with surprise that one of the world's most praised young scholars in literature of the English

Renaissance asked, in response to Kermode's remark about Benjamin Whichcote's role in Cromwell's regime, "who was Benjamin Whichcote?" I told the story in wonderment to another younger scholar, also of international credentials, and the scholar asked, with unperturbed directness, "Who *was* Benjamin Whichcote?"

The third occasion illustrates the breakdown of cultural connection in a different way. Last year I had as guest at an Oxford college one of the world's chief authorities on Wordsworth. We were sitting across the table from one of the world's most distinguished classical historians. The two men did not seem to know each other, so I duly made introductions. The classical historian in a friendly manner asked, "Is this your first visit to Oxford?" The Wordsworthian scholar in an equally friendly way replied, "No", and explained that he was attached to an Oxford college hardly more than a hundred yards away from where we sat. It turned out that both had been at their respective posts for more than twenty years. That they did not know each other's work, we all now find not worthy of comment; that they did not know each other personally is equally surprising; but that, after twenty years and more cheek by jowl at the world forefront of their respective studies, they had never even so much as heard of each other is a mordant commentary on what is happening in our cultural situation.

The last occasion reinforces this observation. At the end of March, just before I came out to Irvine, I gave a party for a visiting Cambridge scholar. At one point I found myself talking to two of the guests, one an economist of international standing, and the other a specialist in comparative literature also of international standing. Precisely the same situation obtained as in my anecdote about Oxford. Both had been on the faculty of a small university for over twenty years, neither knew the other's work, neither knew the other personally, and neither had so much as heard of the other.

Such symbolic situations are now everywhere to be encountered. For there is no longer a culture. There are instead heterogeneous and arbitrarily multiplied cultural fragments with no relation or coherence among themselves. Nietzsche despairingly said that the total character of the world for all eternity is chaos—a dread truth we constantly and desperately attempt to deny. There is no culture; there is rather, in denial of that truth, a myth of culture. To that myth is subjoined the myth of annotation. It is in this subjoining that we find the depth not immediately apparent in the surface phenomenon of footnotes having become a powerful fashion. Footnotes and other annotational apparatus are denials of cultural fragmentation; the greater the actual disintegration of culture, the more in fashion do footnotes become. They are believed to be, are hoped to be, lifelines extending from the individual scholarly work to the fixed stars in a great cultural field, themselves connected still again, in an infinite and reassuring mesh, to other stable points, and so on through the whole proud texture of what faith assures us is one vast patterned fabric of culture.

But it is all in vain. The footnotes and other apparatus, far from being steel cables woven into a gigantic interconnection of meaning, connect to nothing. They protrude only as short and localized outriggers attached to the individual vessel of scholarship. Bobbing about on the vast deeps of chaos, those vessels, with or without outriggers, have no final destinations and few interim ports of call. Indeed, the lighter their cargoes, the more confidently they sometimes seem to ride the waves. But whether empty or laden, whether broadened by outriggers or relying on their own keels for seaworthiness, they each and all float only briefly before they founder and are seen no more.

8

Annotation as Social Practice

Ralph Hanna III

I expect that I appear on this podium for a single reason: at various points I have produced a certain amount of textual annotation, generally as pendant to critical editions of Middle English texts. And over the three days of this conference I've often been pixilated by reminders of this behavior, a forced recognition of the antiquity and conservatism of annotative activity. Yet, like Tom McFarland, I remain oppressively conscious that what I know to say about this subject is nothing more than autobiography, a summary of my conscious practice when I annotated *The Awntyrs off Arthure*, for example.

The issue I want to take up most particularly concerns the status of annotation as "mediation," a claim that I find particularly problematic. At least one way of getting at this problematic is to consider what the scene of annotation is. I think I'm in fundamental agreement with an informal exchange Steve Barney and Jim Nohrnberg had on Saturday: annotation is always a testimony to alienation from a text, always represents a response to a prior culture from which one believes oneself (and consequently, nearly everyone else) distanced. Yet simultaneously, as Jim suggested, annotation also testifies to inclusion: one usually assumes that only canonical texts deserve annotation, and such canonicity depends on the acceptance of the text by some critical community, a community of which the annotator is the designated representative.

Such a view presupposes, I think, two different approaches to "mediation." On the one hand, the annotator is always already mediated: he is produced by the same readerly culture for which he speaks, since only community acceptance of the text on which he works confers upon him the need or power to annotate. And he always is a member of that community, since no one becomes an annotator without the clerical training that constitutes readerly communities in the West. Yet simultaneously, the process of annotation is by no means benign, simply something received: as the rhetorical forms of annotation indicate, and here I take up some issues implicit in Steve Nichols's talk, the process is perceived socially as a form of aggression—an aggression directed at both the community that sanctions annotation and the text that inspires it.

The forms that the receptor community posits for annotation suggest not simply the craft's premediated forms but also a consciousness of the danger of annotation. Here I invoke Tom McFarland again. A receptor community speaks through the decisions of press readers and, beyond them, press editors and typographers (and beyond them, of course, academic reviewers). I, like Tom, have grave doubts whether any substantial deviation from accepted community practice will achieve public acceptance. Moreover, the nature of these acceptable forms, as we heard in several papers, is very old. Tom Toon discussed the way in which Old English annotation presents itself as a series of discrete layers; Anthony Grafton made much the same point in drawing attention to the cloudy and inconsistent nature of Gabriel Harvey's annotations from different sources. The mediated community rules for appropriate annotation simply modernize these layered forms. In the Anglophonic tradition, at least, the annotator is committed to a treatment fragmented and dispersed. (*Piers Plowman* is only the most explicit case, and such explicit dispersal of annotation is not simply a peculiarity of the Kane–Donaldson B Text but had been practiced by Skeat a century ago.)

It's worth passing these community-sanctioned rhetorical forms in brief review. Typically, editors of English texts (unlike medieval annotators of the Vulgate or Map's *Dissuasio*) are required to disperse their annotation throughout the volume. Some annotation, most typically the *corpus lectionum*, belongs at the page foot, below the text. Matters requiring extensive discussion (whether textual cruces, historical and literary allusions, or explanations of obscurities) go into a series of notes placed after the text. Commentary on vocabularly most normally is relegated to a separate glossary at the rear of the volume. And some substantial matters must be treated in a discursive introduction subject to its own rhetorical rules: no edition can be acceptable without a thorough survey of the witnesses and their peculiarities or without a discussion of sources.

(A parenthesis: One might note that these rhetorical rules are rules of inclusion, and do not always provide absolute instructions for practice. Thus, although an annotator must offer a glossary, he can choose its nature: No formal presentation, but elaborate discussion of forms amid the notes? A concordance? A selection? If the latter, every word but only a selection of instances? A selection of words? On what basis? This licensed variation within the given rhetorical format indicates in other ways the socially mediated nature of annotation: such choices are, I think, largely use-driven and reflect conceptions of audience. It's easy enough to imagine an annotator explaining a single text in different ways so as to reflect different social situations in which he finds himself. The differences in Skeat's practice in his Parallel Text Edition and Student Edition are a relevant example.)

Simultaneously, and I think tellingly, the rhetorical rules that govern annotation include one option: no introduction need include either an interpretation of the text or even a review of the scholarship. And although I think it is assumed that the annotator has read all the scholarship, he is not even obligated to include critical studies in his bibliography.

These rhetorical rules seem to me a form, a repression, of guilty knowledge. This is a knowledge, suppressed into a rhetorical dismemberment, of the danger and the aggression inherent in being an annotator. This danger, as my indication of the one true option open to an editor suggests, is the fear that the annotator in fact will become an interpreter, impose his being, in a double attack, on the reader and on the text. The rhetorical dismemberment of annotation exists simply as a sign that this danger has been successfully circumvented: twentieth-century annotators are completely removed from the text page (reduced merely to textual evidence) and are required to fragment their activities into tasks presented as rhetorically discrete, so that they can never appear whole consciousnesses in touch with the text.

But, as I suggest, this rhetorical prescription seems to me merely an expression of guilty knowledge, a way of allowing annotation to proceed as a form of benign mediation, a service profession, which it is not. The easiest way of approaching the claim is to ask what an annotator is doing when he annotates. My practice suggests to me that he is in fact creating himself as reader—and thus creating the reader of his work. For when I annotate, what I am doing is reading through the text with my profoundest attention, asking what it is that a reader should be given so as to facilitate that most attentive reading I can give. When my reading runs into blocks, I have to dissociate myself momentarily and become a researcher. But eventually this split within myself is healed, since I return to write in the most helpful fashion my reading as note or gloss or whatever. Obviously, this procedure testifies to the necessary endlessness of annotation, which troubled Lara Ruffolo in the Friday discussion: I can only create one reader (or one limited range of readers), and the text is open to a multitude of them. Thus, even if I do a superlative job on my text, I can count on the eventual replacement of my annotation as community standards alter and the audience I addressed recedes into the past.

This sketchy documentation of my procedures suggests both why the rhetorical forms of annotation exist and why they are fictive. The forms are precisely the warrant to the reader that I have not overstepped the bounds of annotatorhood, have provided a mediating service. But my act of filling the forms, of course, is quite otherwise. If I've done well, I have produced a single successful reader and her reading of the poem (however tacit this remains in the rhetorical forms of annotation): in effect, rather than serving a community, I have articulated it, created it. In this way, the forms of annotation speak what is not: they exist deliberately to obscure the aggressive act of controlling audience consumption of the text. If my annotation is successful, I have put at least temporary limits on the arena in which community conversation can proceed. The rhetorical rules of annotation exist to obscure this antisocial (yet society-enabling) behavior.

The rules also obscure another aggressiveness—toward my author. This danger has been perceived for centuries: it is inscribed in manuscript page formats that attempt to make it impossible for text and gloss to be confused. And the reality of the danger is oppressively present in textual histories, for example at Chaucer's *Shipman's Tale* 214, where the two manuscripts always taken as sure guides to Chaucer's desires (Hengwrt and Ellesmere) present the author as gloss and a scribal glossator as Chaucer's text. In a similar vein, Jim Nohrnberg has cannily suggested to us the extent to which our most revered cultural text in fact is predicated upon the annotator's status as the truest author.

Since annotation most typically appears in conjunction with a text, as part of a critical edition, I am always flirting with a similar incursion. Thus, in spite of the convention of purely textual text pages, as annotator I am always enveloping my author, always in the act of invading him, of delimiting his possible meaning and relevance.

(Another parenthesis: In my personal case, this involves a very explicit effort, which I learned from Talbot Donaldson, at aggression upon the author. I intervene in the text, with brackets to mark my incursion, to a degree that most readers have found anything from unsettling to odious. I thus always make explicit the bounded conventions behind my very decision to annotate: to say a text is canonical is to say it is a fixed text, accepted by a community in a single form. This assumption I deliberately seek to question, since the community is only as in touch with its text as its last editor was.)

Because my annotation circulates with the author, my invasion is always successful: whatever it was that he meant to do, he becomes imprisoned within my explication. Not only do I aggressively create my audience, I also create my author. And in spite of rhetorical protestations, so do all annotators, as the prevalence of historical "facts" that began life as annotation in critical editions will abundantly testify. Merely as an example, consider the power of notes about tale order in Chaucer's *Canterbury Tales* to shape the author and thus perceptions about him in the readerly community. Identifying oneself with the Bradshaw Shift commits Chaucer and interpretation of him to "roadside realism," while other views provide other poets and other readerly communities.

A brief example, a line that ought to be about annotation and that has been flickering through my mind throughout the conference, may summarize these views that conceive annotation as a necessary aggression. The line is the first in Chaucer's poem *The Parliament of Fowls*: "The lyf so short, the craft so long to lerne." Were I going to annotate this line, I would begin by recognizing that I recognize it, that it's cribbed from another work I know—a purely factual gesture that calls attention to a fact, a relationship of identity. But that would be perhaps the last gesture I would make to the line that wouldn't be embroiled in some kind of assault on either Chaucer or the reader. For, at some point or another, I would recognize that this sententia is identical, not with a single other text, but with a number of other statements, ranging all the way from English proverbs to Hippocrates (*Aphorismi* 1.1); whatever decision about linkage to past utterances I made would involve me in interpreting a whole variety of issues ranging from Chaucer's reading down to how I constitute the text lexically (and not simply in terms of this line but of the whole text).

For example, in *The Parliament of Fowls*, line 2, "Th'assay so hard" would remind me of Hippocrates' subsequent phrase *experientia fallax*. That would probably conduce me to see Chaucer's knowledge of Hippocrates here as direct and primary. In turn, such a decision would suggest to me that "assay" would need a gloss (*pace* some annotators, it could not mean "attempt"). The gloss, in turn, would lead to further lucubrations about the experience/books split in this text and in other Chaucerian dream visions. Moreover, the fact that I recognize the line as a sententia would send me off to rhetorical handbooks for injunctions on beginning a poem in this way and some statement about the rhetorical constitution of Chaucer's text, another interpretive gesture. *Und so weiter.*

But all these might somehow stand as more or less neutral gestures. One other item I'd at least think about annotating certainly wouldn't be. This involves the little word "craft." Should I gloss it? This decision the conventions of Chaucer annotation have usually managed to avoid (albeit by a bit of underhandedness). Typically annotators assume that Chaucer writes something enough like modern English that words descending pretty much intact may be passed over in silence. Whether it's that I'm overly fastidious as a reader, or that I have a strongly developed sense of aggression, I would think a bit before merely accepting the convention. But this moment of thought is instructive: if I gloss this word, in a poem in which perhaps the central issue is the poetic life (viewed through the life of love), I will strongly delimit the way Chaucer perceives his own activity and the way the reader perceives Chaucer's activity. Is "the craft" an *ars* or a handicraft, merely to state two seriously opposed possibilities?

As a way of ending, let me pick up a few points. Throughout my comments I have been forced to acknowledge the social embeddedness of annotation. The annotator is controlled by the same presumptions as the audience he addresses; he allows that audience to stipulate the accepted form his annotations take. Yet simultaneously, the way he fills those forms in effect reconstitutes the audience of which he is a member—but always silently and guiltily. The annotator, if he's a good one, presents a reading that will create the acceptable range of conversation within the group he supposedly serves. This leads me to suggest that questions of annotation always come back to issues of communities and institutions, and consequently questions of power. At least one question one should ponder at length, as Tom McFarland shrewdly invited us to, is precisely that of power: who or what is being served by this activity?

9

For a Political Economy of Annotation

Laurent Mayali

The following is a brief summary of my reflections on the papers presented at this symposium. In Western culture, the relationship of annotation to the text is less a relation of meaning than it is a relation of power. This relation of power has its source in a conception of knowledge in which the written text has become the fundamental legitimizing instance. In our culture it might be said that the text is the dominant image of knowledge. The annotation achieves its political function by fulfilling a need for knowledge that is first of all an essential need for authority.

It is not a mere coincidence that in many modern languages the term "author" used to designate the writer comes from the Latin *auctor*, also the root for the word "authority." In its original Latin meaning, *auctor* does not designate the writer but rather the guarantor, that is, a person who attests or vouches for the truth of a statement or a situation. The text produced by the author/writer guarantees the correspondence between knowledge, the meaning of the text, and the immutable truth. In this perspective the Platonic relationship of knowledge to truth is fundamental. Like truth, which is not produced but merely exists, true knowledge cannot be produced but only reproduced. In our culture, and contrary to Plato's wishes in favor of the spoken word, this guaranteed reproduction of truth is embodied in the text, which in turn becomes a source of power. The annotation is thus a procedure of political appropriation of the power of the text; it is an apparatus for reproducing knowledge in a form that legitimates the annotator, the annotation, and the social structures within which they exist. In order to understand this political relationship between annotations and text, one must begin by reconstructing the historical process of reproducing knowledge.

My intention is not to give a complete account of what makes the privileged relationship to knowledge a fundamental characteristic of Western culture, but rather to explore the cultural reasons that have promoted annotation to its political status in modern society. Originating in the Judeo-Christian religious tradition, these reasons were reinforced in the Middle Ages by the renewal of a legal science in conjunction with the rebirth of literacy.

In his convincing presentation on biblical storytelling, James Nohrnberg clearly shows the importance of filiation in the determination of the identity of the different familial groups in the Bible. The identification of each member of the group is the result of a genealogical process where everyone is assigned to a specific place. This genealogy attests for the existence of the family but also for its coherence based on the mutual recognition of its member. In this structure neither men nor women have places except as father and mother or as son and daughter. Just as there are no parents without children, there are no children without parents. Humanity becomes a large family of which the original parents are themselves the children of God, the almighty father. Thus the real existence of humanity depends heavily upon a form of kinship best illustrated by the bodies of father and child lying side by side in the cave, buried in human earth as opposed to the divine sky. Earth in this cave is thus the place where the human group is attested through the supine bodies of its affiliated members. Likewise, the page has become the place where knowledge exists through the supine bodies of the text and of its annotations (the Justinian compilations of the Roman Law were called "*Corpus* Iuris Civilis"). And as there is no father without a child, there is no text without annotations. Laid down on the page, the text becomes real, and so does its offspring, annotation.

The genealogical principle appears as a principle of legitimization that works similarly in the reproduction of the human species and the reproduction of knowledge. In the intellectual renewal of the Middle Ages, such a principle becomes fundamental for reproducing knowledge. With the development of universities and other centers of learning, knowledge is institutionalized. Its production is the monopoly of a limited group that takes its authority from the faithful commentary of some privileged texts. It is thus not a coincidence if this period appears as the golden age of the annotation, the best illustration of which is given by the success of the different *glossae ordinariae* to the Bible, the laws of the late Roman emperors, and the legislation of the Church.

It is interesting to notice that, at this same moment, genealogies of annotators are constituted. Quite often these intellectual filiations are not separated from the natural ones, as can be seen in a manuscript of the Corpus Iuris Civilis where the copyist of the *glossa ordinaria* tells an edifying story.[1] He begins by giving a genealogy of the most famous glossators from Accursius, the author of the *glossa ordinaria*, back to Bulgarus (Accursius. Azonis. Johannis. Bulgari). Then he tells us that Franciscus, Accursius's son, found the forgotten grave of Johannes Bassianus, the intellectual grandfather of his father, and made him a *pulcherrima sepultura.* Once again, as in the above-mentioned story of the Bible, the tomb becomes the cement of the familial bonds, a place where the family becomes real.

Each *glossa ordinaria* was a mere genealogy for producing a discourse that was in turn recognized as knowledge. Through this process, the annotation was inserted in an educational system. The subsequent normalization and legitimization of the official knowledge was effected by the annotating procedure. At this stage, the annotation's raison d'être was primarily to attest to the authority of the annotator as author. It was thus developed not only as an instrument of knowledge but also as an instrument of power insofar as the annotator sought not only a better understanding of the text but also respect and recognition. Today the modern methods for text editing illustrate in some way such a situation. They aim at the constitution of a set of propositions that are scientifically acceptable according to the standards determined by the discipline. Therefore the multiplication of critical apparatus does not enhance the

1. Vatican, MS vat. lat. 1423, fol. 176ra.

authority of the text itself but achieves the recognition of the annotator within the academic discipline. Through his annotation of a text, the institutional annotator becomes conscious of his or her work and role. But as source of knowledge, it might be said that the text retains its mysterious meaning.

A second characteristic of the Western tradition is the definition of God as the creator. By assigning to the creative act a divine origin, such a definition seems to take it away from the realm of human abilities. The artist is condemned to the role of imitator as the only possible alternative. The artistic creation acts as a fiction, an *imitatio naturae*. During the Middle Ages, imitation is gradually considered as creation. This view appears first in the writing of the canonists. It legitimizes the power of the Pope as *Vicarius Christi* who, *ut Deus*, can do something out of nothing (*de nihilo aliquid facit*). The history of this doctrinal change has been perfectly reconstituted by Ernst Kantorowicz in his stimulating study on the sovereignty of the artist.[2]

The historical relationship between nature and art, the divine creation and the human imitation, is reproduced in the historical relationship between text and annotation. The annotation is born from the imitation of the text. It is a fictive text. But it becomes as real as the text since, according to Thomas Aquinas, this fiction is nothing but a *figura veritatis*. Once introduced within this fictive relationship, the annotation becomes a text by itself and generates in turn its own annotation in an endless process, as an established routine.

The cultural patterns inherited from the Judeo-Christian tradition respecting genealogical legitimacy, nature and art, and text and annotation were reinforced by the intellectual renewal of the Middle Ages. In the eleventh and twelfth centuries, we note the emergence of literacy and the gradual development of jurisprudence. This combined phenomenon gives its final form to the recognition of the text as the privileged source of knowledge. The junction of written knowledge and legal reasoning worked to the benefit of a

2. Ernst Kantorowicz, "The Sovereignty of the Artist. A Note on Legal Maxims and Renaissance Theories of Art," *De Artibus Opuscula XL. Essays in Honor of Erwin Panofsky* (New York: Millard Meiss, 1961), p. 267–279, as reprinted in Ernst Kantorowicz, *Selected Studies* (New York: Augustin, 1965), pp. 352–65.

literate culture. Remarkably, as noticed by Richard Sennett, all the ideas of the text that we inherited from the Middle Ages are based on the notion of authority.[3]

On the one hand, there was a proliferation of written sources. Literacy, according to Brian Stock, "penetrated medieval life and thought and brought about a transformation of the basic skill of reading and writing into instruments of analysis and interpretation."[4] The issue that I want to consider here, however, is somewhat different. As a process of appropriation of the textual knowledge, it might be said that annotation stands indeed between orality and literacy.

In the early Middle Ages, annotations may be regarded as a manifestation of a contemporary knowledge that is essentially oral. In this perspective, the dry-point annotations studied by Thomas Toon are an eloquent illustration of such a phenomenon. During this period a written text is still rare and expensive. Its external form is almost as important as its content. It is a work of art and a display of wealth, a symbol of power. As such it belongs to a small, privileged group. The political authority of the text is displayed on the white page where it lies untouched. It should not be violated by any form of disrespectful comments, neither should the harmonious alternation of written and blank columns be disrupted by an unauthorized hand. Having neither the required authority nor the required legitimacy, the annotator hesitates to take possession of the empty margins. His intrusion through the dry-point annotations is thus tolerated but not yet fully recognized. In a mostly oral culture the relationship between the voice and the text is not yet established, because textual knowledge remains mysterious and magical. It is in any case out of reach for the human being. It is reserved to the gods or their human offsprings, the kings. On the other hand, the voice—spoken sound—has not received a visual materiality. Its reality is not to be seen and read but to be heard.

What a difference between these early medieval texts majestically lying between white margins where some timid annotations are not

3. Richard Sennett, *Authority* (New York: Vintage Books, 1981), p. 16ff.

4. Brian Stock, *The Implications of Literacy. Written Language and Models of Interpretation in the Eleventh and Twelfth Centuries* (Princeton: Princeton University Press, 1983), p. 11.

to be seen but by experienced eyes, and twelfth- and thirteenth-century manuscripts where any remaining blank space is covered with ink! However, the process of appropriation of this newly rediscovered textual knowledge was achieved gradually. The first attempts essentially consisted of cross-references (*allegationes*) among different passages of the text or different texts. The annotator was only rearranging the text according to his own reason. The text was classified but remained itself practically unviolated. Next to these *allegationes*, sparse *notabilia* pointing to the question addressed in the text appeared in the still unused margins, which remain a forbidden place. The first annotations directed toward an explanation or interpretation of the text take place within the shelter of the text as interlinear glosses. Inserted between the lines, they do not stand on their own outside the text. Then, in the second half of the twelfth century, the annotating process will be completed. Interlinear glosses and marginal commentaries are regrouped in apparatuses that begin to circulate without the annotated text. On the page, they have taken the place of the text. The margins shelter a second generation of annotations that are additions to the existing commentary. The annotator has become an author: he is a source of knowledge, his opinions are discussed. What were originally annotations are now cited as independent works.

This gradual process of recognition of both the authority of the annotations and the legitimacy of the annotator was, of course, accentuated in many ways by the birth of a legal science. First, the legal texts bore the stamp of the imperial power. This supreme power was itself legitimized by a written knowledge, since the emperor was himself described as a living archive. His knowledge was the greatest because the "laws were written in the archive of his chest." This text found in the Justinian compilations of civil law was abundantly annotated during the Middle Ages. The jurists could then claim that the absolute power was both generated and legitimized by the knowledge of legal writings.

Second, because of its imperial origin, the legal text was itself a *res sacra*. One of the first known legal annotators, Irnerius, was prompt to quote a passage of the Roman jurisconsult Ulpian contained in the Digest (D.1.1.1: "The law is the art of goodness and fairness. Of that art we [jurists] are deservedly called the priests").

According to Irnerius, then, the jurist was the *sacrarum rerum minister* and, as part of the legal discourse, his annotations might be considered sacred.

Last but not the least, the law was defined as the *Ratio scripta.* The development of legal rationality modified the perception of truth that was defined in legal terms. Legal knowledge was the true knowledge, and the legal order the true order. Doctor, judge, or notary, the jurist annotators could then legitimately claim the power of the author. "Annotatio: id est lex," wrote Johannes Teutonicus, the author of the *glossa ordinaria* to Gratian's Decretum, one of the most important legal works in the Western legal tradition.[5]

5. Johannes Teutonicus, *Glossa ordinaria to the Decretum Gratiani*, D. 50 c. 46, v. *annotatione*.

10

This Is Not an Oral Footnote

Jacques Derrida

My impossible situation was very well described, in his paper for this colloquium, by our colleague Traugott Lawler. It is that of the annotator, caught in the prescriptive double bind of an interdiction and an injunction: "I am forbidden to speak," "I cannot remain silent." I should not speak because of my incompetence and my respect for your competence; nevertheless it is impossible for me to keep silent since I am committed to speak; I have promised this to Stephen Barney, who now urges me to speak. And so I must but I cannot keep my promise.

In order to comment on these first statements, I will propose first of all two remarks, and will let you decide whether they have the status of footnotes or of annotations, or, more important, whether or not they belong to the symposium. Perhaps at the moment when someone as incompetent and as foreign to your community as I am begins to speak, to speak in a language that is neither yours nor his own, nor yet simply a translation (and the question of translation in the broader sense is a crucial one for all that we have discussed up to this point), maybe at that instant the contract of the symposium is broken. You will notice, however, that in saying that I might add a footnote to my first two or three statements, I subscribe nevertheless to the contract proposed by Stephen Barney, since in his "Notes Toward a Symposium on Annotation," I pick up two questions for which I provide at least one example. These two questions are:

1. *Are there good and bad footnotes*?

By offering bad footnotes, I offer you the possibility of deciphering *a contrario* what good footnotes might be. But I believe that the destiny, the fate of a footnote or more generally of an annotation, is to be always bad; and the better it is, the worse it is. I will try to explain why this is so.

2. *What is an oral footnote*?

One could say figuratively that *this* is an "oral footnote," an example of an "oral footnote," if one believed that there could be such a thing, in the strict sense, as a purely "oral footnote." I do not believe that there is such a thing.

In the strict sense, the status of a footnote implies a normalized, legalized, legitimized distribution of the space, a spacing that assigns hierarchical relationships: relationships of authority between the so-called principal text, the footnoted text, which happens to be higher (spatially and symbolically), and the footnoting text, which happens to be lower, situated in what could be called an inferior margin. (I leave aside the possibility of those footnotes that, in the past or today, we have inscribed in the lateral and not the inferior margins of the principal text.)

This relationship of authority inscribed in the topology has a political dimension as well, indeed a theologico-political one. Why theologico-political? If one considers that the absolute model of a text whose very structure precludes its ever being second, secondary, explanatory, a text that is never pedagogical, descriptive, constative, theoretical, interpretive—in other words, it never comes after another text upon which it would depend, however little—if one considers that a text so absolutely performative, self-sufficient, self-interpretive, initial, and inaugural, and poetic in the strong sense of the word, is a divine speech act or divine writing, then the hierarchical relationship between the main text and the annotations—which are sometimes but not always footnotes—reproduces a theologico-political model.

The law of this hierarchy—which implies spacing in general, even in speech acts, even in purely oral statements—binds the author of the main text, the God of the footnoted text, to subordinates, slaves, or foreign annotators. One knows, for example, that in modern times the author of the footnote can, of course, be a translator (a translator's note is a footnote); he can be the editor, but he can also be the author, who thus subordinates himself to himself, who becomes his own auxiliary and hierarchizes his own text in deciding what is to be principal and what is to be secondary—who in other words organizes in his own text a multiplicity of connected hierarchized functions that always correspond to the structure of a political community or to some institutional model (crafts or trades, industry, pedagogy).

Of course—as is always the case as soon as there is a law, *the* law—all deceptions, transgressions, and subversions are possible, and have been so since long before what is called modernity, even postmodernity. The author of the text that seems to occupy the main and highest place can invert or subvert the places himself, or can see himself overturned by the annotator and by the play of the game of the footnote. We know very well—and this knowledge belongs to what could be called the pragmatics of annotation, which does not limit itself to a linguistic, a rhetoric, or a semantic, since it plays in the space with gestures that are not simply speech acts or writing acts but movements in the space—we know that in these given pragmatic situations, it is the footnote that conveys the main message, and the footnote that has the best chance of being read. For example, in a polemical context, if I want to be sure that my reply or my attack will be read and not passed by, indeed read even before the main text, I put it into a footnote for at least two reasons.

First, because of the topological reasons I have already mentioned, the very subordination of the footnote assures a sort of framing, a delimitation in the space that gives it a paradoxical independence, a freedom, an autonomy. The footnote is also a text unto itself, rather detached, relatively decontextualized or capable of creating its own context, such that one can read it quickly and directly for itself. One can even begin, and you know that we often do, by reading the footnotes and by looking to them, rightly or wrongly according to the case, for the strategic preorientations necessary for approaching certain academic books. I am obviously not talking about the Bible here, about poems or novels, that is to say about texts that exclude by structure and by destination not all annotation, but all footnotes by the author. One has no right to exclude all annotative statements from a sacred or from a literary text, from a poem or fiction, that is to say all secondary statements that accomplish a function either explicative, pedagogic, or parenthetic according to very different modes. However, one does have the right to exclude from these sacred or literary texts any footnotes by the author. But this distinction, which I believe to be legitimate, between annotation in general and the footnote, still depends on an overly general concept of annotation, or at least on a feature common to all annotation, namely its theoretico-constative nature (a pure annotation is neither performative nor poetic), its *secondary* nature (an annotation implies the preeminent priority and authority of another text).

These general features (the theoretico-descriptive or constative secondarity) are common to annotation and to many other similar practices that are not annotation: commentary, criticism, exegesis, gloss, interpretation—that is, a certain kind of secondary interpretation, because there is an interpretation of the interpretation, or at least of the *hermeneuein*, that situates the hermeneutic act beside the primary text as a productive, poetico-performative act. But I will leave this problem aside, seeing that it would lead us into an interesting and necessary digression, and would at the same time lure us into an analysis of the concept of digression itself. Despite their digressive nature—and you see that I myself am going from digression to digression—neither annotation nor the footnote is *stricto sensu* a digression; the digression takes place as a detour within the narrative or demonstrative discouse that one has no intention of either abandoning or interrupting, even for an instant, to begin elsewhere, at the bottom of the page, in the margins or between brackets. In the same way, all the incidental remarks, the parenthetical discourse, the comments made in passing, the details, all the self-interpretive structures, all the supplementary or explanatory information that, up to a certain point, share with annotation the general features of theoretico-constative secondariness, are nevertheless not annotations strictly speaking.

(An oral footnote here: when I say "theoretico-constative," I do not exclude the evaluative, prescriptive, or normative value of these secondary discourses. Because, as some of you have already demonstrated, no annotation is neutral: annotations, directly or indirectly, can express judgments, give advice, or provide an order for reading—as we do when we annotate a paper or a dissertation; they can constitute a sort of ethics or politics of interpretation. Inasmuch as they are secondary discourses, however, they remain theoretico-constative in their relation to the text that precedes them structurally, and about which they claim finally and essentially to say what it is already in itself, independent of the secondary discourse, which is there not to enrich or transform the primary discourse, but to say or make manifest or reveal the truth of its being or its meaning. Normative prescriptions or evaluations are at the service of the theoretico-constative unveiling of the truth.)

For there to be an annotation, it seems to me, all that I have mentioned must be present, as well as other distinct predicates: for example, the nonbelonging or rigorous, determinable exteriority of the annotation in relation to the principal, primitive text. This exclusion, which must be imposed by internal or external laws, and sometimes by both, raises a great number of difficulties. For all the difficulties we are dealing with here are related to the limit, the problematic limit between an inside and an outside that is always threatened by graft and by parasite. Internal laws include the heterogeneity of the style of the main text and the secondary text, of the mode of writing, of the rhetoric, even of the language (it is not contradictory to the concept of annotation that it be done in a language different from that of the annotated text). External laws include the typographical or topographical disposition and other indices of this kind. Simultaneously external and internal laws include everything that denotes or connotes both the origin and the destination of annotations, the signature and silhouette of the audience or of the readership with all the marks the signatory and the addressee may leave inside the two texts, the annotated and the annotating.

From this point of view, the concept of annotation, in the strict sense (if indeed it has a strict sense), has limits that are simply the limits imposed by certain laws, institutions, and social conventions that have a history and their own precise cultural limits. The historical model to which most of the papers in this symposium have referred, and that corresponds in effect to this institutive concept of annotation, to this concept that is institutional through and through, is surely foreign to many of the cultures in which addition, note, gloss, and marginal graft are used according to different topological and socioinstitutional structures. Other cultures—even some like the Jewish and Arabic, very close to our own—use an *intertextual* layout of the page and construct a topographical *mise en page* according to rules and hierarchical evaluations that are not at all those that you or we call annotation.

In saying this, I pose the beginning of an answer to another one of the questions posed by Stephen Barney in "Notes Toward a Symposium on Annotation": "How does annotation differ from intertextuality?" My response would be: annotation in the strict sense in no way differs from intertextuality. It is intertextual through and through, from the moment we understand "text" in the classical sense as a notation representing one discourse propped on another. It consists, in effect, of a text related to another text that has meaning only within the relationship. But if annotation is wholly intertextual, in the strict sense it is nothing more than a very narrowly determined mode of intertextuality. Not all intertextuality, of course, has the form of annotation, nor need it necessarily include any form of annotation. In the same way, if one confines intertextuality, as is usually done (but as I am not doing), to a relationship between things written generally on the medium of paper, I believe that one does not have the right to say that an event in general can, strictly speaking, be "footnoted," unless the event in question consists of a text in the classical and in the usual trivial sense of the term, which is possible, though in this case the footnote will concern the text and not the event. In this way I respond in passing to another of Stephen Barney's questions ("Can an event be footnoted?).

Finally I would have liked to propose a rhetorical reading of all these questions, that is, of the program of this symposium and the twenty-seven notes it comprises, notes that offer themselves as an exemplary object of what the symposium is about, and that are so self-comprehensive both for the symposium and in themselves that they include, as one of their parts, particular questions that are larger than the notes and symposium together. For instance, this one: "What's the difference between a symposium and a footnote?" The question remains, do we or do we not abuse rhetorically, when we refer to question as "Notes"? As a rule, annotations or notes say something; they "state" or add something, they answer a potential question by the reader. They do not pose questions: they do not interrogate either author or reader. This may occur accidentally, but it is not the essential purpose of notes, annotations, or footnotes. Whether annotation or footnote, in our culture the note is a remark, a "notice" (as its etymology suggests, I think) whose purpose is to introduce a piece of information: this is why I said it was theoretico-constative or descriptive. In this sense, the note does not pose questions; it informs, it makes things known. The question mark is only a rhetorical feint, a ruse whose aim is the production of knowledge.

I was saying, therefore, that I would like to propose a rhetorical reading of the operation of certain concepts in Stephen Barney's twenty-seven question, that is, in the charter and the constitutional law of this symposium. For example, the concept of footnote is sometimes used in a presumably literal fashion when Professor Barney, the author of the principal text upon which I am now commenting, asks "How can we distinguish footnotes, commentaries, essays, new texts?" However, in the question "What do we mean in saying philosophy is footnotes to Plato and Aristotle?," the same word "footnote" is used in a figurative, metonymic, and therefore already fictive fashion. (There would be much to say about this metonymy, which I find very interesting, but I prefer to leave this matter for the discussion.)

I do not know if I am making myself clear, but I am in the process of going from the first to the second point of a two-part remark in the course of which, commenting on the second of a pair of questions by Stephen Barney ("What is an oral footnote?"), I was trying to explain why, in the strict sense, there is no such thing as an oral footnote, because, in the strict sense, annotation is not footnotes. I was most of all trying to explain the reasons why, in a polemical context, if I wanted to be sure that my reply or my attack would be read and not passed by—indeed, read before the main text—I would put it in a footnote, conferring on it the principal role, so that what is apparently the main text would become an auxiliary pretext for the footnote. Before explaining the second of these reasons, I would like to risk a brief digression on what is happening at this moment.

I am now in the midst of awkwardly improvising an English translation of a text I wrote yesterday in French on the Macintosh SE that the University of California, Irvine has generously put at my disposal during my stay here. Now you may well ask whether the digressive, complicated, parenthetical, sophisticated structure of this discourse, which seems to include notes within notes, infinitely *en abŷme*, derives from the fact that I wrote on a computer. The computer today makes possible the fluid integration of the digression or supplement into the course of linear writing, whereas the rigidity and heaviness of other instruments and props (including the typewriter and tape recorder) limit such an integration, because they limit the reversibility and the insertion after the fact of any supplement. I am not saying that they make this insertion impossible, but they necessitate laborious restructurings. We all know that we sometimes add a footnote (*stricto sensu*) simply to avoid having to retype or restructure the entire text. And prior to the "economics and technology of printing" of which Professor McFarland was speaking a while ago, to account for the tendency to repress or suppress footnotes, there is an "economics and technology of writing, of composing the original," that can tend toward the same result. What is remarkable about computers in this regard is that they protect and extend the authority of phonetic linear writing in giving it a greater capacity for integration, and finally a greater proximity to the voice or speech act *stricto sensu*. The program composed by Stephen Barney, our charter, our common law, asked: "How does a computer annotate?" This is an enormous question that I will not attempt to undertake, because the computer certainly opens up a number of rich possibilities for annotation but also represents, *stricto sensu* and figuratively, a powerful increase in the possibility of integrating and of erasing an annotation or footnote from the main text, whether this integration is the work of the presumed author or of another or of a collective. In destabilizing the limits, borders, norms, the prerogatives of authorship, these possibilities can both proclaim very new, hitherto unheard-of juridico-politico-textual situations, but also recall very old situations where these limits, these frontiers, were not yet concretely defined and legitimized.

I was, then, in the process of giving the second of the reasons for which one can, in a polemical situation and within the limits of a certain type of text, inscribe the main point in a footnote. (Certainly not in a journalistic polemic, since there are, as a rule, no footnotes in newspapers, a feature they therefore share with sacred or poetico-narrative-literary texts. There can be, in exceptional cases, footnotes in newspapers, but one does everything one can to avoid these parasites, while in an academic dissertation these parasites, these footnotes, find themselves at home. In this general parasitology that is a scholarly, academic discourse on annotations, we must distinguish, in a long footnote that could run throughout the text, between domestic and foreign parasites, the good and the bad, the legitimate and the others.) The note can contain the main point because academics generally rush to read the footnotes, because they usually find the highest concentration of titles and proper names therein. This is quite useful, even if often dangerous and almost always unjust, for orienting oneself without wasting too much time, for getting an overview of the field, and for calculating the strategic positions.

What I am saying here about these aggressive or defensive footnotes, about these titles and names, confirms what Professor McFarland was saying about "reference or dialogical notes," and about all the anxiety with which they can be charged. For instance, suppose that the text I am now reading were published one day after being revised and rewritten; and suppose that I want to make a disagreement with Professor McFarland very visible. This is not at all the case, but if it were, I would rather say in a note that, since anxiety and dialogicity and reference are characteristics of any text, these predicates are completely extrinsic and therefore useless for defining the essence or the concept of the footnote. I would say the same for the definition of annotation as "a combination of six sources of authority and power." If, as the author of this definition correctly notes, "not all these sources are mobilized in every publishing decision about annotation, but all are potentially dynamic factors, and more than one, even if its effect is not immediately discernible, is always active," then none of the sources is indispensable for defining the kind of authority or specific power that annotation displays. Consequently, the combination of these six sources is an empirical and even empiricist summation that tells us nothing about the essence of annotation itself, nor even about the legitimization, the power, the authority that it manifests or bestows.

My "defensive," amicably polemical footnote in answer to Professor McFarland would actually be a cryptic citation of Stephen Barney, who, in his notes on the symposium, speaks metonymically of philosophy as footnotes to Plato and Aristotle. Because the charge against empiricism—which I could have multiplied against Professor McFarland, for example, when he cites René Wellek among the three most learned figures living today (why three, why Wellek, and is this intended to illustrate or to protest against *radikale Unwissenheit* or against what Hazlitt called "the ignorance of the learned"?)—the charge against empiricism has a long Platonic-Socratic genealogy, and my antiempiricist objection belongs to this tradition. When Socrates asks his interlocutor, "Tell me what science is for you," and the interlocutor, instead of giving an essential definition, replies, "Well, there's geometry, grammar, music, architecture, medicine, and gymnastics," Socrates must repeat and annotate the sense of the question: "I didn't ask for a list of sciences; I asked you what was the essence of science, what makes a science a science, what makes all of those sciences sciences? I asked you to think of an essential definition of the scientific, not to enumerate its multiple phenomena. The richness of your empirical knowledge is really a *radikale Unwissenheit*." (He would, of course, have said this in Greek.)

I have not yet said anything pertinent, but you see that, if I were forbidden to speak because of my incompetence, I could not remain silent. In annotating myself, I remember that I began by describing the double bind in which I was caught: I cannot or should not speak, but I promised that I would do so. I must and cannot; in truth, I should and should not keep my promise. But these two injunctions of the double bind compel me equally, and it is this relation to the law, to being "before the law," that I would like to situate here. I note two things in passing. First, what I just mentioned about being before the law (thus, everything I have said up to now) belongs to what could be considered a footnote to what I published a few years ago on a text of Kafka entitled *Vor dem Gesetz*, "Before the Law," and to which I would like to return in the discussion, because it poses some very interesting juridico-topological questions. Second, another self-annotation on a self-annotation: all I am saying here could be read as a footnote to another text that has just appeared in French and will be published next year in English under the title *How to Avoid Speaking*. Among other subjects, it deals mainly with the negative theology of prayer; to simplify matters somewhat, it could be said that it analyzes the whole mystical tradition of negative theology, from Neoplatonism to Dionysius or Meister Eckhart, indeed to a certain Wittgenstein, as a powerful annotation to silence and prayer of the law that commands silence and prayer.

If I had the time, I would here grant a privilege to all the figures of the law and of the double bind in order to define the general field of all these "secondary" discourses (commentary, interpretation, exegesis, etc.) among which annotation *stricto sensu* is nothing more than a particular species, and the footnote a subspecies. All these secondary discourses are before the law not only because their definition, their status, in the strict sense, depends always on legal or legitimizing norms, that is, on theologico-political or pedagogico-political or scientifico-political institutions. As institutions, they constitute limits that have their own history and historical conditions that are by definition stabilizing, stabilized, but therefore essentially not natural and subject to transformation and destabilization. But all these secondary discourses are before the law for a more fundamental reason: secondariness is their common law. They can only respond; they cannot speak first. They are discourses of "respondents." Before them, in front of them, there has been and there will have been an originary text or speech act. The original is the law. It is a text that, because in principle (for it *is* the "principal," the first, *en archē*) it is nonsecondary, suffices to itself, is independent and self-sufficient in its structure. It is "unannotatable," to quote once more from a note by Stephen Barney. Structurally, it does without any secondary text and constitutes by itself its own commentary.

Yet we see how this law text, which makes the law, produces at the same time a double bind: it says to the reader or auditor, "Be quiet, all has been said, you have nothing to say, obey in silence," while at the same time it implores, it cries out, it says, "Read me and respond: if you want to read me and hear me, you must understand me, know me, interpret me, translate me, and hence, in responding to me and speaking to me, you must begin to speak in my place, to enter into a rivalry with me." The more a text is "unannotatable," the more it generates and cries out for annotation: this is the paradox and the double bind. An infinitely "unannotatable," text provokes infinite annotation. In this way the order says, "Read me, be satisfied with reading me, I am here in front of you"; yet it also says, "If you want to read me, you must write, you must do something other than reading." Read me and don't read me. You know this typical situation in the genesis of the pathological double bind. It is sometimes illustrated in statements such as "be free" or "do not read me."

But since this archaic law, this absolute archive of the law, never presents itself, is never accessible in its presence as such, but only in its trace, which is always already secondary, the difference between the primary and the secondary is always postulated, never given in person except in the phenomenon of the finite secondariness.

If I had the time and were not afraid of taking advantage of your patience, I would tell you why I have insisted since the beginning on the double bind and on the difference between the strict sense and the less strict sense, on the difference in "stricture" in the meanings of all those words that constitute secondary discourse. It would be in order to introduce something I will not speak about, something I would not have dared to name, if Stephen Barney had not invited me (in one of his notes and, yesterday, orally), that is, my experience or treatment of annotation in *Glas*. Here, therefore, very schematically presented, are some notes; if you wish, we could return to them in the discussion.

1. *Glas* is a book on the double bind and on *stricture* (a word that exists in English in another sense, but that did not exist in French), a book in which the logic of *stricture* substitutes itself for the logic or dialectic of opposition.

2. Before *Glas*, I had often tried to destabilize the order of annotation by proposing typographical layouts, topographies that prohibited one from deciding what was the principal text and what was secondary. I did this, for instance, in a text entitled "Tympan" at the beginning of *Marges* (a brief text by Michel Leiris in one column, with a text signed by me facing it, so that one cannot decide which text precedes or comments on, annotates, or responds to the other, nor even if there is the slightest connection between the two). The whole book also deals, in different modes, with grafts and parasites. I did the same again in *La Dissémination*, especially at the beginning of "Double Séance," where a text from Plato's *Philebus* and a text by Mallarmé form a kind of angle such that one cannot establish any kind of hierarchy between them, objective chronology never sufficing to establish a hierarchy (I try to analyze

this subject in *La Carte postale, de Socrate à Freud et au-delà*). Inside *La Dissémination*, in "La Pharmacie de Platon," there is a footnote that responds in advance to Stephen Barney's question on the subject of *Finnegans Wake*. This footnote says approximately this: it will be quickly understood that this whole text—"La Pharmacie de Platon"—is nothing more than a reading of *Finnegans Wake* (which the text elsewhere never mentions at all).

I have always been interested in footnotes or minor texts in philosophy (*parerga*, hors d'oeuvres, exergues in which appear conflicts of forces in institutional politics, problems of canonization and legitimization).

Some final notes. *Glas*: Dramatizes the double bind and the logic of *stricture*.

On the one hand:

1. *Self-annotation*: it comments on itself, explains itself, interprets itself, describes itself directly and figuratively in all ways, including typographically and physically (two columns, two bands, double binds). There is no possible metalanguage on the subject, and annotation is always the structure of a metalanguage. Here, there is nothing but annotations, and no possibility for annotation.

2. All modes of secondariness are tried and mimed and made parasitic and grafted, tattooed (inserted on the body). (Exegesis of sacred texts, commentaries, paraphrase, scientific texts, philosophical theses, farces and satires, "anatomy of criticism," Rabelais, Joyce.)

3. The text has no beginning and no end, no hierarchy, but a text on religion, on proper names, on authority, law, theft, hierarchy.

4. It is an absolutely secondary text, twice secondary (Hegel and Genet, for example), secondary with respect to absolute knowledge (absolute note) as text (Hegel, for example), but it is at the same time not secondary.

5. The text is a continuous annotation on something that lies between discourse and nondiscourse: the syllable "GL": *glose*, *glossa*, *glotte*, Hegel, Genet's mother Gabrielle, the scene of *Gl*aviau, *gl*adiolus . . .).

6. The text plays on play, the fortuitous—*alea*—and necessity, mimesis (cratylism and the arbitrariness of the sign).

7. It mimes and plays on structures of the nonacademic or non-Western gloss (Rabbinical, Talmudic, Islamic; but these are also themes).

8. The two columns face each other and annotate each other, but they are both equally principal texts without any relation to each other, as if they did not belong to the same book: a deconstruction of the unity of the book.

On the other hand:

This book that produces but also records an effervescent destabilization, a turbulence, must also negotiate with the norms that it perturbs. It had to deal with such internal norms as intelligibility, grammaticality, the laws of publishing, printing, marketing. Once published, it entered into negotiation with other, external norms it had sought to perturb: it underwent translation, glossing, a scholarly apparatus—notes, commentaries, translator's notes, essays at the same time playful and serious, matters of academic legitimization like my foreword to the "Glassary."

. . . . The footnote in *La Carte postale*: the two parts that make and do not make a book have a different relationship to the footnote, and so on—one in the fictive (literary) part of the envoi, and another, not signed by the author of the book but by the signatory of the envoi as "editor of the correspondence"; regular notes in the second part (form of the *thesis* but on the Freudian *athesis* in *Beyond* . . .

Contributors

Peter W. Cosgrove's essay draws from his recently completed doctoral work at Columbia, a dissertation on eighteenth-century historiography emphasizing Gibbon. His piece on the aesthetics of music has appeared in *Eighteenth Century Studies*. He teaches at Dartmouth.

Jacques Derrida, of the Ecole des Hautes Etudes en Sciences Sociales, also teaches part of each year at the University of California, Irvine. Recent books of his that have appeared in English are *Glas*, *Truth in Painting*, *Postcard*, and *Limited Inc.*

Anthony Grafton's recent work has focused on his monumental studies of Joseph Scaliger. He teaches history at Princeton.

Currently chair of his department at the University of California, Riverside, **Ralph Hanna III** has collaborated with Traugott Lawler in work on Trevisa, Chaucer's *Boece*, and now *Jankyn's Book of Wikked Wyves*. He has published many works on Middle English literature and textual criticism.

Traugott Lawler's recent work, aside from editing John of Garland and the collaborations with Ralph Hanna, includes his book *The One and the Many in the Canterbury Tales*. He teaches English and is Master of Ezra Stiles College at Yale.

Among **Thomas McFarland's** many books on the Romantic period, *Romantic Cruxes* is the newest. He teaches at Princeton.

Laurent Mayali, professor of law and rhetoric at Berkeley, has published extensively on medieval law, and directs the Robbins Collection of canon and civil legal materials. His recent books include *Droit savant et coutumes: l'exclusion des filles dotées* and, coauthored, *Repertorium manuscriptorum veterum codicis Justiniani.*

Since the publication of his prize-winning *Romanesque Signs*, **Stephen G. Nichols**, who chairs the Department of Romance Languages and serves as dean at the University of Pennsylvania, has continued his work in medieval literature and theory, especially in the Romance languages. His most recent book is *The Legitimacy of the Middle Ages.*

James C. Nohrnberg is best known for *The Analogy of 'The Faerie Queene'.* He teaches at the University of Virginia, and has been publishing a series of articles on the Bible.

A specialist in Old English at the University of Michigan, **Thomas E. Toon** has been working on the social context of early English manuscript production and language change, and is author of *The Politics of Early Old English Sound Change.*

Index